DAMN THE REVOLUTION!

FOUR REVOLUTIONS THAT HAVE HAD A SERIOUS
IMPACT ON HUMAN CIVILIZATION

COLECCIÓN CUBA Y SUS JUECES

From the Same Author

Historia de la Química Industrial
Total Quality and Productivity Management
Performance Management
Strategic Planning
Management Development
Process Improvement Teams
Quality Strategies
Gestión de Futuro

Contramaestre
Baraguá
Poetas y Memorias de Cuba
Jimaguayú
Guáimaro
Colonial Cuba
Republican Cuba
Exiled Cuba
Three Days in March
Raíces cubanas
Álbum de Cuba
Rescatando a Martí
Un Festín de Palabras
Damn the Revolution

EDICIONES UNIVERSAL, Miami, Florida, 2017

There was once a beautiful land
with pristine beaches and transparent rivers,
sprinkled with majestic mountains
and fertile green valleys,
where men and women were trying
to build dreams and happiness.

It so happened that some of them
became intolerant and destructive
and covered the ground red,
scattering the birds from the skies
and turning the dreams into terror.

This book is dedicated to the
young men and women who
escaped the nightmare,
and worked harder than ever
to build a future elsewhere.

Ever since, into their golden years
they have warned others who want to listen
with a truth much higher than their grief :
damn the revolution !

All Revolutions end up eating their own children
Georges Jacques Danton in France, April 5, 1794, aged 35.
Francisco Indalecio Madero in Mexico, February 22, 1913, aged 39.
Leon Trotsky Russian killed in Mexico, August 21, 1940, aged 47.
Camilo Cienguegos in Cuba, October 28, 1959, aged 27.

RAUL EDUARDO CHAO

DAMN THE REVOLUTION !

Four Revolutions that have had a serious
impact on Human Civilization

Copyright © 2017 by Raúl Eduardo Chao

Primera edición, 2017
EDICIONES UNIVERSAL
P.O. Box 450353 (Shenandoah Station)
Miami, FL 33245-0353. USA
Tel: (305) 642-3234 Fax: (305) 642-7978
e-mail: ediciones@ediciones.com
http://www.ediciones.com
SINCE 1965
Library of Congress Catalog Card No.: 2016959887
ISBN-10: 1-59388-279-3
ISBN-13: 978-1-59388-279-2

Printed in the United States of America

Front Cover:
Eugene Delacroix, *Liberty Leading the People* (fragment)
Back Cover:
Jean-Pierre Houël, *Storming La Bastille* (fragment)

All rights reserved Under Internacional and Pan American Copyright Conventions.
No part of this publication may be reproduced, stored or introduced
into a retrieval system, or transmitted, in any form, or by any
means, without the prior written permission of both the
copyright owner and the above
publisher of this book.
The scanning, uploading, selling and/or distribution of this book,
by any means, including the Internet, without the permission
of the publisher is illegal and punishable by law.

Contents

Introduction	**10**
The French Revolution	**13**
A Condensed Timeline	15
Narrative	17
The Mexican Revolution	**81**
A Condensed Timeline	83
Narrative	85
The Russian Revolution	**149**
A Condensed Timeline	151
Narrative	157
The Cuban Revolution	**229**
A Condensed Timeline	231
Narrative	237
Epilogue	**315**
Appendices	**317**
Index	**337**

Introduction

The term *Revolution* comes from the Latin word *Revolutio*, which means "*a turn around.*" Most dictionaries define it as «*a change in the way a country is governed, usually to a different political system and often using violence or war.*» (Cambridge English Dictionary & Tresaurus) or «*the usually violent attempt by many people to end the rule of one government and start a new one.*» (Merrian-Webster Dictionary and Thesaurus). In common ordinary language most people understand by Revolution «*a fundamental change in political power or organizational structures that takes place in a relatively short period of time when the population rises up in revolt against the current authorities.*»

Hundreds, if not thousands of revolutions have taken place in human history, particularly if the definition is extended to include as revolutions those deep changes characterized by one of these modifiers: cultural, ideological, economic, industrial, psychological, social, political, proletarian, nonviolent, technological, commercial, digital, sociological, cognitive, agricultural, poetical, and many others.

In this book we define and will limit the term *Revolution* to large scope socio-political changes that are not *coups d'états*, civil wars, revolts, rebellions and relatively peaceful transitions, nor are they the result of plebiscites or free elections that make no effort to substantially transform institutions or recognize new authorities. Thus non-violent regime changes, peaceful radical changes in political authority, non-aggressive movements that attempt to resolve situations of social or political disequilibrium, regardless of how radical they might be, will not merit the term *revolutionary* within the scope of this book.

Even with those restrictions there are hundreds of events in human history that qualify as revolutions. [1]

---

[1] According to historians, the earliest known to us is probably the **Set Rebellion** during the reign of pharaoh Seth-Peribsen of the Second Dynasty in Egipt in 2730 BC. One of the latests would be the **January 25 Egyptian Revolution** of 2011 that toppled the government of Hosni Mubarak and set the Muslim Brotherhood in power in Egypt.

There have been hundreds of scholarly researchers in the social, political and historical sciences that have studied the phenomena of revolutions from every possible angle. Most of them concentrate in the issue of *why*, *when* and *how* revolutions occur. Others look in detail on how revolutions *develop* once they start and what do they have in *common*, if anything. Finally there are many studies on the *consequences* of revolutions; are they inevitable, are they good or bad, do they retard the progress or advance the course of civilization and human happiness?

The Hispanic world, a good terrain where revolutions have frequently flourish, has had its share of scholars on the issue of revolutions, the most notable being José Ortega y Gasset (1883-1955) with his *The Revolt of the Masses*, first published in 1930.[2]

Given the monumental amount of studies and documentation on revolutions that exist today, this book will simply take a phenomenological approach to five such events for the purpose of illustrating the genesis, the development and the likely consequences of revolutionary happenings.

Behind every revolution there is a simple two step process: first some deteriorating situation make people feel that things are not as good as they could be. It could be strained economic conditions, novel social constraints, deteriorating access to basic resources, scarcity, authoritarian impositions by the rulers, ineffective governance, increased corruption or a combination of some of these. The second step is the awareness of an opportunity to take a massive approach to correct the course of events; the emergence of a convincing leader, the coming out of a nucleus of credible activists, an effectual support for deliverance from outside, one riot that explodes out of control.

Five revolutions have been chosen for this analysis: the **French**, **Mexican** an **Russian** revolutions; to those the author wishes to add the **Cuban revolutions of 1933 and 1959**, which, at a much smaller but not unimportant scale, illustrate very well the *why*, the *how* and the *social and political price* of having revolutions.

---

[2] Ortega was one of the first students of revolutions that characterized them as «*sorry manifestations of the masses, due to their having decided to rule society without the capacity for doing so.*»

The Third Estate (the people) carrying on its back
the First Estate (the clergy) and the
Second Estate (the nobility).

The French Revolution
1789 - 1799

«*Terror is naught but prompt, severe, inflexible justice;
it is therefore an emanation of virtue.*»
MAXIMILLIEN MARIE ISIDORE DE ROBESPIERRE
ADDRESS TO THE NATIONAL CONVENTION, 1794

The French Revolution: a condensed timeline

1787
    Harvests have failed and starvation stalks France; the peasantry are in open and continuing revolt across the country.

1788
    August 8. Louis XVI convokes the *État-Général* on suggestion of former finance minister Jacques Necker, to hear grievances.

1789
    May 5. Opening of the *État-Général* at Versailles.
    June 17. Representatives of the *tiers état* form a National Assembly swearing not to leave until a new constitution is established.
    July 9. National Assembly declares itself Constituent Assembly.
    July 14. Armed citizens storm and capture the Bastille.
    July 15. Lafayette appointed Commander of National Guard.
    August 26. National Assembly decrees *Declaration of the Rights of Man and the Citizen*.
    October 5. Women lead delegation to King in Versailles. Louis XVI is forced to return to Paris.

1790
    February 13. Religious orders and nobility are abolished.

1791
    June 27. Louis XVI and family try to escape but they are captured in Varennes.
    September 13. Louis XVI accepts the French Constitution.
    October 1. The Constituent Assembly dissolved and the Legislative Assembly starts.
    November 9. The Constituent Assembly orders all *émigrés* to return under pain of death. The King vetoes the ruling.

1792
    August 10. Jacobin masses storm the Tuileries Palace, massacring the Swiss Guard. The King is imprisoned.
    August 19. Lafayette goes into exile in Austria.
    August 22. Royalist riots in the Vendée, France. Henceforth the struggle is between bourgeois and proletariat, rather than nobility and bourgeoisie.
    September 2. Danton instigates the massacre of about 1,200 Royalists held in Parisian prisons.
    September 20. Revolutionary French forces defeat the invading force at Valmy. Henceforth the Revolution would enjoy victory in its military conflicts.
    September 21. The Convention elected by the Legislative Assembly commences, abolishes monarchy; the Republican Calendar is established.
    December 11. The Trial of Louis XVI begins.

1793
    January 21. Louis XVI is executed.
    April 6. The *Committee of Public Safety* is established by the Legislative Assembly. Danton presides.

April 24. Marat put on trial for complicity in the September massacre but is acquitted.
May 27. Uprising of the *Paris Commune* against the Convention.
June 3. Expulsion of the *Girondists* (the party of compromise) from all offices. The Commune of Paris becomes the center of power.
June 24. The *Jacobin Constitution* accepted by the Convention.
July 13. Marat, "the people's friend," is murdered by Charlotte Corday. She is executed on July 17.
August 23. *Levée en masse* (conscription into the army) is decreed.
September 17. The *Law of Suspects* is approved. Start of the *Terror*.
October 14. Marie-Antoinette is tried and executed.
October 24. 22 *Girondists* are tried and executed.
November 10. The *Festival of Liberty and Reason* takes place in Paris.

1794

March 24. Robespierre, the *Committee of Public Safety* and the *Jacobin Club* denounce the *Hébertists* and *Dantonists* on framed-up charges and execute all their popular leaders. Robespierre becomes virtually the dictator.
May 18. Robespierre decreed that the new religion of France is that of the *Supreme Being*.
June 8. The day of inauguration of the *Feast and Religion of the Supreme Being*.
June 10. The Convention calls for the arrest of Robespierre. Robespierre first attempts insurrection and later suicide; both flop, is arrested and executed. After about 150 of his supporters are done away with, the *Terror* is over.
Summer. Parisians react to the end of the *Terror*. The limit on the price of bread is removed. Reactionary gangs beat up revolutionaries in the streets.
November 12. The *Jacobin Club* is suppressed by the Convention.

1795

January 1. Catholic Churches are re-opened for worship.
June 8. The Dauphin disappears. Nobody knows if he died in prison or has been rescued by a Catholic family. Not knowing if they will have a Louis XVII, the Comte de Provence assumes title of Louis XVIII.
August 22. The Directory is established.
October 5. Royalists attempt a coup and Napoleon Bonaparte makes his name suppressing the move with decisive action killing people with his cannons.
October 26. The Convention dissolves itself in favor of a dictatorship of the Directorate.

1796

February 2. Napoleon assumes the command of the French army in Italy.

1799

June 18. The Directorate resigns.
November 9. (*18th Brumaire*) Napoleon Bonaparte named "First Consul," now the effective dictator.

1804

December 2. Napoleon is consecrated as Emperor of France by the Pope Pius VII.

The French Revolution
1789 - 1799

For over 200 years the French Revolution has been characterized as one of the most important historical events of all time. It has been proclaimed as one of the brightest of human events, the engine that gave rise to modernity, the event that laid down the definitive foundation of human development, the sacred initiation of a novel but definitive secular religion, the definitive episode that laid down the groundwork of the *Rights of Man and the Citizen*, the historical groundwork of the ideals of *Liberty, Equality and Fraternity*, the epic feat that transformed and saved human civilization from the excruciating pathway in which it was submerged.

During the last two centuries the world has blindly confirmed the optimistic myth that 1789 marked the start of a better human experience. France, the birthplace of the revolution, retains to this day the gripping music and lyrics of the Marseillaise. Tourists in France come every July 14th to celebrate the storming of the Bastille and when they watch the French army sporting the tricolor marching down the Champs Elysees, many feel the same mesmerizing thrills that the natives experience. Every year Paris explodes as visitors and citizens evoke the pride and patriotism of the populace who changed the course of human history in 1789.

Is this real? Was the French revolution the first and definitive strike against totalitarianism? Does humanity owe that much to the *Jacobins* and the *sans-coulottes*?

In 1790, a few months after the Bastille, Edmund Burke in England wrote his *Reflections on the Revolution in France*.[3] He found the events in 1789 Paris pointless and brutal and condemned the atrocities without reservations. Half century later, in 1856, Alexis de Tocqueville, the critical liberal thinker, addressed the issue

---

[3] **Edmund Burke** predicted that the *French Revolution* would end disastrously because its intangible foundations, presumably rational, ignored the complexities of human and societal realities. He addressed the revolution's inattention of practical solutions rather than the metaphysics of their nature: «*What is the use of discussing a man's abstract right to food or to medicine? The question is upon the method of procuring and administering them.*»

with rare elegance in his *The Old Regime and the Revolution* [4] and was not convinced that the French Revolution had lived up to its reputation.

The important question is therefore: Was the French Revolution a romantic but failed and foible attempt to improve humanity? Did the revolution spin out of control as *Liberté, Egalité,* and *Fraternité* inevitably gave birth to the soaring figure of Robespierre and his Reign of Terror? Did the revolution ended up murdering itself?

These and the previous questions can only be answered by carefully and thoughtfully looking at the developments of the ideas and events during the years prior, during and after the revolution.

In the year 1700 France was in the midst of what was later called the *Ancien Régime*. Its territory covered 200,000 square miles and supported 20 million people, the second largest population in Europe. Louis XIV (1638-1715), a member of the House of Bourbon best known as the *Sun King*, and his minister Jean-Baptiste Colbert were the top authorities of the French people. They had a staff of about 10,000 officials in their service. Internal communications were slow; the road system inadequate and most people moved large distances by ship or river boats. The realm consisted of three different estates: the clergy, the nobility, and the commoners, generally known as the first, second and third estate. The three estates met occasionally in an assembly called the *Estates General*. These meetings had the purpose of make petitions to the King; they had no power and could not pass laws of any kind. Close to half the wealth of the country was in the hands of the Church; the King nominated French bishops (not the Pope) and generally consulted with the noble families who had endowed and protected the local monasteries, the cathedrals and most local church buildings.

Each noble had its own lands, subjects and military forces. Towns and cities had an almost independent political and economic status, controlled by merchants and guilds. Politically Paris was at the top, but economically Lyon had the strongest banking power and wealth.

---

[4] *Alexis de Tocqueville* prefaced his study with these words: «*Here I am at the threshold of this memorable revolution; this time I shall not cross it: perhaps soon I may be able to do so. I will not then consider its causes, I shall examine it for itself, and I shall finally dare to judge the society that sprang from it.* »

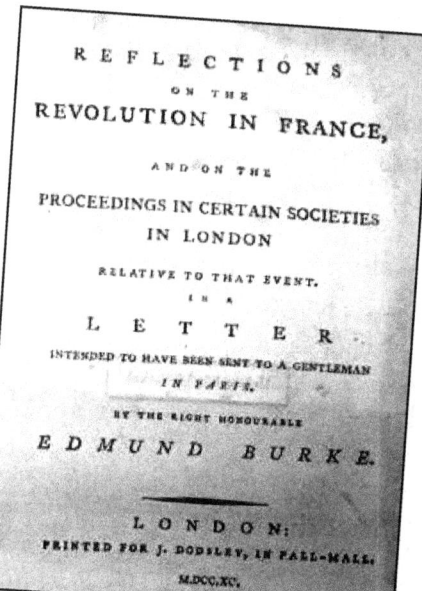

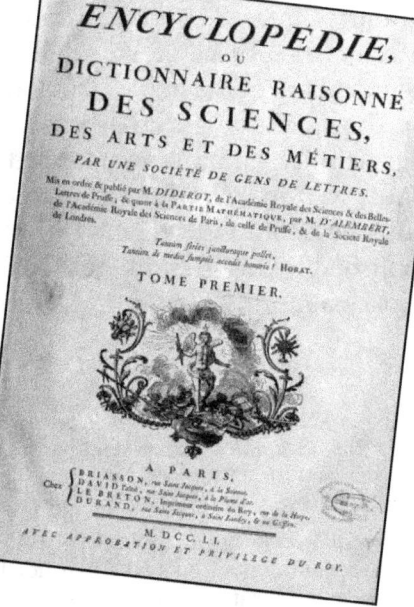

British historian ***Edmund Burke*** and his book *Reflexions on the Revolution in France*; ***Diderot*** and ***D'Alembert***, the main writers of the *Encyclopedie Française*.

About 95% of France's population lived in rural areas; probably 90% of them were peasants. The main path to their social mobility was to do well in the marketplace. The core of French society, however, was in the hands of guilds people (in modern terms we could called them middle class, mostly conservative) and village working men and women (sort of today's lower classes, mostly liberal minded and feeling neglected). They did not see eye to eye in many important issues like loyalty to the crown, obedience of royal regulations, conscriptions to the kingdom armed forces and upward mobility.

Most members of the working classes spoke local dialects; what is known today as the French language was only clearly spoken by the aristocrats.[5]

During the reign of Louis XVI, who believed his authority emanated from the hands of God and never contemplated to be answerable to his people, France had wars with Spain, the Ottoman Turks and the Dutch. The King had no qualms about draining the country's treasure. On the contrary, in 1682 he renovated and expanded the Palace of Versailles, to where he compelled to move all members of the noble class [6] at an extraordinary cost to France.

The splendor and luxury to which the French royal family and the nobility became accustomed did not end after the death of Louis XIV in 1715. He was succeeded by Louis XV, his five year old grandson, who reigned until 1774. Following the pattern established by his grandfather, Louis XV made war in 1718 to Philip V of Spain, in 1733 to the Austrian Empire, in 1740 during the dis-

---

[5] In the XVI century **Emperor Charles V**, ruler of the *Spanish Empire* and the *Holy Roman Empire* (today's Germany, the low Countries, Switzerland, Northern Italy and the eastern side of France) had famously said: «*I speak Spanish to God, Italian to women, French to men, and German to my horse.*»

[6] *Versailles* was begun by Louis XIII in 1623. Much of its early cost was paid by the royal family. Louis XIV expanded it an referred to it as the *King's house*, hence paying for it from the country's purse. After Versailles was declared the location of the French court and the center of the French government, the support and maintenance of the Chateau skyrocketed. Life at Versailles was determined exclusively by position, royal favour and above all pedigree, i.e., one's birth. The Chateau was a sprawling cluster of lodgings for which courtiers vied and manipulated. On each floor, each of the 350 living units of varying size, were arranged along tiled corridors and given a number. The Noailles family, to which General Lafayette belonged, for instance, took over so much of the Southern Wing of the Chateau that the corridor leading to all the lodgings on that floor was nicknamed *Noailles Road* by courtiers of the time.

pute about the Austrian succession and in 1763 when France lost its North American empire to the British.

In the meantime, the ideals of the *Enlightenment* stated to take hold in France. French *philosophes* [7] included, first of all, Voltaire (1694-1778), a best seller author [8] that exerted enormous influence across Europe; a tireless antagonist of the Church of Rome who ended up in exile in England on several occasions. On the list was also Jean-Jacques Rousseau (1712-1778), whose essay *The Social Contract*, or *Principles of Political Right* was a catalyst for governmental and societal reform throughout Europe; Charles-Louis de Secondat Montesquieu (1689-1755) the proponent of the separation of powers, Denis Diderot (1713-1784) and Jean Baptiste le Rond d'Alambert (1717-1783), editors of the grand *Encyclopédie*, whose aim was to «*change the way people think.*»

In 1789, unlike in France, the feudal regime [9] had been weakened and had already disappeared in most of Europe. One part of the estate, the prosperous elite of merchants, manufacturers, bureaucrats and professionals, often called the *bourgeoisie*—felt they had earned the right to political power and only in France they did not possess it. The other part of the third estate, the rural workforce and the peasants who owned land, had achieved an improved standard of living and education and wanted to acquire the same rights as the aristocratic landowners and to be free to augment their wealth. Furthermore, since the early 1700s, advan-

---

[7] French term for *philosophers*, the aclaimed intelectuals of the XVIII Enlightenment in France who applied reason to the study of many areas of knowledge like philosophy, history, science, politics, economics, sociology and government. They endorsed progress and tolerance, distrusted organized religion and in particular the Catholic Church, as well as all feudal institutions. Most of them contributed to *Denis Diderot* and *Jean le Rond s' Alembert's* **Encyclopédie** (1751-1772), a gigantic editorial effort (requiring over 1,800 printers and artisans) consisting of 28 volumes, almost 72,000 articles before it merited "*privilèges de publication suspendus*" by the Parlament of Paris in 1759. The **Encyclopédie** had to go underground until 1765 with Neufchâtel, Switzerland, as the place of publication, although the printing presses continued to be located in Paris.

[8] Some of Voltaire's books reached printed editions of 200,000 copies, a level not ever seen by any author in Europe.

[9] The political system by which peasants (vassals to the crown) received a piece of land in return for serving the king, especially during times of war. Vassals were expected to perform various duties in exchange for their own fiefs, or areas of land.

The gardens and the interior of the *Chateau de Versailles*, at the top of the period of royal opulence in France.

ces in the sciences had reduced the mortality rate among adults with an unprecedented increase in population of France during the rest of the century: by the end of the 1790s the residents had doubled. France was then the most populated country of Europe; it had increased 6 million during the century to reach 26 million inhabitants. Compounding the problem of an ever increasing population was the fact that there had been a general rise in prices throughout the West during the century. By the end of the 1790s there was an additional quandary in the French economy: the French treasury was faced with the heavy expenditures caused by the wars of the 1700s. Louis XVI, now the King of France, sought to raise money by taxing the nobles and clergy, who had hitherto been respected and exempt. He resorted to the argument of every enlightened despot before him.

> «In times of crisis, the King's role is to rule, the role of the followers is to obey. The King best knows how to save the state from disasters.»

This provoked a steep reaction throughout France from the until then privileged second and third estates.

On June 7, 1788, the French revolted in Grenoble. Poor harvests and the high cost of bread resulted in an uprising sparked by the attempts of Cardinal Étienne Charles de Loménie de Brienne, the Archbishop of Toulouse and Controller-General of Louis XVI, to abolish the Parliament in order to enact a new tax to deal with France's unmanageable public debt. The third estate could not tolerate the callous refusal of the privileged classes, the Church and the aristocracy, to relinquish any of their fiscal privileges. The King responded by sending troops to the area to put down the revolt. They were received by townspeople on the roofs of the *Jesuit College* hurling down a rain of roof tiles on the soldiers.[10]

On August 8, the crown decided to call the *Estates General*, which had not been assembled since 1614. On August 24 Jacques Necker,[11] assumed the title of Director General of Finances and began to devise a plan for a successful meeting of the Estates General. Through the rest of the year a poor harvest augured a rising level of hunger, desperation and violence throughout France.

---

[10] The event is known as the ***Journée des Tuiles***, the Day of the Tiles.

[11] ***Necker*** was a protestant and a Swiss citizen; Louis XVI aparently tried to keep intact the support of the Catholic clergy and the aristocrats by appointing a very capable foreign economist that would not compromise him.

The **Estates General meeting** of 1789; **Louis XIV** of France, the king who built Versailles; his son **Louis XV**, the elegant king of France; **Jacques Necker**, the economist who could have preventred the French Revolution; **Joseph Sieyès**, the writer who asked and responded the question *What is the Third Estate?*

The man who had to be presiding the Estates General in 1789 and face this economic and political crisis in France did not have the stamina or the ambitions of his grandfather Louis XIV or his predecessor Louis XV. He received from the House of Bourbon «... *a heavy legacy, with ruined finances, unhappy subjects, and a faulty and incompetent government.*» He naively thought, however, that «... *the French people still had confidence in royalty, and his accession to the throne would be welcomed with enthusiasm.*»

An *Assembly of Notables* took place in November of 1788 to organize the upcoming *Estates General*. Following the tradition of 1614, it decided that each Estate would have one vote, giving the Clergy and the Nobles a combined majority 2 to 1 votes. Louis XVI agreed to those conditions but in order to please the Third Estate proposed that it would have twice the number of participants as the Clergy and the Nobles.

The Third State was not amused by that gesture of Louis XVI; just before the first meeting of the Estates General, a 30 year old Roman Catholic clergyman educated at the Seminary of Saint Sulpice in Paris published a pamphlet entitled *Qu'est-ce que le tiers-état?*, What is the Third Estate? The author was the Abbé Emmanuel Joseph Sieyès (1784-1836), Vicar General of the cathedral of Chartres. The answer that the Abbé Sieyès gave to his own question was very simple: [12] The Third Estate, the common people of France, was a complete nation in itself and had no need for the "dead weight" of the other two Estates.

The elections of representatives to the *Estates General* took place during February of 1789. According to tradition the elected members had the option of sending to the organizers their own *Cahiers de Doléances*, writings with summaries of their complaints and dissatisfaction with the *status quo*. Thousands of *Cahiers* inundated the offices of the organizers.

It was decided that on May 5 the *Estates General* would open their deliberations in Versailles. As the representatives prepared themselves to travel to Versailles, news broke out about riots that were occurring in Paris at the factories of *Jean-Baptiste Réveillon*, a wall paper manufacturer, and *Dominique Henriot*, a saltpeter ma-

---

[12] The exact words of the Abbé Sieyès were: «Qu'est-ce que le Tiers-État ? *Tout*. Qu'a-t-il été jusqu'à présent dans l'ordre politique ? *Rien*.Que demande-t-il ? *À y devenir quelque chose.*» (What is the Third Estate? *Everything*. What has it been until now in the political order? *Nothing*. What does it ask? *To become something*).

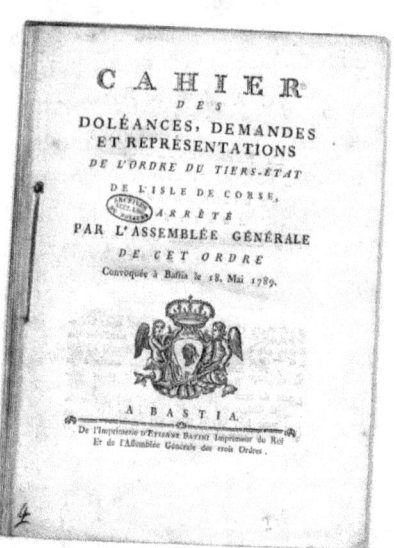

Honoré Gabriel Riqueti. **Marquis de Mirabeur**, a member of the Second Estate (Nobility) who became leader of the Third Estate; a **Book of Doleances** (complaints) that people could bring to the Estates General; a scene from the **riot at the Reveillon** factory, one of the first acts of violence at the onset of the French Revolution.

er, on April 27 and 28, both in the St. Antoine district of the capital. The riots at *Réveillon's* had been unusual in pre-revolutionary France; the factory was functioning in the absence and without the normal control of a guild. The rioters spared *Réveillon's* factory building but not his personal home.[13] In the case of *Henriot's*, who had called the workers "*la canaille*" (riffraff, rabble, scoundrel), the rioters were initially complaining about the price of bread and burned down the facilities.[14] In both instances the rioters were shouting «*Vive le Tiers État*».

Up until that moment, there were no other major riots in any city in France, in spite of the government failure to manage the food crisis.[15] «*The revolution was not yet in people's heads*,» according to Tocqueville; ordinary folks retained very old and ingrained notions of the polity that manifested itself in earlier times of trouble and after the revolution would characterize French citizens for many years to come. As a measure of precaution, the government began to move troops to the perimeter of Paris.

On January 24, 1789, the Estates General had been summoned by a royal edict sent to all provinces. It announced:

« *We have need of a concourse of our faithful subjects, to assist us surmount all the difficulties we find relative to the state of our finances .... These great motives have resolved us to convoke the* **Assemblée des**

---

[13] They made their way to **Reveillon's house** on rue de Montreuil and, after a long struggle against the guards, broke in, vandalized the furniture, smashed the windows and burned his belongins. Soldiers coming to the rescue were met with a shower of stones that killed several of them. As the rioters stormed the house and went to the *caves* in the basement, some drank themselves to stupor with fine wines while others mistakenly drank acids and dyes intended for the wallpaper factory and died in horrible convulsions.

[14] At both factories workers were paid 15 sous a a day at a time when the price of a 4 lb. loaf of bread was 14 sous. Unlike other bread riots in Paris, in 1789 there had been no governmental price fixing, pillage of baker's shops or destruction of merchants granaries.

[15] The only known exceptions were: at **Brignolles**, near Toulon, the seigneur M. de Montferrat was attacked by a crowd that dismembered him with an axe; at **Aubagne**, near Marseille, the leader of the *vignerons* drafted the *Cahier de Doléances* without any imput from the people and was severely beaten; at **Toulon** the townspeople revolted, took over the *Hôtel de Ville*, pillaged the bishop's residence and tossed his carrier into the harbour; in **Aix-en-Provence** the crowds attacked and burned the houses of the mayor, the tax assessor, the royal Intendant and the town tax collector.

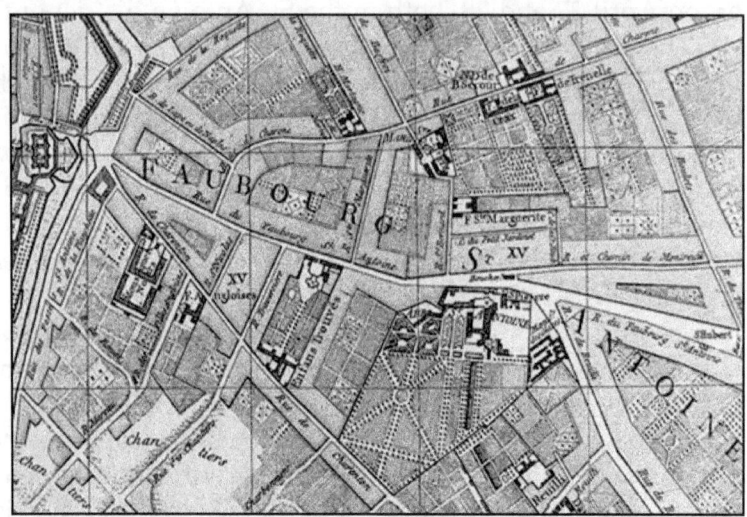

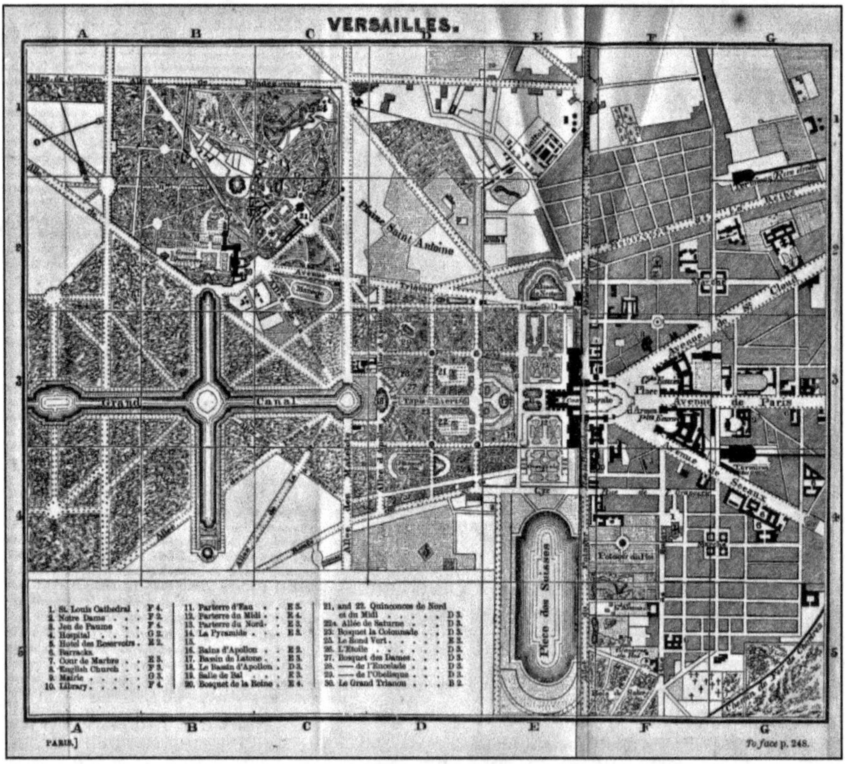

The *Faubourg* (neighborhood) *of San Antoine*, where most of the revolutionary riots started in 1789. A *plan of Versailles* in 1789, showing the main building and the gardens.

États of all the provinces under our authority... we promise to address the grievances of our people...»

The *Letters de Convocation* of January 24 included a *Règlement* prescribing the methods of the elections to the three Estates.

The First Estate elected 303 delegates, representing 100,000 Catholic clergy; the Church owned about 10 percent of the land and collected its own taxes (tithe) on peasants. The lands were controlled by bishops and abbots of monasteries, but two-thirds of the First Estate delegates were ordinary parish priests; only 51 were bishops. About a third of the 282 deputies representing the Second Estate were nobles, mostly with minor holdings. The Third Estate representation was doubled to 578 men, representing 95 percent of the population of France. Half were well educated lawyers or local officials; some were even nobles that decided to represent the people and not the aristocracy.[16] Nearly a third were in trades or industry; 51 were wealthy land owners.

In total, the number of delegates elected was about 1200, half of whom were from the Third Estate. The nobles in the Second Estate were the richest and most powerful people in the kingdom, very loyal to Louis XVI. Not so in the First Estate, where a large amount of priests and nuns elected low level parish priests over noble Bishops. The landless and working city men were under represented in the Third Estate.

In terms of the *Cahiers de Doléances*, the main grievance returned was about taxes, which people considered a crushing burden on their economy; the second was the privileges assigned to the nobles, particularly those that excused them from taxation; the third was an almost unanimous complaint about the ubiquitous tolls and duties levied by the nobility on internal commerce and travel through the country's roads.

On May 5 1789, amidst wide-ranging celebrations, the Estates General opened in one of the courtyards of the *Hôtel des Menus Plaisirs* in the town of Versailles near the royal château. The Clergy and Nobility sat in their full regalia, while the deputies from the Third Estate were far from the podium, as dictated by the protocol. Soon a serious problem arose as Charles Louis François de Paule de Barentin, the Keeper of the Seals of France, addressed the

---

[16] These were passionate revolutionaries. Eventually, having been elected by the Third Estate did not save them from the guillotine during the Terror as we shall see later.

The salon to play tennis, used as meeting room of the *National Assembly*; the Church of St. Louis in Versailles, both scenes of the initial events of the French Revolution.

deputies: Louis XVI had assigned one vote to each Estate (voting by orders) but the delegates of the Third Estate had expected that there would be one vote per delegate.

After a serious floor discussion Louis XVI decided to grant one vote to every delegate rather than three votes in total, one vote per Estate.[17] This concession, wrung from the monarchy by endless deliberations, was viewed as a sign of weakness rather a magnanimous gift from the King. It was the first mistake —of many to follow— on the part of Louis XVI, which was constantly giving the impression that he was utterly bored by the proceedings.

Facing such a critical issue, even after the King's concession, the assembled delegates reached a serious impasse. Necker, the astute financier, did not have the instincts of a good politician and did not know how to continue when the delegates were all shouting to each other. The leadership of the meeting fell into the hands of Comte Honoré Mirabeau, a noble who had been elected by the Third Estate, and the Abbé Sieyès, a clergyman that had also been elected by the Third Estate. Both Mirabeau and Sieyès invited the representatives of the Third Estate to meet separately and began to call themselves the *Communes*.

Having lost their track, the representatives of the Estates General wasted almost a month bogged down in discussions about credentials. On June 13 two radical moves dissolved the proceedings. The *Communes* redefined themselves as a *National Assembly*, leaving out the nobles and the clergy. They began to meet separately at the *Salle des États*. Louis XVI resisted and decreed voided all reforms, agreements and decisions taken at the *Salle des États*; furthermore, he order the *Salle* emptied and locked. The Third Estate, now baptized as the *National Assembly*, moved its deliberations to the *Jeu de Paume*, a nearby tennis court in the Saint-Louis district of Versailles, from where they were also expelled by the King's guards. Under the leadership of Honoré Mirabeau they moved to the Church of Saint Louis, a parish built by Louis XV in the heart of Versailles in 1743 which the members of the National Assembly renamed the *Temple de l'Abondance*.

---

[17] The clergy and the nobility had their own grievances against royal absolutism but the most pressing problem on the floor of the Estates General was the need for more taxation. Voting by Estate the crown would be able to secure new taxes 2 to1. If each delegate had one vote, the Third Estate could prevent increases in taxes, to the detriment of the First and Second Estates, who were tax-exempted and had nothing to lose if taxes were increased.

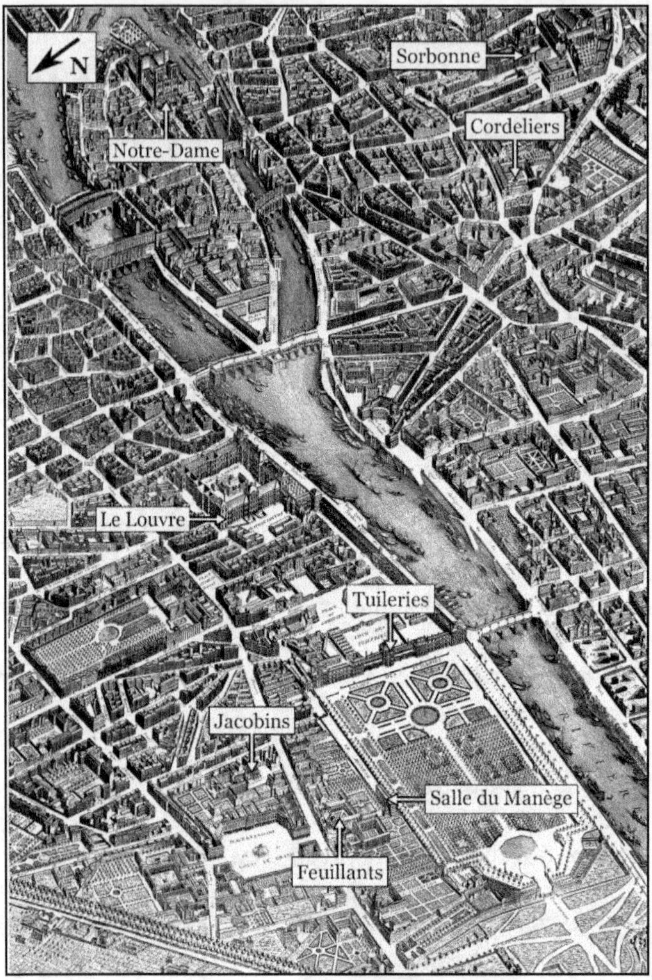

A *map of central Paris* at the time of the French Revolution;
French King *Louis XVI* making a toast for the Revolution, June 20, 1972.

The delegates of the Third Estate, while meeting at the indoor *Jeu de Paume*, had taken a collective oath «*not to separate, and to reassemble whenever circumstances require, until the constitution of the kingdom is established.*» This *Serment du Jeu de Paume* came to have a major significance in the revolution that was about to occur in France. The oath was a revolutionary act, an assertion that political authority derived from the people and not from the monarch. It signified that French citizens did not owe loyalty to Louis XVI; the National Assembly's refusal to yield to the king's will, forced the crown of France, for the first time, to make political concessions.

Within days of the *Serment du Jeu de Paume*, on June 27, Louis XVI ordered the clergy and the nobility to join with the Third Estate in the *National Assembly*, attempting to give the false impression that the National Assembly had been organized with his blessing. In the days that followed, the actions of the National Assembly drew heavily from the July 4, 1776 *United States Declaration of Independence* adopted by the *Second Continental Congress* meeting in Philadelphia declaring the thirteen colonies a sovereign state.[18] Nevertheless, concerned by the boldness of the Third Estate, Louis XVI ordered the army to send reinforcements to the garrisons in the outskirts of Paris. In the capital, hundreds of belligerent demonstrators gathered at the *Palais-Royal* to listen to speeches from disaffected citizens complaining about the stage of siege of the city.

Within a few days the Estates General ceased to exist. The newly designated *National Assembly* moved from Versailles to Paris and became on 9 July 1789 the *Assemblée Nationale Constituante*, the National Constitutional Assembly; it declared itself to have full authority and power to decree law. Their primary task was to draw up and adopt a constitution. It would dissolve on 30 September 1791 to be succeeded by the *Assemblée Législative*, a unicameral Legislative Assembly.

---

[18] One of the most graphic representations of the influence of the *1776 United States Declaration of Independence* on the *Serment du Jeu de Paume* is the magnificent 1789 painting by Jean-Louis David. **Thomas Jefferson** is shown standing on a table at the center of the painting, declaiming in the fashion of a French Jacobin, while to his left the Jacobin *Jean-Sylvain Bailly*, leader of the meeting is pointing to Jefferson, as if asking the members to pay attention to his words.

Two views of the **Bastille**: in peaceful times and the day of the **Fall of the Bastille**, July 14, 1789, a not so important event that nevertheless became the most important image of the start of the French Revolution in 1789 Paris.

On July 11 Jacques Necker was dismissed by Louis XVI, who regretted that his popular minister had failed in his passionate effort to find a solution to the budgetary crisis.

A few days later, no one could have anticipated that the situation could get much worse. Parisians, many from the class of artisans and journeyman workers from the *Faubourg St. Antoine*, were alarmed by the gathering of troops, angry at the dismissal of Necker and irritated by the price of grain. They decided to take the situation under their control and set a siege and took command of the *Bastille*, a fortress in eastern Paris, known formally as the *Bastille Saint-Antoine* that would play an important role in the French internal conflict; for most of its history it had been used as a state prison by the kings of France.[19]

The mobs initially took 3,000 rifles and some cannons from the *Invalides*, a few kilometers downriver in Paris. They then marched to the Bastille and demanded that it be opened and its gunpowder delivered to them. The Swiss Guards inside fired on the crowd. About 100 persons were killed. The assailants prevailed and took with them several tons of valuable gunpowder held within the fortress. Only seven prisoners were found inside and were released; the Bastille's governor, Bernard-René de Launay, was killed by the mobs. The Bastille became one of Europe's most famous symbols of cruel and arbitrary power.

Shortly thereafter, on July 16 and upon the insistence of the *Assemblée Nationale Constituante*, Jacques Necker was recalled to his post as Director General of Finances and Minister of State.

On the night of August 4, 1789, The National Constituent Assembly, following a proposal by the Viscount of Noailles, abo-

---

[19] The **Bastille** had been built in 1357 to defend the eastern approach to the city of Paris from the English threat in the *Hundred Years' War*. It was a very strong fortress with eight towers that protected the strategic gateway of the **Porte Saint-Antoine** on the eastern edge of Paris. Its design was very influential in both France and England and was widely copied. It figured prominently in France's domestic conflicts, including the fighting between the *Burgundians* and the *Armagnacs* in the 15th century, as well as the *Wars of Religion* in the 16th. The fortress became a state prison in 1417; this role was expanded under **Louis XI** in the 1460s to incorporate debtors to the state and upper class delinquents. The fortress had played a key role in the rebellion of the *Fronde* which was fought beneath its walls in 1652. The fortress was eventually demolished and many pieces of stone were transported around France as souvenirs and displayed as icons of the overthrow of despotism. Most of the stones were recycled and used on bridges and palaces in and around Paris. Nothing was left of the Bastille except some remains of its stone foundations; they were relocated to the side of the Boulevard Henri IV near the Seine river.

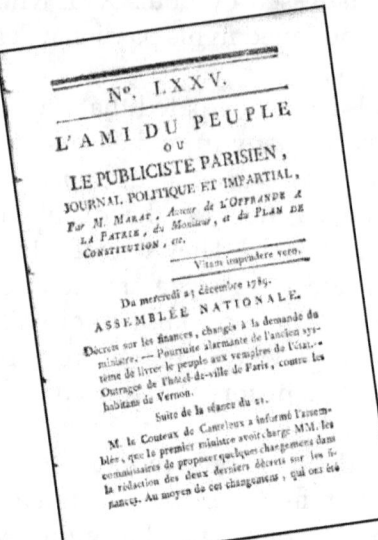

Jean-Paul Marat, political theorist and amateur scientist who became best known for his role as a radical journalist and politician during the French Revolution and his pamphet *L'Ami du People* (the people's friend); Typical revolutionaries at the front of one of the many protests marches at the start of the Revolution.

lished the feudal system entirely, both the seigniorial rights of the Second Estate (the nobility, with the support of the Duke d'Aiguillon) and the tithes gathered by the First Estate (the Catholic clergy, with the support of the Bishops of Nancy and Chartres). The old judicial system that had jurisdiction on the 13 regional parliaments, was suspended the following November 1789, and finally abolished in 1790. The records show that on the span of a few night hours...

> «Without debate the Assembly enthusiastically adopted equality of taxation and redemption of all manorial rights except for those involving personal servitude, which were to be abolished without indemnification. Other proposals were approved with the same speed: the equality of legal punishment, admission of all to public office, abolition of venality in office, the purchase of a public office, conversion of the tithe into payments subject to redemption, freedom of worship, prohibition of plural holding of benefices, privileges of game-laws, seigneurial courts, the purchase and sale of posts in the magistracy, pecuniary immunities, favoritism in taxation, and unmerited pensions..... including all privileges of provinces and towns which were offered as a last sacrifice. The aristocratic society was destroyed from top to bottom, along with its structure of dependencies and privileges. For the old structure they substituted the modern, autonomous individual, free to do whatever was not prohibited by law... »

The Assembly was carried away by its enthusiasm and the atmosphere inside the Assembly was so heady and the decision so radical that confusion reigned in the provinces for months afterwards as to the true meaning of the laws.

As to the rest of the year 1789, a few events would become of extraordinary importance for the future of the revolution. On September 12, Jean-Paul Marat (1743-1793), a reputable and wealthy Swiss physician, political theorist and journalist who had become the hoarsest voice of the revolution, published an eight-page pamphlet called *L'Ami du Peuple* (The Friend of the People), proposing outrageous social entitlements for the poor and the middle classes that enraged aristocrats, particularly those who opposed an egalitarian distribution of property.[20] In his pamphlet, *Offrande à la Patrie* ("Offering to the Nation"), he had argued that that society should provide fundamental needs such as food, education and

---

[20] **Marat** was a radical supporter of the *sans-culottes* (radical common people of the lower classes; originaly a term of contempt applied by the aristocrats but later adopted as a popular designation by the revolutionaries) and the *Commune of Paris* (the government of the city of Paris from 1789 until 1795).

The ***famous March of Women towards Versailles*** to force the royal family to return to Paris and do something to alleviate the scarcity of food; The revolutionaries taken an ***oath of loyalty to clerics*** as the only choice they had to continue their ministery legally.

shelter to all people if it expected all its citizens to follow its laws. His views were so radical that by 1790 he was forced into hiding, often in the sewers of Paris, where he contracted a debilitating chronic skin disease (possibly *dermatitis herpetoformis*) which forced him to take medicinal vinegar baths; as we will see later, bathing in a tub full of vinegar would be the reason for his death in 1793.[21]

A second important event in 1789 took place in October 5 and 6 of that year. Parisians, led by a large number of women, marched upon Versailles and forced the royal family to move back to Paris, where they took up residence at the *Tuileries*. Louis XVI was from there on considered by many a prisoner of the mobs in Paris. The National Assembly, still in Versailles, declared in the spirit of constitutional monarchy its inseparability from the king and its meetings were transferred to a building on the garden side of *rue de Rivoli*, half way between Louis XVI residence in the *Tuileries Palace* to the *Place Louis XV*, later known as *Place de la Révolution* (today Place de la Concorde).

Finally, a third important event was the expropriation of all Church property, which were paid for in *assignats*, a form of paper money which was easily falsified and promptly became useless.

As 1790 began, the National Assembly prohibited and declared null all monastical vows, disbanded and abolished all religious orders and confirmed voided all aristocratic and hereditary titles. From there on the Marquis de Lafayette would simply be called Citizen Lafayette.

On July 12, the National Assembly adopted the *Civil Constitution of the Clergy*. It granted itself the right to appoint all church officers, from archbishop down, and established a Gallican Catholic Church, subordinating the Roman Catholic Church in France to the French government. Some support for this measure came from figures within the Church, such as the revolutionary priest Henri Grégoire. King Louis XVI was initially opposed, but ultimately acquiesced to the measure. The circle that started in August 11, 1789 with the abolition of the tithes, on November 2, 1789 with the confiscation of Church property and on February 13, 1790 with the

---

[21] **Marat** was inmortalized by Jacques-Louis David famous painting *The Death of Marat*, where he is shown as he was murdered inside his bathtub by a women of the right called Carlotta Corday.

The ***Fête de la Federation*** in 1790, a massive holiday festival commemorating the first anniversary of the Fall of the Bastille. It provided an illusory image of national unity; ***Gilbert the Motier, Marquis de Lafayette***, known in the US simply as Lafayette, member of the Estates General upon returning to France, co-author of the Declaration of the Rights of Man, Commander in Chief of the National Guard; the ***French National Guard flag*** in 1790.

dissolution of the orders and congregations, was now closed on April 19, 1790 with the subordination of all religious authority, credo and dogma to the National Assembly.

As the first anniversary of the storming of the Bastille approached, the National Constituent Assembly declared a *Grande Fête de la Fédération* on the *Champ de Mars*, in celebration of the anniversary of July 14.[22]

By way of prelude to this patriotic fête, on June 20, the Assembly, at the urging of the popular members of the nobility, abolished all titles, armorial bearings, liveries and orders of knighthood, destroying the symbolic paraphernalia of the *ancien régime*. This further alienated the more conservative nobles, and added to the ranks of the émigrés.

One of the participants in this grandiose celebration was Marie-Joseph Paul Yves Roch Gilbert du Motier, Marquis de Lafayette (1757-1834), the French aristocrat and military officer who fought for the United States in the American Revolutionary War.[23] He had been appointed by Louis XVI as Commander in Chief of *la Garde Nationale*, the new French National Guard,[24] or, as it was initially called, the *Bourgeois Guard*. The formation of this outfit had been discussed by the National Assembly on July 11, 1789 in response to the rapidly spread anger and violence throughout Paris. The National Assembly created this paramilitary organization on July 13. In the early morning of the next day, the search for weapons for this new militia led to the storming of the *Hotel des Invalides* and then the storming of the Bastille.

---

[22] The ***Champ de Mars*** is the large public greenspace in Paris, located in today's seventh arrondissement, between the Eiffel Tower to the northwest and the École Militaire to the southeast.

[23] When ***Lafayette***, the hero of Yorktown, as he was known in America, went back to France he also became a French hero. He was welcomed by Louis XVI in Versailles and congratulated on his military victories and was admired all over the country for his ideas on freedom and equality.

Lafayette participated in the meeting of the *Estates General* and joined the *National Assembly* when the negociations failed. He worked on the *Declaration of the Rights of Man and of the Citizen* which was adopted on August 26th, 1789 by the *National Constituent Assembly*. Louis XVI named him commander in chief of the National Guard, the military hand of the newly created Assembly. In France, and on a legendary visit to the United States, Lafayette always used the blue, white and red French cockade as a personal symbol.

[24] The ***National Guard*** existed from 1789 until 1872. It was separate from the French Army and existed both for policing and as a military reserve.

The *seal of the Jacobines*; a portrait of Charles Maurice de **Talleyrand**-Périgord, French bishop, politician and diplomat who survived during the revolution and became an important supporter of Napoleon; a view of the **Jacobin Club** meeting building near the Palace of the Tuileries.

On July 14, 1790, Lafayette led his troops, dressed for the most important of events, on the *Champ de Mars* next to Louis XVI and his family; an obscure and intriguing bishop of Autumn, Charles de Talleyrand [25] performed a mass in an altar erected and profusely decorated for such occasion, and all participants swore an oath of «*fidelity to the nation, the law, and the king.*» The celebrations went on for several days.

Later in 1790 the first signs of trouble began to emerge in a society that had so drastically changed itself. Several small counter-revolutionary uprisings broke out across France trying to turn all or part of the army against the revolution. The inspiration came from the royal court, which was «*encouraging every anti-revolutionary enterprise while avowing none.*» Mirabeau, a noble himself, was trying his best as peacemaker, reminding the royal family that they were living in the Tuileries, under the generally benevolent guardianship of Lafayette and his National Guard. He also reminded the revolutionaries that what was keeping peace in the country was the consent of Louis XVI to preside over the revolution even if it offered no guarantees that the revolution would always vouch for him. At the time, everyone knew that the guards protecting Louis XVI and his family from occasional popular outbursts, were also fending off any efforts by royalists, particularly the Austrians, to spirit them out of Paris.

It was during those uncertain years after the fall of the Bastille that political clubs began to emerge inside and outside the Constitutional Assembly. Foremost among them was the *Club of the Jacobins*. By august 10, 1790 there were over 150 such Clubs across France. The *Jacobin Club* was heterogeneous and it initially included both prominent parliamentary factions, the radical *Mountain Group*, whose members sat at the left side of the meeting room and the more moderate *Girondists*, who sat at the right. In the early times of the French revolution, up until 1792, the *Girondists* domi-

---

[25] **Charles Maurice de Talleyrand-Périgord**, prince de Bénévent, Prince de Talleyrand, was an impious French bishop, crafty politician and cynical diplomat. He worked at the highest levels of successive French governments, most commonly as foreign minister or in some other diplomatic capacity. His career spanned the regimes of Louis XVI, the years of the French Revolution, Napoleon, Louis XVIII, and Louis-Philippe. Those he served often distrusted Talleyrand but, like Napoleon, found him extremely useful.

A view of the *carriages* that took the condemned to the guillotine down the rue de Saint Honoré, a meeting of the *Girondines*, the moderate political group during the revolution.

nated the *Jacobin Club* [26] and led the country. One of its most notable leaders was an English American political activist, philosopher and revolutionary called Thomas Paine, one of the founding fathers of the United States.[27]

By October 1790, Louis XVI was feeling very insecure for himself and his family and decided to explore a possible coalition with foreign powers to end the Revolution. He wrote a letter to his cousin Charles IV of Spain, complaining of the *Civil Constitution of the Clergy* and began to make overtures to the Austrians, whose royal family included his wife Marie Antoinette.[28]

After a religion-neutral end of the year 1790, when the National Assembly discouraged any references about the birth of Christ during the holidays, the year 1791 started with an abolition of all guilds which provided training for those entering into the artisan crafts; the responsibility was completely absorbed by the state. By June all worker unions, strikes and *compagnonnage* (apprenticeship with a master) were prohibited by *Le Chapelier Law*, a legislation advocated and drafted by Isaac René Guy le Chapelier, one of the founders of the *Jacobin Club* and its first president.

Louis XVI was hysterical and could no longer wait for a coalition of royal European houses to come into French territory to rescue his family. He decided to snick out of France. He was par-

---

[26] The name **Jacobins**, formally called the *Société des Amis de la Constitution*, came about because they initially met at a Dominican Convent located in the rue St. Jacques (in Latin *Jacobus*); it was originally named the *Club Breton*, formed at Versailles during the Estates General by deputies from Brittany. Among the early members were Mirabeau, Sieyès, and Robespierre, who met in secret at very unlikely and concealed places. The name *Jacobins* was given to the group in ridicule by its enemies.

[27] **Paine**, a close friend of Benjamin Franklin, was the author of two of the most influential pamphlets at the start of the war of independence of the United States; *Common Sense* (1776) and *The American Crisis* (1776-1783). He was a *corsetmaker* by trade, a *journalist* by profession, and a *propagandist* by inclination. According to President John Adams, «*Without the pen of the author of Common Sense, the sword of Washington would have been raised in vain.*»

[28] **Marie Antoinette** (1755-1793) had been born *Maria Antonia Josepha JohAna von Habsburg-Lothringen, Archduchess of Austria*; she was the fifteenth and second youngest child of Francis I, Holy Roman Emperor and Empress Maria Theresa. Despite her initial popularity as the young wife of the French King, most French people eventually came to dislike her, accusing *L'Autrichienne*, (the Austrian woman, a nickname given her upon her arrival to France by the daughters of Louis XV), of being profligate, promiscuous, and disloyal, harbouring sympathies for France's enemies, particularly her native Austria.

The **arrest of Louis XVI** at Varennes and the arrival of the caravan that took him to Temple (the building on the right), the **former monastery of the Templars**, converted during the revolution into a royal prison.

ticularly reassured of support by other European governments after March 10, 1791, when Pope Pius VI had publicly condemned *The Declaration of the Rights of Man and of the Citizen* and the *Civil Constitution of the Clergy*.

What turned out as a disastrous attempt of the royal family to escape from Paris began to build up during the first days of June of 1791. The King was short of cash to undertake the adventure and was financed by the Swedish Count Axel von Fersen and the Baron de Breteuil, who had garnered support from Swedish King Gustavus III. On June 21, the dauphin's governess, the Marquise de Tourzel dressed as a Russian baroness, the queen and the king's sister Madame Élisabeth played the roles of governess and nurse respectively, the king was clothed like a valet, and the royal children as two run of the mill aristocratic children; so disguised, the royal family began their attempted escape from the Tuileries.

Having such a large number of people in the journey, they required and obtained the use of a large carriage. It was their first and second mistake; the outsized vehicle was very conspicuous in the vicinity of the Tuileries and needed several changes of horses before reaching the frontiers to Austria. A third mistake was to arrange to meet a force of 10,000 regulars of the old royal army who were considered to still be loyal to the monarchy at Montmédy, a commune in the Meuse department in Lorraine in north-eastern France, close to the Austrian Netherlands border in what is now Belgium territory. Such a large concentration of troops arose the suspicions of revolutionaries that something serious was happening in the area. A fourth mistake was made when Louis XVI instinctively responded positively when Jean-Baptiste Drouet, the postmaster of Sainte-Menehould, a town of the road to Montmédy, recognized the king from his portrait printed on an assignat in his possession and addressed him as «*your majesty*.»

A detachment of revolutionary cavalry from Varennes, barely 50 kilometers from the Austrian border, was immediately dispatched to intercept the large and slow moving coach being used by the royal family; they arrested the entire party within sight of the advanced scouts of the two Swiss and four German mercenary regiments who were waiting for Louis XVI and his family. A final mistake had been not leaving the Tuileries with the support of Lafayette, who would have probably escorted the royal family as they ran towards the border.

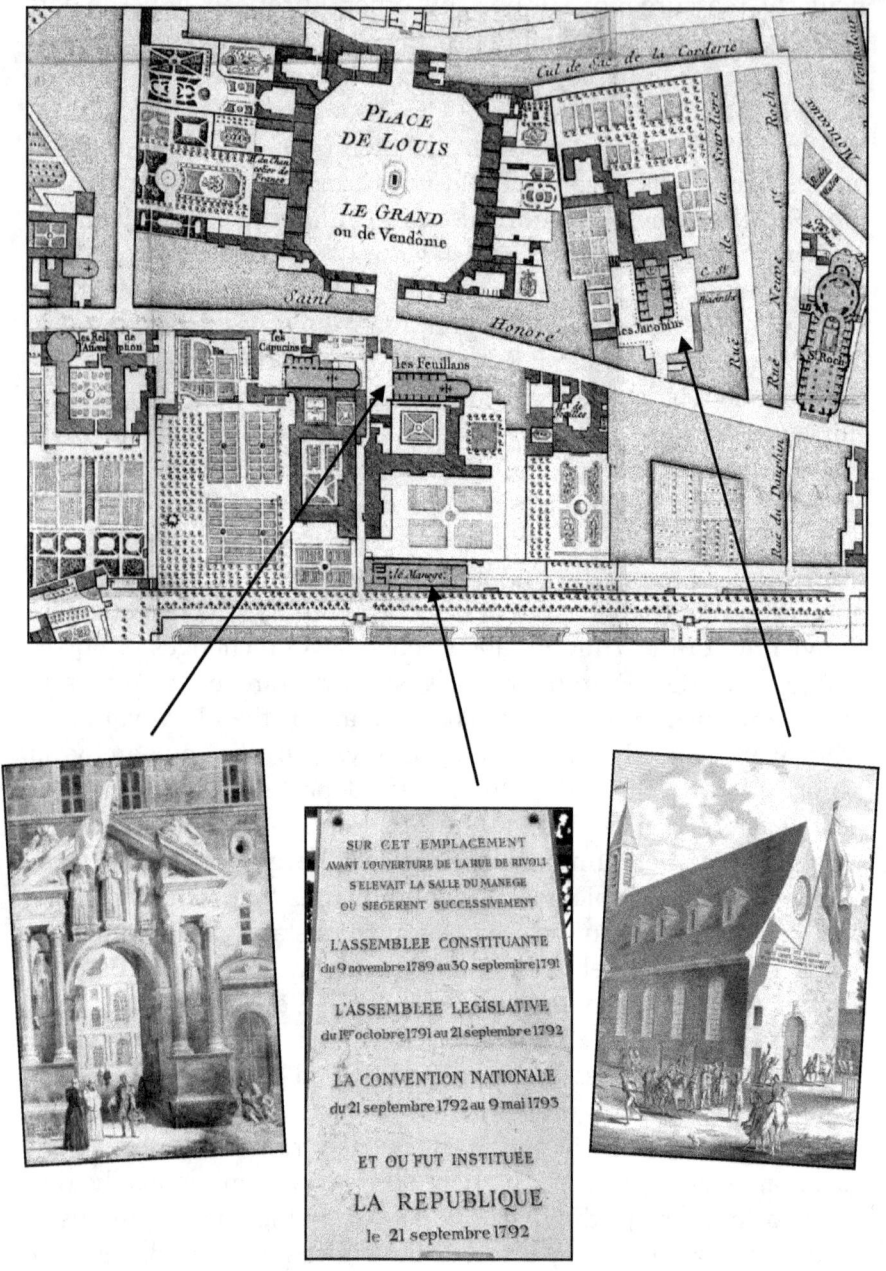

The area near la *Place Vendome* and the Northern border of the Garden de les Tuileries; on the left, the entrance to the *Convent of the Cordeliers*, in the center, the *plaque* along the fence of the garden showing the location of the Convention National, on the right, the *Salle des Jacobins* in 1794.

When the royals were returned under guard to Paris a revolutionary crowd was waiting for them at the Tuileries. They felt betrayed by the attempt of Louis XVI to escape France; his credentials as a constitutional monarch were seriously undermined by the escape attempt. The *Cordeliers* [29] and the *Jacobins* lobbied the National Constitutional Assembly to declare the King a prisoner and no longer a guest in the Tuileries. The *Cordeliers*, demanding the immediate formation of a republic, organized a violent demonstration in the *Champ-de-Mars* on July 17; the National Guard dispersed them, after inflicting 50 deaths and the Club was temporarily disbanded by orders of Lafayette. After the *Champ-de-Mars* massacre, a large group of Jacobins disassociated themselves from both the Jacobins and the Cordeliers and formed the Club of the *Feuillants*.[30]

On August 27, upon knowing of the humiliation of Louis XVI after the incident at Varennes, the rulers of Austria and Prussia agreed to stop the revolution in France at any cost. A week later, on September 3, the French Constitution of 1791 was proclaimed by the Constituent National Assembly, which met for the last time on September 30. France now had a constitutional monarchy and

---

[29] The **Cordeliers** were formally *La Société des Amis des Droits de l'Homme et du Citoyen* (The Society of the Friends of the Rights of Man and of the Citizen), a left leaning political Club within the National Assembly. The name indicated that they met at a Franciscan monastery (Franciscan priests tied their robes with a cord around their waist), hence they were *Cordeliers*. *Jean-Paul Marat* and *Georges Danton* were notable members of this club. After the failed flight to Varennes the Cordeliers began to meet at the Salle du Musée in the Place de Thionville, today the *Place Dauphine* on the *Île de la Cité*.

[30] The **Feuillants** were a split within the *Jacobin Club* composed mostly of moderate revolutionaries who wanted to preserve the position of the King and turn France into a constitutional monarchy. On July 16, 1791, they published a pamphlet disassociating themselves from the proyected July 17 demonstrations on the *Champs-de-Mars*. They regularly met at a monastry of *Feuillant monks* on rue Saint Honoré. The Feuillant monks were an ascetic branch of the *Cistercian monks* that had renounced the use of wine, fish, eggs, butter, salt, and all seasoning, eating solely barley bread, herbs cooked in water, and oatmeal. They consumed their food kneeling on the floor, walked barefoot in their monasteries, tended their gardens without tools, kept silent all day and slept only four hours a day on the floor or on bare planks with a stone for a pilow. During revolutionary times in France, the Feuillant monks had 24 abbeys in the country but less than 200 members. Most of them rejoined the Cistercian order in Italy when the French order was suppressed by the revolution.

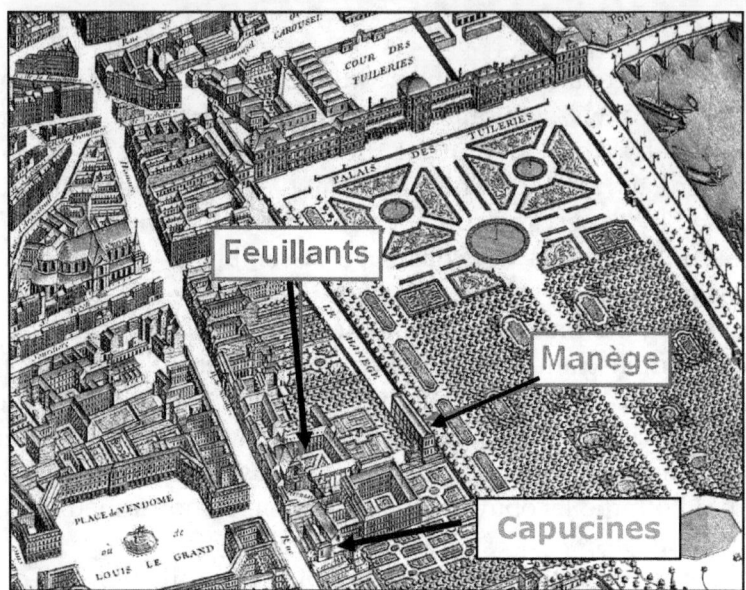

The indoor riding academy called the ***Salle du Manège*** ("Riding Hall"), was the seat of deliberations during most of the French Revolution, from 1789 to 1798. Before the revolution it was home to the royal equestrian academy. It was built by Louis XV. Soon the *Assemblée Nationale* extended its occupation to two adjacent convents, those of the ***Capuchins***, (it housed the Revolutionary printing presses), and of the ***Feuillants***, (which received the archives of the Assemblée).

On the right the image of ***Claude Rouget de Lisle***, author of *La Marseillese*.

a unicameral legislature; Louis XVI had veto powers over the action of the legislature. Only about 50,000 citizens were qualified to elect deputies provided they paid their taxes. All other citizens of France were considered "*inactive*" and were liberated from tax burdens.

The *Constituent National Assembly* turned itself into the *Legislative Assembly* on October 1, 1791. Its first order of business was to declare war against any country opposing the French Revolution. Jacques Pierre Brissot, a Parisian deputy, member of the *Girondines*, began to urge war against Austria. Maximilien Robespierre, formerly a public prosecutor at Versailles and a leader of the *Jacobins*, argued against war, fearing that France was ill-prepared. His opinions influenced many revolutionaries and Jacobins in the belief that the royalists wanted to plunge the country into war because a military defeat would mean the end of the Revolution.

On April 20, 1792, the King, with the consent of the Legislative Assembly, declared that France was in a state of war with Austria. It prompted Claude Rouget de Lisle (1760-1836), an engineer, captain of the army and royalist, to pledge his support to the king and refuse to take the oath of allegiance to the new constitution. Instead, he composed the words and music of *Chant de Guerre pour l'Armée du Rhin*. The song would later be known as *La Marseillaise* and become the French national anthem.[31]

By June of that year the tensions on the streets of Paris increased over a law ordering the deportation of all priests that had not sworn loyalty to the state over the Church; Louis XVI vetoed this law, as well as the dismantling of the king's *Constitutional Garde* (6,000 men), and the stationing of 20,000 troops loyal to the Assembly in the area of the Champ de Mars de Paris. Furthermore, Louis XVI challenged the Assembly by dismissing his *Jacobin* ministers and replacing them with more moderate *Feuillants*. When the Assembly objected, Lafayette sent a strong letter to the Assembly condemning the Jacobins.

Lafayette's actions provoked the revolutionary crowds. A march of 10,000 men and women from the neighborhoods of St.

---

[31] **Rouget** died in poverty in Choisy-le-Roi, forgotten by the general public even after Louis Philippe d'Orleans had awarded him the *Legion of Honor*. In 1915 his ashes were transferred to the *Invalides*, when the French government needed to raise the moral and patriotism of its citizens in the midst of World War I.

Antoine and St. Marcel invaded the Tuileries on June 20, demanding the return of the Jacobin ministers. Louis XVI timidly tried to calm the rioters by showing up on a balcony donning the *bonnet phrygien*[32] that had become the symbol of the revolutionaries and making a toast to the health of the Parisian people.

Things went from bad to worse when the Duke of Brunswick, commanding general of the Austro-Prussian Armies, warned Parisians publicly to obey Louis XVI or risk severe punishments from his army. The Assembly was offended. The Parisians began to arm themselves with rifles, knives, home-made catapults, stones and pistols. On July 29, at a meeting of the Jacobin Club, Maximilien Robespierre called for the overthrow of the king. Several battalions began to march on Paris. The *sans-culottes* from the St. Antoine neighborhood attacked the Tuileries and overwhelmed the Swiss Guards. Louis XVI, realizing that his French Garde was sympathetic to the Revolution and were shouting *Vive la Nation!,* decided to seek refuge at the Assembly building a few hundred feet down the gardens. He and his family ran through the Tuileries garden dressed only with their nightgowns. His troops, however, remained in position, trying to defend the palace; they were attacked, many of them were killed and the Tuileries was taken and pillaged. [33]

As the royal family were experiencing the end of the respect with which they were accustomed, Maximilien Robespierre began to encourage the notion that France needed a new type of army officers and popular militias rather than the soldiers and officers produced by the aristocratic *École Militaire*. The recruitment of such a new promotion for the army ranks began immediately. Robespierre, for the first time, called for the end of the monarchy.

---

[32] The **Phrygian cap** is a soft conical hat with the top pulled forward; it was first used by the Phrygians (Greeks and Armenians) during the 4th century BC. In modern times it has been used in many national symbols, for instance, the Cuban coat of arms.

[33] Halfway between the Tuileries Palace and the Legislative Assembly building there was **a set of steps** that provided access to the garden fron the rue de Rivoli. These 13 steps were 22 feet across and on the 4th level from the garden level a young recruit watched in horror the royal family runing for their lives as they fled their home. The soldier would write in his diary that «*I could not believe that the populace could be so malicious that would forever disgrace the royal family by forcing them to run half dressed through the streets of Paris. If I were in charge of the government I would not have allowed that to happen.*» The name of this young recruit was Napoleon Bonaparte.

Contrary to what he had said after the arrest of the royal family at Varennes «*je ne suis ni monarchiste ni républicain*» (*I am neither monarchist nor republican,)* Robespierre began to press on the process to do away with the Bourbons. Under his inspiration the Assembly striped Louis XVI of his powers and declared him a prisoner of the nation. It also decreed the formation of a new assembly to be called a *Convention Nationale Française*, a French National Convention, which would write a new constitution to replace that of 1791. Six ministers were elected by the Assembly to oversee the national election of representatives to the *Convention Nationale*. The Assembly also authorized the arrest throughout France of suspected enemies of the Revolution and prohibited the publication of any and all Royalist newspapers.

The royal family were now imprisoned in the tower of the Temple, a former monastery of the Order of the Templars.[34] On August 13 Robespierre proposed to the Assembly the creation of a People's Tribunal to judge the king and other members of the monarchy. Two large groups of citizens refused to continue obeying the orders from the Assembly and declared themselves against the republic: the *Chouans*[35] and the citizens of the *Vendee*,[36] both in the western region of France.

Chaos ensued. Lafayette went into exile in Austria after failing to persuade his army to march with him upon Paris to dissolve

---

[34] The **Templars** or *Pauperes Commilitones Christi Templique Salomonici, l'Ordre du Temple* or *Templiers* in French, were formally named the **Poor Fellow-Soldiers of Christ and of the Temple of Solomon**, commonly known as the *Knights Templar*, or simply the *Templars*, a Catholic military order in existance since medieval times. They were among the wealthiest and most powerful of the **groups that protected** the financial and security viability of the **Christian faith**. The Temple was demolished by Napoleon to prevent pilgrimages by royalists.

[35] In the West of France, under the inspiration of Jean Cottereau, known as Jean Chouan, hundreds of insurgents, calling themselves the **Chouans** (mostly Catholic peasants), declared for the king and against the *Civil Constitution of the Clergy*. They confronted the National Army first in a guerrilla warfare and later in full scale battles.

[36] The **Vendée** is a department south of the Loire river in west-central France, on the Atlantic Ocean. There, tens of thousands of insurgents and civilians, were massacred by the French National Army in response to their revolt against the imprisonment of the king and the *Civil Constitution of the Clergy*. Prior to the massacre, religious orders were suppressed and church property confiscated and destroyed. The region was eventually "pacified" by virtue of a complete physical destruction. Many historians consider the actions of the French republican government during the War in the Vendée as the first modern ***genocide***.

A view of the grounds of the *Convent of the Templars*, taken over by the revolutionaries. On the top right of the picture, the building used as royal prison; the summary trials of *Vendéens and Chouans*, two large ethnic groups opposed to the revolution; a painting of the *Battle of Valmy*, the first military campaign won by the revolution against Prussian troops on September 20, 1792

the Convention. Prussian armies and French émigrés invaded France. By September of 1792 there were rumors that Verdun had fallen into Prussian hands. The revolution seemed to be collapsing. Prompted by Robespierre, the French National Army responded with unusual cruelty. There were massacres in Paris; over 1,500 prisoners were killed by soldiers and angry mobs. The capital was targeted by the Prussians for occupation; the defenders, however, defeated the Prussian troops in the Battle of Valmy. It was the first victory of a citizen army and a turning point in favor of the revolutionaries. Thousands of volunteers began to swell the revolutionary ranks. The myth of troops singing "*Ça Ira*" [37] while in battle defending the revolution spread all over France. Witnessing the Battle of Valmy was a young German writer and poet that had been conscripted into the Prussian army, Johann Wolfgang von Goethe.[38]

The Battle of Valmy was not only a serious setback to the most effective European army of its time, it became a decisive boost to the revolutionaries in France. On September 20, 1792, a single chamber elected by all Frenchmen twenty-five years old or more succeeded the Legislative Assembly. Due to the abstention of aristocrats and anti-republicans as well as the fear of victimization, the voter turnout across France was low – 11.9% of the electorate. On the whole, the electorate returned the same sort of men that had been in the Legislative Assembly. Once the election to the National Convention became known, the Legislative Assembly formally surrendered its authority.

In the absence of the royal family the Convention held its sessions in the Tuileries Palace, first in the *Salle du Manège*, and finally in the *Salle des Machines*, which had galleries for the public, who often influenced the debate by interruptions or by applause. For legislative and administrative issues the Convention appointed committees with extensive powers. The most famous of these

---

[37] "*Ça ira*" (French: "it'll be fine") became the emblematic song of the French Revolution after 1792. Interestingly, the music was a popular **contredanse** rhythm called *Le Carillon National*, often played by queen **Marie Antoinette** on her **harpsichord**. History has it that the title and theme of the song were inspired by Benjamin Franklin; when asked about the progress of the American Independence War he would reply: "*Ça ira, ça ira*" ("It'll be fine, it'll be fine").

[38] Goethe wrote in his diary: «*From this place, and from this day forth begins a new era in the history of the world, and I can all say that I was present at its birth.*»

A pinting showing **Robespierre** (sitting), **Danton** (cnter) and **Marat** (right) at a friendly meeting during revolutionary times. They ended up hating each other; *Danton on the way to the guillotine*; the statue of **Danton** erected at the Boulevard de Saint Germaine in Paris after the revolution.

committees became the *Comité de Salut Public*, the Committee of Public Safety.

Two main groups characterized the deliberations of the Convention: the *Gironde* and the *Mountain*. The *Girondins*, sometime also called the *Brissotin*, represented the interests of the provinces rather than Paris; they were in the minority and had a conservative approach to governance. Their name was derived from the Gironde, the region of France were many of the deputies of this faction originated. The *Montagnards*, comprised a majority of the deputies; they were much more radical, and held strong connections to the *sans-culottes* of Paris. They drew that name because they sat on the high bleachers when the Convention was in session. The first issue of the Convention was the trial of Louis XVI. On the first session Robespierre prevailed over all other speakers and expressed: «*Louis must die so that the nation may live.*»

From the opening session of the Convention the *Girondins* showed no inclination to bring the king to trial; on the contrary, they genuinely wanted to save the king's life. They could not overcome the oratory of Robespierre who on December 2 declared: «*If the king is not guilty, then those who have dethroned him are.*» Within a matter of hours the Convention declared the King guilty of summoning the aid of foreign powers against the revolution and guilty of causing the ambush of *sans-coulottes* at the Tuileries on August 10, 1792. One of the most vocal members of the *Montagnards*, who became notable on these debates, was Georges Jacques Danton (1759-1794), [39] the first president of the *Committee of Public Safety*. He was perceived by the *Girondists* as...

> « an eloquent, dazzling, patriotic member of the Mountain who was unable to apprehend the fearful nature of the crisis, too full of vanity and exclusive party-spirit, and too fastidious to strike hands with those who had a different opinion.»

---

[39] **Danton's** role at the onset of the Revolution has been disputed; many historians describe him as «*the chief force in the overthrow of the monarchy and the establishment of the First French Republic.*» Others consider him «*a moderating influence on the Jacobins who sought leniency for the enemies of the Revolution.*» He was the first president of the *Cordeliers Club* and during the massacre of the *Champ de Mars* of July, 1791, he fled to England as an exile. He became a member of the *Paris Commune* upon his return in September, 1791 and became Minister of Justice on August 10, 1792 when the royal family had to take refuge on the building of the Legislative Assembly. During the Convention he became a member of the *Mountain*, a close friend of Marat and a distant friend of Robespierre, whom he did not trust.

The royal family after the notification of the ***death pennalty for Louis XVI***; a drawin showing the ***execution of Louis XVI***; a scene at the **Place de la Revolution** (today's Place de la Concorde) where most executions took place viewed by thousands of people.

On August 28, a list of *Adversaries de la Révolution* was drawn up, the gates to the city were sealed, and many Parisians began to be subjected to domiciliary visits, ostensibly in a search for muskets. By the evening of the 31st, every prison in Paris was full to overflowing, and on 2 September, with a wave of rumors and fears, the *Paris Commune* ordered a mayor massacre in which over 1,200 prisoners (200 of them Catholic priests) were murdered as they were released from their prisons.

By December of 1792 a new group had emerged in the National Convention, the *Enrages*. They demanded that the aristocrats and the rich be stripped of all their privileges. They were attacked by both the *Girondists* and the *Jacobins*, who still defended what was until then a central principle of the French Revolution: the right to own property. While the Convention prepared a trial for Louis XVI the English House of Commons urged taking up arms against France to protect the life of Louis XVI.

On January 21, 1793, Louis was found guilty as charged. The penalty was to be guillotined on the *Place de la Republique*.[40] Georges Danton voted for the death of the king; his voice resonated on the floor of the Convention...

> «*Let the kings of Europe dare to challenge us! We will throw at them the head of our king.*»

Within days Louis XVI was guillotined. Emboldened by his own fame, Danton proposed the creation of a *Tribunal Révolutionnaire*; on one hand he was taking away from the disorderly popular mobs the weapons that were used in the September 2 massacres, on the other hand he was creating the instrument what would institutionalize *La Terreur* in France. The *Girondists* swore never to forgive him; the fury of their attacks became unremitting. Danton decided to suppress them politically. In the meantime Robespierre began unsuccessfully pushing on the Convention a new version of the *Declaration of the Rights of Man and of the Citizen*, placing certain restrictions on the right of property.

The chaos in Paris continued unabated. Marat was arrested and liberated by orders of the *Tribunal Révolutionnaire*. The *Girondines* failed in their attempt to clear the Commune of Paris from *Enrages*. The *Jacobines* threatened to begin to kill *Girondines* and demanded their immediate arrest. A new Constitution was approved on June 24, 1793. It prescribed the right to work, the right to

---

[40] Formerly the **Place de Louis XV**, which was Louis XVI father.

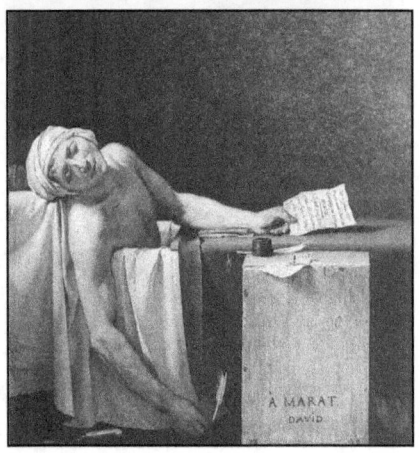

The ***Festival of Reason*** in 1793, organized by the revolution hoping to do away with all religions; ***Charlotte Corday***, murderess of Marat; the fampous painting by David showing ***Jean-Paul Marat***, after his assassination on July 13, 1793; ***Charles-Henrui Sanson de Longval***, the only executioner during the entire revolution. He was always at the foot of the guillotine.

education, de-emphasized private property in relation to liberty and social order and specifically enunciated the sacred right and duty of a people to revolt. A few days after the new Constitution was announced, Charlotte Corday, a *Girondine* member of a minor aristocratic family, assassinated Jean-Paul Marat, by then a well known radical member of the *Jacobines*. She indicated as her reason her revulsion at the September massacres and the execution of Louis XVI. Marat, to her, was a "hoarder" (a capital crime in revolutionary France due to the food scarcity that the revolution had created) and a monster. In four days she was executed by guillotine.[41]

On the last days of 1793, the Convention decreed a *proscription en masse* of the entire French male population (between 18 and 25, unmarried or widower without children) to defend the revolution. All women were ordered to wear a tricolored ribbon and the calendar was changed to a non-Christian system. Marie Antoinette was guillotined on October 16, as well as a large group of *Girondines*. The Cathedral of Notre Dame was turned into a secular meeting room and a *Festival of Reason* was celebrated there on November 10.

The year closed with a non-Christian celebration on December 25, when Robespierre [42] announced...

«*a new set of principles for the revolutionary government that will apply during the wars against the French enemies. The new principles will cease to apply when constitutional government is reinstated and the enemies of the revolution have been defeated.*»

---

[41] As it was tradition after every **public decapitation**, a man named Legros, assitant to Charles-Henri Sanson, the official and only executioner by guillotine during the entire French Revolution, lifted her head from the basket and slapped it on the cheek. According to historian Albert Camus in his *Reflections of the Guillotine*, Charlotte's severed hear "blushed." Harper's Weekly, declared «*Charlotteis the one assassin whom history mentions with applause.*»

[42] By his own choosing, Robespierre was beginning to be addressed as «**the incorruptible Maximilien Robespierre.**» A profusion of signs around Paris attempt to popularize his motto: «*La révolution est basé à la fois sur la vertu et la terreur;la vertu sans laquelle la terreur est le mal, la terreur sans laquelle la vertu est impuissante.*» (the revolution is based on both virtue and terror; virtue without which terror is evil, terror without which virtue is powerless.)

A view of the *Fête del Être Suppreme* at the Champ de Mars on June 8, 1794, organized by Robespierre and his revolutionaries to supress any religious celebrations; The *Abbé Henri Grégoire*, constitutional Catholic Bishop of Blois and strong supporteer of the revolution. He never retracted his oath of support and when he died was burried at the Cemetery of Montparnasse by students since the Church had excommunicated him; a painting of *Camille Desmoulins* at the Palais Royal.

In the meantime, The National army continued to lose ground to its enemies.[43]

The personality of Robespierre continued to inspire the Convention during most of 1794. The seizure and distribution of all property belonging to those suspected of collaboration or sympathy with the enemies of the Republic was approved. All known *Enragés* were guillotined in front of their families. The uninhibited extremism of the revolution finally reached beyond rational limits when the *Committee of Public Safety* ordered the arrest and execution of Georges Danton and all known Dantonists, including Camille Desmoulins.[44] On April 5, 1794, the revolution began to devour its children; Danton, Desmoulins and most Dantonistes were guillotined.[45] Two months later, in preparation to the *Fête de l'Être Suprême*, a "secular" (Festival of the Supreme Being), the Abbé Gregoire [46] proposed and the Convention approved to esta-

---

[43] Out in the field, one of the few victories ocurred during the December 19 in the recovery of the city of Toulon by revoutionaries. A 24 year old captain became the heroe of the day. His name was Napoleon Bonaparte.

[44] **Lucie Simplice Camille Benoît Desmoulins** (1760-1794) was a journalist and politician, a childhood friend of Maximilien Robespierre and a close friend and political ally of Georges Danton. He was inspired and enthused by the political reforms expected from the Estates-General. On July 11, 1789, he leapt onto a table outside the *Cafe du Foy* (one of many cafés in the garden of the *Palais Royal*, frequented in large part by political dissidents) and delivered an impassioned call to arms. Casting off his customary stutter in the excitement, he urged the volatile crowd to «*take up arms and adopt cockades by which we may know each other.*» The cockades were made by Parisian women in the traditional colors of Paris: red and blue. The forces that followed the appeal from Desmoulins attacked the *Hôtel des Invalides* to gain arms and, on July 14, participated in the Storming of the Bastille.

45 **Danton** was accused of using his position within the Revolution for personal gain as well as various financial misdeeds. He was not shy to talk about his financial success during the Revolution; his detractors found several acquisitions of funds and property that he could not adequately explain. Most of the accusations against him, however, were based on trivial or non-existing evidence.

[46] The ***Abbe Henri Gregoire*** (1750-1831) was a French Roman Catholic priest, the bishop of the city of Blois and a radical revolutionary leader. He was the first priest to take the loyalty oath required under the new *Civil Constitution of the Clergy* on December 27, 1790. He delivered a speech in which he demanded that King Louis XVI should be brought to trial. Regretting this act, he attempted to save the life of the monarch by proposing that the death penalty should be suspended. Throughout the *Reign of Terror* he appeared in the streets in his episcopal dress and said daily Mass in his house. Grégoire coined the term *vandalism* in reference to the destruction of property that occurred during the Revolution.

The ceremony of US Marines paying tribute to **Lafayette** at the Picpus Cemetery in 1889 Paris. Years later, after WWII, Chales de Gaule, in gratitude for US participation in the liberation of France, agreed to sell that space to the US nation after a request by General Bradley. Since then, the US flag has flown there. Picpus, the only private cemetery in all of Paris, only contains the remains of people and families assassinated by the French Revolution. Lafayette was burried there because his wife, **Marie Adrienne Françoise de Noailles,** was a member of an aristocratic family victim; her sister and mother were murdered during the Terror in 1794.

blish French as the national language.

Most citizens of Paris were in terror during all of 1794. The revolutionary government could not cope with the amount of corpses produced by the guillotine. The stench of rotten bodies permeated the city. The *Cimetière des Saints-Innocents,* opened in the XII century and already holding more than 2 million corpses, found no space to dig more tombs and began to bury the cadavers at much less than the prescribed depth. A new place to dispose of the victims was set up on the grounds of a convent of nuns in the south eastern part of the city.[47] Three gigantic pits were dug up and bodies of the decapitated began to be thrown in at random.

According to witnesses:

> «*The condemned were sent to* **Temple**, *the medieval fortress built by the Templars, to the dungeons of the* **Chatelet**, *a fetid castle located at the place where the sewers of Paris oozed into the Seine, or to the* **Conciergerie**, *the old prison on the west of the Île de la Cité. From there they were taken in carts, three to five at a time, once or twice every day, along the rue St. Honoré, to the* **Place de la Revolution**. *All along the route, people in droves went to watch the guillotine to do its grisly work. The Place de la Revolution was everyday packed to the rim. Hundreds of* **sans-culotte women** *screamed obscenities to the condemned. Spectators could buy souvenirs, read a program listing the names of the victims, or even grab a quick bite to eat at a nearby restaurant called* **Le Cabaret de la Guillotine**.
>
> *Some people attended on a daily basis, most famously the* **Tricoteuses**, *a group of morbid women who sat beside the scaffold and knitted in between beheadings. Most of the condemned pronounced defiant last words before being executed; some others danced their way up the steps of the scaffold pretending they had no fear. Children often attended guillotine executions; some of them even played with their own miniature guillotines at home, decapitating dolls or small rodents provided by their revolutionary parents. Small, functioning guillotines also found their way onto some upper class dinner tables, where they were used as bread and vegetable slicers. The entire town of Paris seemed to have collapsed into a stupor of insensitivity.*

---

[47] It became known as **Picpus Cemetery**. The nuns were relegated to a building with a chapel and told not to go outside. They began a continuous day and night vigil of prayers for the victims of the revolution, which lasted well into the XX century. Picpus became the only private cemetery in Paris when some of the families of the nobles interred there bought it from the Paris Commune. The noble families included the Noailles, the last name of the wife of the Marquis de Lafayette. For that reason Lafayette, honoring his wife, asked to be buried at Picpus. His tumb is still there. After World War II, at the petition of General of the US Army Omar Bradley, the French government sold to the US an area of about 100 sq ft where Lafayette was buried. There forever flies the American flag.

Parish of **Saint-Paul Saint-Louis**

The old **Cemetery of the Saint Innocents**, founded in 1550, where many of the guillotined were initially burried. There were so many victims executed that other places had to be found in 1792; two views of the **Saint Paul and Saint Louis Church** on *rue Saint Antoine*. From their steps, priests gave discrete and secret absolutions to the victims of the guillotine as the carts carrying their corpses went by. It was a ceremony that lasted all through the revolutionary period and particularly during the days of the Terror.

Paris great executioner during the revolution, Charles-Henri Sanson de Longval (1739-1806), became a celebrity because of the speed and precision with which he could orchestrate multiple beheadings in a single morning. [48] *He was also very skillful when reacting to desperate acts that some of the condemned would improvise at the last minute. People got to be so callous during the Terror that some gangsters and other hoods would get tattoos with grim slogans such as "My Head To Sanson."* [49]

After the guillotine decapitation was over, the head and the body were placed together in a large wooden cart that had its sides and floor covered with a thin metal plate. The cart would start its trip towards the designated cemetery; the route back was generally through rue de Rivoli and the rue Saint-Antoine, where the parish of Saint-Paul Saint Louis was located. [50] *On the steps of the church there was always a priest dressed like a common citizen blessing the corpses of the dead of the day. With a license from the archbishop of Paris, the condemned could confess their faults to someone who orally transmitted the confession to the priest on the steps of Saint-Paul Saint Louis. The priest was with his blessing providing absolution to the sacrament of confession.*

As the cadavers reached the cemeteries their bodies were thrown into common graves and a document was signed by the guard in charge of the records of the Committee of Public Safety, stating the names and ages of the guillotined. Most of the common grave pits of the cemeteries could hold 3 to 4,000 bodies.»

The months of July and August were called *Thermidor* in the new republican calendar. On July 27, 1794 (9 Thermidor of year II), Robespierre and all of his political allies were charged in the National Convention of «*crimes contre la République*» at a time when the French Revolution was living its most tragic and critical days.

---

[48] He kept his post for 40 years after the revolution was over; by his own account he executed **over 3,000 people**, including the King and the Queen. Upon his death, his sons inherited his position (the Sansons were a six generation family of executioners); the family owned and maintained all their work equipment.

[49] In the face of so many executions there were speculations over whether the heads of the guillotined remained conscious for a few minutes after being cut off. Certain that it was so, **Sanson** would lift the severed heads by the hair and pointed them in the direction of the headless bodies so that the condemned, in a final act of cruelty, would be aware of the end of his or her life. An insensitive doctor, *Dassy de Lignieres*, even asked one of the condemned to blink or leave one eye open after the execution to prove if it could still perform. The general thinking nowadays is that the brain could continue to function under oxigen deprivation or *hypoxia* for 2 to 3 minutes in some cases. The last execution by guillotine in France took place in September of 1981, when the French abolished capital punishment for good.

[50] The Parish of **Saint-Paul Saint Louis** is still functional; the location is in the Marais, the 4th Arrondisement of Paris.

Marie Jean Antoine Nicolas de Caritat, **Marquis de Condorcet**, outstanding French philosopher and mathematician, commited suicide after been branded a traitor by the revolution; **Jean Lambert Tallien** the deputy who challenged Robespierre and got him arrested; The **arrest of Robespierre** at a session of the Assembly; **Robespierre attempting suicide** at the Hôtel de Ville. He was mediclly treated and ended in the guillotine.

The members of the National Assembly who accused Robespierre and his closest allies in the hall of the Convention were conservative elements set out to end the Terror; they were hoping that once Robespierre was out of the way the government policies would no longer favor the social and political radicalism espoused by him and would return towards constitutionality and classical liberal economic policies. The fact that Robespierre had ordered the death of Danton and Desmoulins,[51] was also important in the decision *pour se débar-rasser du tyran* (to get rid of the tyrant).

Above all, Robespierre had turned into a detestable man which, in the words of Condorcet,[52] *«never had a first-class idea in his head or a good feeling in his heart.»* In fact, he had developed a reputation of a coward; his colleagues knew that he used to disappear whenever there was a crisis in the Legislative or the National Assemblies. On August 9, 1792, for instance, when the belfries were sounding at midnight, and members of the Assembly singing la *Marseillese* were leading the way to the Tuileries to arrest Louis XVI and take him to *Temple*, Robespierre did not come out of his desk until the king was put under lock and key and rendered powerless.

By the middle of July of 1794 Robespierre had lost the trust of his fellow Jacobins, enthralled also by the account of one member of the Assembly called Carnot:

> *«At a dinner-party near Paris, on a very hot day in July, the guests took off their coats, and left them in the drawing-room. I could not stop the temptation of looking into Robespierre's coat pocket; there I found a list of forty names, my own being among them. Of course I skipped the party and made my way at once into a place of safety.»*

On July 26 Robespierre mounted the tribune, and spoke of the bad state of Republican spirit, and of the need of giving new vigor to the guillotine. The speech fell flat, and the usually obsequious Convention became defiant. The following morning, as one of

---

[51] Both **Danton** and **Desmoulins** were killed in the prime of life, one being 34, and the other 35; both were very popular with members of the Assembly.

[52] Marie Jean Antoine Nicolas de Caritat, **marquis de Condorcet** (1743-1794), was a French philosopher, advocate of woman's rights and educational reform. He greeted the French Revolution with enthusiasm and became a Girondine. He was a good friend of Thomas Jefferson and Benjamin Franklin, contributed heavily to the writing of the 1793 French Constitution and voted against the death penalty for Louis XVI. He was *«too loved to be executed,»* and was probably assassinated after being branded a traitor to the Revolution.

Antoine-Laurent de Lavoisier (1743-1794), French nobleman, father of modern chemistry, was tried, convicted and guillotined on May 8, 1794 at age 50, accused of treason (for his noble origin) by Robespierre; two ***sketches by David*** upon the death of Robespierre at the guillotine; the rioters in front of the ***Hôtel de Ville*** de Paris demanding the execution of Robespierre.

Robespierre's followers was reading a report, one of the assambleists, Jean-Lambert Tallien (1767-1820), entered the chamber and interrupted him saying...

> «If this Convention dares not strike the tyrant, I will; and with this weapon I will do it!»

At these words he drew out a dagger. All hell broke loose. Robespierre tried several times to speak, but because of the raucous he could not be heard. He turned and appealed to each party, but none would pay the least attention now to his words. A voice above all others came out of the room:

> «Le sang de Danton l'étouffe.» (The blood of Danton is chocking him)

Before he could respond he was taken to prison. Within hours some National Guards rescued him and he was declared an outlaw by the Assembly. He took refuge at the *Hôtel de Ville*. The building was surrounded. Some of the followers that were protecting him escaped by jumping out of the windows. As he fell in the hands of his persecutors Robespierre tried to blow out his brains, but failed, breaking his lower jaw instead. They were all tried, and condemned to death, and were guillotined that same afternoon in the *Place de la Revolution*. With their execution *La Terreur*, the Reign of Terror, came to an end. On November 12 the National Assembly ordered the Jacobin Club to be closed.

After the death of Robespierre on *10 Thermidor*, An II (July 28, 1794), the French Republic began to recover from the major military threats from the Alliance, its internal revolts in the Vendée and the Southeast, and the Terror. On September 18 the Convention entered a new phase called *The Thermidorian Reaction*[53] issuing a decree stating that it would not pay salaries or expenses of the Church. The ashes of Marat and Rousseau were transferred to the Pantheon. The 1793 Constitution was decreed void. By April a Peace Treaty had been signed with Prussia. Supporters of Robespierre were disarmed. In May the *sans-coulottes* continued to revolt but this time they were aggressively confronted. Later treaties

---

[53] In practice the **Thermidorian Reaction** was a coup d'état within the French Revolution against the leaders of the *Jacobin Club* who had dominated the *Committee of Public Safety*. It was triggered by the vote of the *National Convention* to execute Maximilien Robespierre, Louis Antoine de Saint-Just, and several other leading members of the revolutionary government. This ended the most radical phase of the French Revolution.

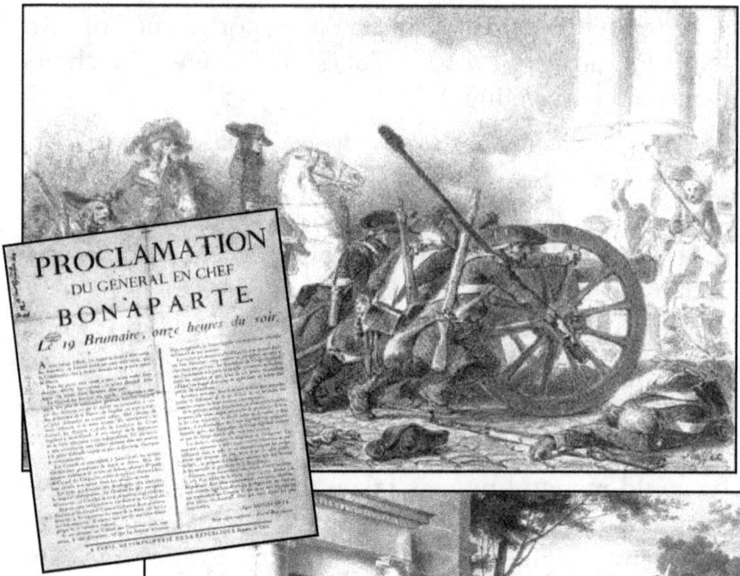

PROCLAMATION
DU GÉNÉRAL EN CHEF
BONAPARTE.
Le 19 Brumaire, onze heures du soir.

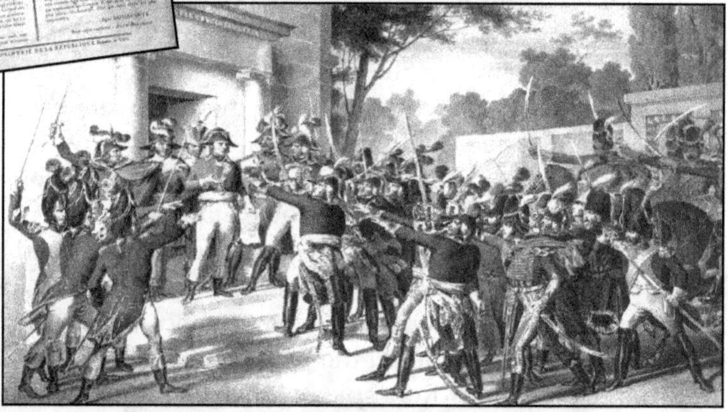

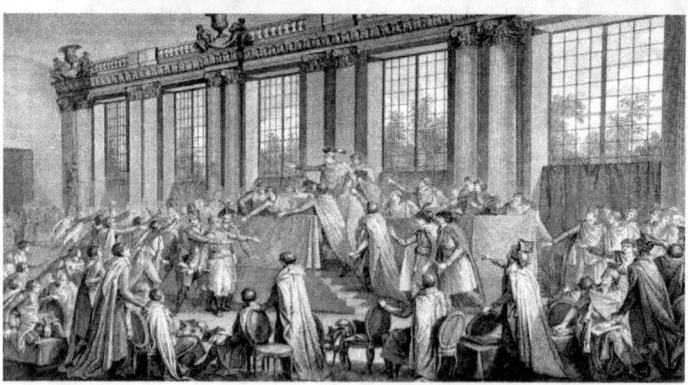

Napoleon Bonaparte dissolving a riot in front of the *Church of St. Roch* in Paris using cannon force; ***Napoleon on 18 Brumaire*** (November 9, 1799), the bloodless *Coup d'État* that brought him to power as First Consul and marked the end of the French Revolution; the scene at the ***National Assembly*** during the 18 Brumaire.

with the Netherlands and Spain were agreed to. The *Chouan* rebels, assisted by the British, continued their armed opposition and were defeated.

A new Constitution of Year III was approved on August 22 granting the vote only to those who paid taxes. It established a bicameral system, a *Council of Five Hundred* and a *Council of Elders* with 250 members; both to be elected every five years. The executive consisted of a group of five men chosen by both the *Council of Five Hundred* and the *Council of* Elders. It became known as the *Directory*[54] and replaced the functions of the *Committee of Public Safety*. It lasted until it was overthrown by Napoleon in November 1799 and replaced by the *Consulate*.

On October 5 a group of rioters took to the streets and entrenched themselves at the *Church of Saint-Roch* in rue Saint-Honoré. Napoleon Bonaparte, about to be appointed Chief of all Armies of France,[55] remembering the escape of the royal family from the *Tuileries* to the *Manege*, emplaced four cannons in front of the church and ended the revolt after causing numerous deaths and dispersing the rioters from Church property.

As the year 1796 began, the *Directory* suppressed the *Assignats* as a valid money of France. They became a curiosity, ruining all dealers that were paying 15% of their face value. France continued to be a sea of chaos. After the revolution the only road to peace seemed to be the establishment of a tyrannical dictatorship. It would come to pass with the coup d'état of *18 Brumaire* (9 November 1799) in which General Napoleon Bonaparte overthrew the *Directory* and replaced it with the *Consulate*.

---

[54] The **Directory** was in practice an ineffective dictatorship. It failed to restore financial and political stability in France and used military force to overturn election results. Several revolts flared up again in western France, particularly in the *Vendée*. The religious schism increased and the *Directoire* decided to take severe and unpopular measures toward those clerics who had not sworn allegiance to the revolution, the so called refractory priests. Most historians think it was «*a government of self-interest rather than virtue that forfeited its claim to be a constitutional government by clinging to power by such illegal acts as purges and fraudulent elections.* »

[55] **Napoleon Bonaparte** was appointed *Chief of all Armies of France* the following October 26, 1795.

Official portraits of *King Louis XVI* and *Queen Marie Antoinette*; contemporary drawings of the *execution of Louis XVI* (January 21, 1793) and the *execution of Queen Marie Antoinette* (October 16, 1793).

Marie Antoinette on her way to the guillotine. Pen and ink by Jacques-Louis David, 16 October 1793; *Alexander Lenoir* opposing the destruction of the royal necropolis in the Basilica of Saint Denis during the Reign of Terror, 1793. Vitrails of the ***Chapelle du Petit-Luc*** in Lucs-sur-Boulogne in the department of la Vendée, near the Loire, showing the worst massacre perpretated by the revolutionary forces during the revolution, on February 28, 1794. More than 1,200 old people, men, women and children died in the hands of the revolutionaries in a single day, all having taken refuge in the Chapel.

A Final Word about the French Revolution

The French Revolution, though it seemed a failure in 1796 and appeared nullified by the fall of Napoleon in 1815, had far-reaching results. It was unequivocally a watershed event that changed Europe and the Western world permanently, following in the footsteps of the American Revolution, which had occurred just a decade earlier. On one hand the revolution collapsed in the midst of the Terror in 1794 and its benefits and legacy were nullified by the dictatorship and absolutist government of Napoleon Bonaparte after 1802. On the other hand, however, it seems fair to agree that it had an extraordinary influence on the making of the modern world.

The positive contributions of the revolution can be summarized as follows:
- In France first, and later across the entire western world, bourgeois and landowning classes emerged as the dominant power and developed into what is now the middle class. The strict French class system that had long placed the clergy and nobility far above the rest of the French citizens, despite the fact that many of those citizens far exceeded nobles in wealth and reputation, ceased to exist.
- Feudalism died; land was freed and the old aristocracy-centered society was destroyed.
- The Church lost it power and was restored, at least nominally, to a civil and spiritual but not a political authority. Among other things, people were freed from tithes and other incurred fees mandated by the Church.
- In principle, social order and contractual relations became regulated by the emergence of democratically elected representative legislative bodies that codified the laws.
- The French Revolution gave a great stimulus to the growth of modern nationalism, with republicanism its most permanent option.
- Even after the demise of revolutionary ideas and the fall of power into the hands of a tyrannical dictator like Napoleon, the French people endured a fundamental transformation in self-identity; thousands of citizens gained firsthand experience

in the political arena: they participated in governance in novel ways; they joined political organizations, marched for their political ideas; democracy became a goal and a tradition.
- The French Revolution invented the concept of *revolutionary revolt*, a popular movement that can destroy the foundations of old *régimes* and achieve the reform of obsolete institutions that can satisfy new standards of reason and fairness. It also invented the concept of *public opinion*, undermining the existing notion that political, social and economic decisions rested exclusively on a privileged class that needed not seek concurrence from the general population.

There is still debate, however, over whether the revolution was worthwhile given the high cost in personal life and fortune as well as the waste of lost opportunities for development of the French society and the evident disregard for human talent that became part of the revolutionary credo. It has also been argued that the revolution simply interrupted a long term process that was predictably and inexorably going to produce modern France. Such a process had its roots in the Enlightenment and was bound to bloodlessly build a new France, completely wiping away seigniorial dues, aristocratic titles and rights, burdensome taxation and tithes and many other hangovers from the decaying feudal government of old regime France.

The negative balance of the French revolution included:

- To a large extent many of the so called accomplishments of the French Revolution which ardent supporters claim as being the result of events after 1789, like the seigniorial dues, were well on the way to being replaced with rents and contracts by 1789.
- The wartime atmosphere of the revolution took quite a toll on the French treasury. The costs of waging war, supporting allies, and maintaining the French army quickly depleted French treasure, already weakened by royal extravagance.
- The accomplishments of the French Revolution were merely temporary, given that the next leader after the Revolution was Napoleon, who imposed a dictatorship and voided the sovereign democracy of the Revolution. The era of Napoleon was closer to the *ancient régime* than the best times of the revolution.
- Immersed in the consuming battle to achieve equality and remove oppression, France missed a good part of an *Industrial Revolution*

that was transforming the economy and bringing the Western world into an improved modern society. French industry struggled for years after the Revolution to regain a foothold in a drastically different environment that took place everywhere except in France.
- In its haste to eliminate potential enemies, the Revolution did not spare lives even if they were not enemies but victims of jealousy, vendettas or false denunciations. It resulted into an enormous loss of talent. Antoine de Lavoisier (1743-1794), for instance, the father of modern chemistry, was labeled a traitor by Robespierre and was executed on May 8, 1794, along with 27 co-defendants that opposed the Revolution's intolerance against progress.
- France lost thousands of her countrymen as they emigrated to escape political tensions and save their lives. Hundreds of Frenchmen settled in Great Britain, Germany, Austria, Prussia and even the United States.
- Power became centralized in Paris, with its strong bureaucracy and an army supplied by conscripting all young men. French politics were permanently polarized—new names were given, "left" and "right" for the supporters and opponents of the principles of the Revolution.
- The often repeated claim of the revolution paying more attention to the poor and sick is absolutely false; by 1815, at the end of the Napoleonic era, there were over 40% fewer hospitals in France than before the revolution. The redistribution of wealth was also a dramatically false claim of the revolution; by 1802, nobles and aristocrats were able to either preserve or reclaim a large percentage of their land and wealth that had been confiscated by the revolution.
- In 1789 the economic growth of France started a period of stagnation that lasted throughout the revolution and only began to recover after the end of the Terror. Only two medium size buildings and one fountain in the Tuileries gardens, for instance, were build in Paris from 1789 to 1796
- The French Revolution, in its radicalism, attempted to reject and erase France's past history, both to avoid comparisons with the earlier periods but also to create uninformed new men and women that would not question the legality and appropriateness of revolutionary decisions.

The French these days are divided over the benefits and shortfalls of the revolution. Around the world its balance of good and bad are also debated by modern historiographers. Conservatives accept that reform was necessary but believe that the revolution was a blunder from which the Terror and tyranny inevitably followed. Liberals support most of the achievements but disown the excessive violence undertaken by mobs that usurped the power of the state. In 1972 China's Premier *Chou En Lai* was asked whether the revolution had been good or bad and, after musing for a few moments, he declared «*It is too early to tell.*»

After the Marseillese, thousands of innocent deaths, years of fear and merciless terror, the rise of a tyrannical Napoleonic empire and a return to the monarchy of the Bourbons, more or less as it was before the revolution started.

Photos above: two samples of *Assignats*, the paper money with which the state paid the Catholic Church and the nobles for the properties it confiscated. Within a few years they were totally worthless.

«Sufragio efectivo, no reelección.»
Slogan of the political campaign of Francisco I. Madero
in the 1909 elections against Porfirio Díaz
Detail of a Mural by Juan O'Gorman

The Mexican Revolution
1910 - 1920

«El que quiera ser Aguila que vuele; el que quiera ser gusano que se arrastre, pero que no llore cuando lo pisen.»
EMILIANO ZAPATA SALAZAR (1879-1919)
COMANDANTE DEL EJERCITO LIBERTADOR DEL SUR

The Mexican Revolution: a condensed timeline

1904
There was hope for an end to the Porfirio Díaz 36 year old regime. Francisco Madero entered local politics.

1910
April 15. The nominating convention for the *Partido Nacional Antirreeleccionista* was held. The night before Porfirio Díaz ordered Madero's arrest.
June 26. The Primary elections were held and there was strong evidence of fraud.
October 6. Madero called for an armed revolution to start on November 20.

1911
October 5. Madero drafted the *Plan de San Luis Potosí*, which declared the elections void.
May 25. Díaz resigned his office. General elections were set for October 1. Madero received 98% of the votes and was sworn into office on November 6.
September. Zapata began an armed rebellion against the government of Madero.

1912
Pascual Orozco led a rebellion against the government of Madero. Mexico City and the government of Madero were defended by Victoriano Huerta.
Emiliano Zapata composed the *Plan of Ayala*, asking for «*the return of the land the haciendas had stolen...the expropriation of one-third of all hacienda holding for villages without land titles, and the confiscation of the property of those who oppose the plan.*»

1913
February 9. There was a *Coup d'État* attempt against Madero. Huerta was appointed as general. Beginning of the **Ten Tragic Days.**
February 18. Huerta arrested Madero and ended his government. Huerta named himself acting President of Mexico.
February 21. Madero and his vice President, Pino Suárez, were assassinated, under the orders of Huerta.
Rebellion by Álvaro Obregón, Francisco Villa, Emiliano Zapata, and Venustiano Carranza.
March 26. Carranza vowed to return constitutional rule back to Mexico; he issued the *Plan de Guadalupe* and proceeded to establish his own government in the north.

1914
Spring. Carranza controlled northern Mexico and all railroads connecting Mexico to the United States.
April 21. President Wilson ordered the U.S. Marines to land at the port of Veracruz.
March and *July.* Carranza and Villa were now in a conflict that almost ended their partnership.
July 8. Villa acknowledged that Carranza was the First Chief of the armed

1914 (continuation)

resistance. Carranza agreed to send arms, ammunition, and coal to Villa's troops. Zapata continued his fight against the Huerta government.
July 15. Huerta resigned as President.
August 15. Obregón's troops entered Mexico City.
August 20. Carranza's troops entered Mexico City.
December 6. Emiliano Zapata and Francisco Villa met at Mexico City.

1915
Civil war between the forces of Carranza, Villa, and Zapata. President Wilson threatened U.S. intervention.
Obregón destroyed Villa's army at Celaya but loses his right arm in battle.

1916
October 19. The United States and a number of Latin American countries recognized the Carranza government.
Villa raided Columbus, New Mexico in retaliation.

1917
January 6. Carranza created a law regulating an agrarian reform and land distribution.
December 1. Constitutional Convention at Querétaro: universal manhood suffrage, no reelection of the president and state governors, direct elections, free education, freedom of religion, restriction on monopolies.

1918
March 11. Carranza was elected President.

1919
April 10. Zapata continued to fight Carranza, was ambushed and shot dead.
June 1. Obregón announced his candidacy for the presidency.

1920
April 2. Carranza attempted to arrest Obregón in Mexico City.
Obregón managed to flee to safety in Guerrero.
May 7. Carranza fled Mexico City, heading towards Veracruz and exile.
May 20. Carranza was shot and killed.
December 1. Obregón elected president of Mexico. He restored order after a decade of political upheavals, crime and civil wars.

1923
July 20. Villa was assassinated in Parral, Chihuahua, as seven men fired over 40 shots into his 1919 Dodge touring car. His skull was stolen from his grave three years later.

1924
December 1. Obregón retired and Plutarco Elías Calles was elected president of Mexico. He limited the number of clergy, prohibited church schools, restricted alien ownership of land and regulated the petroleum industry.

1928
July 17. Obregón was assassinated in Mexico city while dining with friends.

The Mexican Revolution
1910 - 1920

On December 12, 1684, *Edmond Halley* (1656-1742), a young English scientist, visited Isaac Newton, the foremost expert in planetary theory at the prestigious *London Royal Society* to persuade Newton to work with him in the study of the motion of comets and other celestial bodies. Newton agreed and soon after Halley received his first appointment at Oxford University as a Professor of Geometry and Astronomy and later as Royal Astronomer in 1720. In 1726 Halley predicted that a comet that had been seen from earth four times since 1456 would show up again in 1758. Halley did not get to see his prediction come true and died on January 14, 1742. His prediction came true on Christmas day sixteen years later, when the comet was visible again, exactly as he had predicted.[56] It was then baptized the *Halley's Comet*. It cemented forever the name and prestige of Edmond Halley.

The Halley Comet made a new pass and was especially close to earth in 1910, right on schedule as Halley had predicted: every 75.8 years. In anticipation, the world press created quite a stir. For many people everywhere, from Germany to Argentina, Cuba, India and the USA, the close approach was seen as a sign of impending doom. The comet was 24 million miles long, hence it was clearly visible to the naked eye on the sky for six hours on the night of May 19, 1910. [57]

Comets like Halley had been blamed for the death of kings, the fall of empires, even the biblical flood. Legend has it that Pope

---

[56] His precise words were «*In the year 1456 ... a Comet was seen passing retrograde between the Earth and the sun... Hence I dare venture to foretell, that it will return again in the year 1758.*»

[57] Its last pass was in 1986, when it was studied for the first time in detail by spacecrafts. It was found to contain a mixture of volatile ices, such as water, carbon dioxide, and ammonia, and some dusty, non volatile material. It was seen in New York city at 3:09 am, on March 24, 1986, very low in the horizon in the southeast sky. It was traveling at 13,000 mph, roughly 14.3 miles away from the earth.

Callixtus III excommunicated Halley's comet as an agent of the devil upon its arrival in 1456. In 1910, in Mexico city, the press reminded the reading public that Roman Emperor Julius Caesar was assassinated in A.D. 44, the same year a comet appeared in the sky; four centuries later, the comet of year 453 AD reportedly presaged the death of Attila the Hun. In February of 1910, Mexico's *Excelsior* newspaper reported...

> «Comets distemper and inflame the air and exhaust the juices of the Earth.... As the inevitable effects of both, we must expect sickness, diseases, mortality, and more especially the sudden death of many Great Ones as Halley's comet shows up in the skies of Mexico.»

The bad news that people took for granted in Mexico was reinforced by similar reactions in the USA: Coal miners in Pennsylvania and silver miners in Colorado refused to go underground as the date approached for fear of being trapped. Pineapple workers in Hawaii fled to the beaches for protection from the comet's fiery tail; thousands in San Francisco's Chinatown climbed into wooden barrels filled with rain water. A sect in Oklahoma known as the *Select Followers* viewed Halley's as a sign of the vengeance of Jehovah. The local sheriff arrived just in time one night to prevent the sacrifice of a virgin. Thousands of Chinese rioted in Peking in what became known as the *Halley's Comet Rebellion*. King Edward VII of England died in May of 1910, renewing the suspicion that comets heralded the death of rulers. In one strange coincidence Mark Twain, as he had predicted, died on April 21, 1910, a day after Halley's closest proximity to the sun.

It took less than 15 seconds for Halley to travel from Veracruz to Mexico City. Near El Paso hundreds of Mexicans gathered about crucifixes erected on the hills, trying to calm the fury of the comet with music, incantations and prayers. As the comet passed them without visible catastrophes, dancing and feasting replaced the religious ceremonies; elders, however, continued to tell the young that Halley's, sooner or later, meant famine, plague, suffering and death of someone ruling Mexico.

In the Roma neighborhood of Mexico City, a *corrido* became popular:

Cometa si hubieras sabido	Oh comet, if you had but known
lo que venías anunciando,	What it was you prophesized.
nunca hubieras salido	You never would have come,
por el cielo relumbrando.	lightening up the sky.

For many Mexicans the world of Don Porfirio Díaz (1830-1915) and his wife Doña Carmelita (1864-1944), by the grace or the disgraceful presence of Halley's Comet, was coming to an end; the day of judgment was at hand. The Lord had almost certainly sent a group of revolutionaries led by a man named Francisco Madero, to be their judge and executioner. It was not wise to ignore the ominous warning of a comet like Halley's on the sky. The ruling of Porfirio Díaz was most certainly doomed.

By 1910, José de la Cruz Porfirio Díaz Mori (1830-1915) had served seven terms as President of Mexico. He had risen to the rank of General leading republican troops against the French-imposed Emperor Maximilian,[58] seizing power in a coup in 1876.

Porfirio was a *mestizo*; his mother was Petrona Mori, the daughter of a Spaniard and an indigenous woman. His father was José de la Cruz Díaz, a modest innkeeper who died of cholera in 1833 when Porfirio was three. The Díaz family was devoutly religious, and young Porfirio began training for the priesthood at the age of fifteen when his mother sent him to the *Colegio Seminario Conciliar* in Oaxaca. He was about to be ordained in 1846 when most seminarians volunteered as soldiers in the Mexican-American war that followed the annexation of Texas to the USA.[59] Porfirio never saw any action in the war but realized his vocation was in the military and not in the priesthood. In 1847 he met Benito Juárez, the governor of Oaxaca.

---

[58] **Ferdinand Maximilian Joseph** (1831-1867), Archduke of Austria, was the first and only monarch of the Second Mexican Empire. He was the younger brother of the Austrian emperor Francis Joseph I. After a distinguished carrer in the Austrian Navy he accepted to be emperor of Mexico at the request of Mexican monarchists, falsely believing the Mexican people had voted him their king. In reality the offer was a scheme orchestrated by conservative Mexicans trying to overturn the government of Benito Juárez. He was married to *Carlota*, the only daughter of Leopold I of Belgium. After the French troops protecting him from a confrontation with Juárez abandoned their posts, Maximilian was executed in 1867 by Juárez' army in Querétaro, Mexico, when he was surrounded, starved and betrayed into capitulation.

[59] The forced **annexation of Texas** into US territory took place after decades of Comanche, Navajo and Apache raids (mostly to acquire livestock) against settlements in the sparsely populated areas of northern Mexico, which prompted the Mexican government to sponsor American migration to Texas to turn the area into a buffer zone. Texas residents eventually created a republic not recognized by Mexico. When the US annexed the Texas republic a territorial conflict ensued resulting in the loss of much of Mexico's northern territories.

Portraits of four important personalities at the start of the Mexican Revolution: the mexican dictator **Porfirio Díaz Mori** (1830-1915), dictator of Mexico for 35 years; **Antonio López de Santa Ana** (1794-1876), the *Napoleon of the West*, a Creole who fought to defend royalist New Spain and then for Mexican Independence; **Benito Juárez** (1806-1872), constitutional president of Mexico for five terms who resisted the French occupation of Maximilian in 1862; **Francisco Indalecio Madero** (1873-1913) and his wife Sara Pérez. Madero served as the 33rd president of Mexico nd was the man who challenged Porfirio Díaz, sparking the Mexican Revolution in

Six years later, in 1853, Antonio López de Santa Ana (1794-1876), became President of Mexico through a successful *Coup d'État*.[60] Porfirio and Juárez became allies. Juárez went into exile in New Orleans while Porfirio joined a band of guerrillas to fight Santa Ana. After the defeat of Mexico in the Mexican-American war, Santa Ana, unable to find refuge in the USA, went into exile in Kingston, Jamaica, returning to Mexico at the invitation of Mexican conservatives. He was for the last time elected again President of Mexico and declared himself as dictator-for-life with self granted titles of *Most Serene Highness, Benemérito of the Nation, General of the Division, Grand Master of the National and Distinguished Order of Guadalupe, Grand Cross of the Royal and Distinguished Spanish Order of Carlos III, and President of the Mexican Republic.*

In 1855 a group of liberals led by Benito Juárez overthrew his government and Santa Ana fled to Cuba, where he lived until 1874, when he moved to Staten Island in New York. As the extent of his corruption became known, he was tried *in absentia* for treason; all his estates were confiscated by the government.

In New York, at age 74, Santa Ana became an entrepreneur. He joined forces with a man called Thomas Adams to import *chicle* [61] from Mexico. Adams became a millionaire when he formed the *Adams Chewing Gum Company*. Santa Ana, on the other hand, was ruined as he invested in a company trying to replace *latex* or natural rubber with *chicle* in the manufacture water-repealing garments and boots. He also became passionate about cockfighting and spent thousands of dollars on price roosters. He returned to Mexico at age 82 and died at his home in Mexico City. He was buried with full military honors; his grass covered coffin is now at the *Panteón del Tepeyac Cemetery*.

---

[60] ***Santa Ana*** was known as the Napoleon of the West. He was an American-born wealthy Spaniard landowner (a Creole), the general who had several times defended Mexico against foreign invaders. As a skillful soldier and cunning politician, he dominated Mexican history in the earlier part of the nineteenth century to such an extent that historians often refer to it as the *Age of Santa Ana*. The history of Mexico from 1822 to 1855 might accurately be called the history of Santa Ana's revolutions.... he played a major role in all the political events of the country and Mexico's destiny became intertwined with his own.

[61] ***Chicle*** in a natural gum collected, like latex, by tapping with zig-zag gashes the surface of certain Mexican trees of the Manikara genus. It was first used by the Aztec and the Maya as a chewing but not ingesting substance that could stave off hunger, freshen breath and keep teeth clean. The word *chicle* comes from the Nahuatl term for gum, *tziktli*, meaning sticky stuff.

Sebastian Lerdo de Tejada (1823-1889), a former Catholic seminarian in Puebla who became a just and liberal president of Mexico, good friend of José Martí; a portrait of ***Porfirio Díaz*** in 1872, four years before he became President of Mexico for the first time; a painting showing the popular ***entrance of Porfirio Díaz in Puebla*** on April 2, 1867, when he was a popular and well respected general of the Mexican Army.

In the meantime Porfirio Díaz began to ascend in the military. He served in the long struggle against French occupation as general of an infantry brigade and became well known after his capture by the French armies and a heroic escape. Upon the defeat of the French, President Benito Juárez offered him the position of Secretary of Defense and Commander in Chief of the Army. He became the top general in the Mexican army fighting the French and Emperor Maximilian; trying to overcome his inevitable defeat, Maximilian offered him the command of the imperial army if he would join their cause. Díaz refused. Finally, on 2 April 1867, he went on to win the final battle for Puebla.

When Juárez returned to the presidency of Mexico in 1868 and began to restore peace, Porfirio resigned his military command and went home to Oaxaca. It did not take long, however, before the ambitious Díaz became unhappy with the Juárez administration and in 1871 he led a rebellion against the re-election of Juárez.

He was defeated in Zacatecas but Juárez died of a heart attack on July 18, 1872 and his successor, Sebastian Lerdo de Tejada, offered Porfirio an amnesty and he retired to Tlacotalpan, Veracruz, where he was elected to Congress in 1874.[62] He led a revolt against Lerdo de Tejada in 1876. This attempt also failed and Díaz fled to the USA. In November 1876, Díaz returned to Mexico when on November 16 he fought the *Battle of Tecoac* and defeated the government forces. On May 12, 1877, Porfirio was elected president of Mexico for the first time. He violated his campaign promise of *no re-election* and did not surrendered his control over the state for the next thirty three years.

On February 17, 1908, in an interview with a US journalist from the staff of *Pearson's Magazine*, Porfirio Díaz stated for the record:

«*Mexico is ready for democracy and elections. I have no desire to continue in the Presidency. This nation is ready for her ultimate life of free-*

---

[62] **JoséMartí** knew Sebastian Lerdo de Tejada and was an outspoken lerdista during his residence in Mexico City. He even published an editorial in one of the leading newspapers in Mexico asking readers to back Lerdo's reelection bid in June 1876. When Mexico's highest court later invalidated Lerdo's reelection and the conservative Porfirio Díaz seized power through a military coup, Martí and his family were forced to flee the country. On the eve of leaving Mexico and with Díaz attacking journalists and other dissidents, Martí expressed his contempt for the new regime: «*There goes our restored liberties. There goes our individual rights. There goes the Mexican Constitution.*»

Front cover of Madero's book *La Sucesion Presidencial* (The Presidential Succession); Madero at a ***train stop*** during his 1910 presidential campaign against Porfirio Díaz; one of Madero's numerous political rallies with the theme ***Sufragio Efectivo: No Reelección***
(Effective elections; no reelection).

dom. I will retire and allow other candidates to compete for the presidency.»

Several opposition groups united to find suitable candidates who would represent them in the upcoming presidential elections. Bernardo Reyes, the governor of Nuevo León, was chosen as candidate for the presidency; at that point Porfirio Díaz began to perceive him as a threat to his legacy and sent him on a mission to Europe. According to the Mexico press, it soon became known that Porfirio believed that...

> «Reyes would not be in the country for the elections... and there would be no electoral contest after all. Since I am responsible for bringing several billion dollars in foreign investments into Mexico, I think I should continue in my position until a competent successor is found.»

Porfirio Díaz finally found a competent successor in an aristocratic Mexican statesman, writer, landowner and bank investor: Francisco Indalecio Madero González (1837-1913).[63] He was an unusual politician, who had never held office until he ran for president against Porfirio Díaz in the 1910 elections. In one of his books entitled *The Presidential Succession*, he asked voters to prevent the sixth reelection of Porfirio Díaz and bankrolled the *Anti-Reelectionist Party* (later called the *Progressive Constitutional Party*, eventually called the *Maderistas*.) Mexicans liked him far and above Porfirio Díaz since «*he was someone of independent financial means with a strong ideological determination, brave enough to oppose Díaz when it was dangerous to do so.*»

Madero's slogan in the 1910 election was «*Sufragio Efectivo, No Re-Elección,*» a real election, not a mere reelection. He started his campaign organizing mass meetings and whistle-stop tours with all the hoopla of the North American elections, which he sought to emulate. Díaz, on the other hand, was passively complacent until the popularity of Madero rattled him and his followers.[64]

When the government announced the official results, Díaz was proclaimed to have been re-elected almost unanimously, with Madero gathering only a minuscule number of votes. The massive electoral fraud was compounded with the imprisonment of Francisco Madero four days before the election; his entire staff and

---

[63] **Madero** had been educated at Mount St. Mary's College in Maryland, the Sorbonne in Paris and UCLA at Berkeley.

[64] Many times **Porfirio Díaz** repeated to his close allies the dismissive comment that «*this election resembles one microbe confrontation with an elephant.*»

Pascual Orozco Vázquez (1882-1915), first on the left, Mexican revolutionary leader who, after the triumph of Madero, rose against him and joined the *Coup d'État* by Victoriano Huerta on March 3, 1912. The second from the right in this photo is Pancho Villa; Francisco Madero wounded at the **Battle of Casas Grandes**, Chihuahua, in March 1911; **Madero entering Mexico city** in June of 1911.

5,000 members of his party were also jailed.

After his family secured his release from prison, Madero fled to San Antonio, Texas,[65] declared himself the legitimately elected President of Mexico and published the *Plan de San Luis de Potosí*, calling for Mexicans to overthrow Porfirio Díaz. The Plan written during his time in prison, proclaimed the elections of 1910 null and void, and called for an armed revolution to begin at 6 pm on 20 November 1910, against the illegitimate election of Porfirio Díaz. It was the spark that would launch the Mexican Revolution.

Madero and his men entered the Mexican territory in February of 1911; their first encounter was an attack on Casas Grande, Chihuahua. By April the insurrection had spread to 18 of the 32 Mexican states, including Morelos, where the leader of the revolutionary movement was a 31 year old peasant of Nahua and Spanish ancestry with very limited education called Emiliano Zapata.

Porfirio Diaz could no longer ignore the consequences of his decision to remain in the presidency of Mexico after 36 years. Claiming that he had heard the voice of the people, he replaced his cabinet and agreed to the restitution of lands taken from the dispossessed and the release of political prisoners. Madero insisted in his demand that Porfirio resign the presidency but wanted to accomplish that goal peacefully, with Díaz voluntarily leaving his post. His fellow revolutionaries, *Pascual Orozco* (1882-1915) from Chihuahua and *Francisco Villa* (1878-1923), from Durango, disagreed and went ahead with an attack on *Ciudad Juárez*, at the time the largest border town in Mexico. In May of 1911, the city was surrounded by 3,000 revolutionary fighters; inside only 500 Federal troops and 300 civilian voluntaries were garrisoned. In a few days the city surrendered, which enabled the revolutionary forces to bring in weapons and supplies from across the river in El Paso. Much of the city was destroyed and the population left *en masse*. By the end of May Porfirio Díaz agreed to resign. On June 7, 1911, Francisco Madero entered Mexico City in triumph; he was greeted by huge crowds shouting *¡Viva Madero!* Somehow everybody knew that it was the beginning and not the end of the revolution.

---

[65] **Madero's father** was able to post bond to give Madero the right to move on horseback during daytime about the city of Monterrey. On October 7, 1910, Madero escaped from his guards and took refuge with some members of his party in the countryside around Monterrey. His friends smuggled him across the **US border**, hidden in a baggage car by sympathetic railway workers.

In October of 1910, Madero escaped from prison, went to the US and in San Antonio, Texas, wrote **El Plan of San Luis**, published in San Luis Potosí. The plan declared invalid the elections recently held and affirmed the national powers missing, also naming himself interim president; he promised to call new elections and made a call for all the towns in the country to rise up in arms on November 20 at 6:00 PM, which indeed occurred.

Emiliano Zapata, on November 25, 1911, denounced the Plan de San Luis as a betrayal of the revolution and issues his own **Plan de Ayala**, calling for land reform and freedom. In the two photos below, the manuscript handwritten by Otilio Montaño Sánchez, Zapata's mentor, since Emiliano had difficulty writing.

As Mexico struggled to work out its most pressing problems, Madero was busy preparing for new elections after the fall of Porfirio Díaz. The elections took place and Francisco Madero won by a landslide. Mexico was overjoyed, but by the time Madero took possession of the Presidential chair on November 6, 1911, much of his governing and fighting coalition had disintegrated. He had snubbed General Pascual Orozco, Jr. by not appointing him to the cabinet, and worse, he had ditched Francisco Vázquez Gómez, his first Vice President choice, in favor of José María Pino Suárez. Orozco and Emilio Vázquez Gómez (Francisco's brother) ended up rebelling against him. Still, the Mexican public was excited by a fresh start and cheered the new President.

General Bernardo Reyes, having returned from Europe, rose up against the government in December 1911. He was considered part of Porfirio Díaz' old guard and few Mexicans rallied to his cause. He deposed his arms by the end of the year. Emilio Vázquez Gómez (1858-1926), a close supporter of Madero in 1910, turned against him; he gathered a group of disaffected former followers in Chihuahua and took Ciudad Juárez by surprise. Madero sent General Pascual Orozco to quench the rebellion, which he did without a struggle. Soon, however, Orozco revolted and had to surrender to troops sent by Madero under the command of Victoriano Huerta. There were followers, disaffected, traitors and unscrupulous vandals all over. Very few people were to be trusted.

Shortly after Madero assumed the presidency on June 7, 1911, Emiliano Zapata issued on November 25, 1911 his *Plan de Ayala* in opposition to Madero's *Plan de San Luis Potosí*, and revolted against the new government pledging alliance to Pascual Orozco, rather than to Francisco Madero.[66] The *Plan de Ayala* stipulated that all *hacendados* ("usurpers" according to the Plan) had to return the lands they owned to its rightful owners, i.e., all landless citizens. Anyone who owned property could later argue in an agrarian court and provide proof of their ownership once the re-

---

[66] ***Emiliano Zapata*** was not an educated man. The text of the *Plan de Ayala* was dictated by Zapata and handwritten and proofread by his mentor Otilio Montaño Sánchez, a school teacher that was acting as his mentor. The Plan's motto was «*Reforma, Libertad, Justicia y Ley.*» Montaño was considered an "*intellectual*" by Zapata. Years later, in 1917, Montaño was accused of heading a rebellion, found guilty and executed by firing squad with a sign around his neck reading "*So die all traitors to the fatheland.*"

Angel Ortiz Monasterio (1849-1922), the officer that is considered the founder of the Mexican Navy, loyal follower of Madero; *Lauro Villar Ochoa* (1849-1923), combatant agains the forces of Maximilian, defender of the National Palace in Mexico; *General Félix Díaz* (1868-1945), enemy of Madero, fought agains him in 1913; *Bernardo Doroteo Reyes* (1949-1913), loyal porfirista, fought against Madero in 1910, shown as he exited the Tlatelolco prison in 1913.

volt was victorious. Eventually, one-third of all lands would be given back to the villages and people of Mexico for their own use. The *Plan de Ayala* raised Zapata's popularity and support from the peasantry throughout the South of Mexico South, dramatically increasing the membership of his *Ejército Libertador del Sur*.[67]

Zapata hoped there would be some major regime changes when Madero came into power, but in spite of his best efforts he was not able to work with Madero and his opposition to the Madero government increased with time. Throughout 1912 opposition to the Madero government grew practically from all sides. Pascual Orozco was one of the main leaders of the opposition, along with Felix Díaz and Bernardo Reyes. Orozco had been a member of the Revolution and of the Madero government. He led a rebellion against Madero in 1912. At this time Mexico City and the government was defended by Victoriano Huerta. In late October 1912, Felix Díaz led an armed rebellion against Madero; the insurrection failed and he was arrested on October 23, 1912.

On February 9, 1913, General Bernardo Reyes and Felix Díaz were released from prison by rebel guards; their followers surrounded and captured the National Palace. With the aid of Ángel Ortiz Monasterio,[68] the National Palace was retaken by government troops but at the cost of serious wounds to the leader of the government forces General Lauro Villar.[69] With Villar out of his

---

[67] **Emiliano Zapata's** *Ejército Libertador del Sur* promptly made an alliance with northern revolutionary armies, under **Venustiano Carranza (1859-1920)** and **Pancho Villa (1878-1923)**. As we shall see later, together Zapata, Carranza and Villa were able to depose Victoriano Huerta (1850-1916) as President of Mexico and brought a temporary degree of order to the country. Zapata eventually came to be in disagreement with Carranza and took up arms once again. Carranza ultimately put a bounty on Zapata's head, resulting in his assassination on April 10, 1919, as shown in the 1952 film ¡*Viva Zapata!*, where Emiliano is portrayed by Marlon Brando.

[68] **Ángel Ortiz Monasterio** had been a 24 year old *Alférez de Navío* (Junior level officer) of the Spanish Navy when he commadered the *Virginius*, a ship carrying men and weapons to Cuba in October of 1873, during the Cuban Independence War of 1868. Legend was that with only 10 men he took 165 prisoners.

[69] **General Lauro Villar Ochoa** (1849-1923) successfully defended the **Palacio Nacional** with troops under the orders of *Ángel Ortiz Monasterio*, a former vice Admiral loyal to Madero that had joined the Mexican Army and assumed the position of Chief of Staff of Madero. It was one of the initial events of what has been called *la Decena Trágica* (Mexico's Ten Tragic Days, February 9 to 19, 1913).

President Madero and VP Pino Suárez as they left the ceremony commemorating the 1857 inauguration of the monument to Juárez on February 5, 1913; soldiers loyal to General Felix Díaz, opponent of Madero, as they were taking a break at la *Ciudadela* in Mexico City in 1913.

active role in the army Madero decided to replace him with Victoriano Huerta, a move he would live to regret before the end of the year.

Nothing worked out for Madero during the first days of 1913. Although he was the first president of Mexico with a wealthy background, he had the stigma of having driven Porfirio Díaz out of office and conservative Mexicans were not convinced of his political philosophy. When he refused to implement the economic and political reform plans he had promised, like the breaking down the *latifundios* (the large estate land holdings), his supporters became disenchanted. He knew he was facing serious difficulties. Mexicans were to a great extent flustered, the treasury was depleted and Madero, in his actions, was only slightly less enterprising than the hated *Científicos*[70] of the Porfirio Díaz' era.

Revolts were occurring with unprecedented frequency in the new Madero era and they had become increasingly difficult to squash. The November 1911 Zapata revolt in Morelos was contained by Gen. Felipe Ángeles, but was not suppressed; the March 1912 Pascual Orozco revolt in Chihuahua was restricted by Gen. Victoriano Huerta, but Orozco and his *Colorados* remained at large; the November 1912 revolts of Gen. Bernardo Reyes in Nuevo León, and the December 1912 revolt by Gen. Félix Díaz in Veracruz were the only ones brought under control when the two generals were imprisoned in Mexico City.

Mexico City was awash with rumors that the overthrow of Madero was imminent. The worst indication of things to come, however, were the incidents after the release of General Bernardo Reyes and Felix Díaz by prison guards.

On the night of February 8, 1913, the cadets of the *Escuela Militar de Aspirantes*, a Military School located at Tlalpan entered the city in trolley cars. At 5:30 in the morning, they had gathered before the civilian penitentiary, demanding the release of General Félix Díaz. After a brief encounter where the commander of

---

[70] The **Científicos** were a group of politicians, intellectuals and business people loyal to Porfirio Díaz that had a strong influence in government policies during the last years of Porfirio's era. It was a time of economic constrictions, rebelions and a crash of the value of silver in world markets. The *científicos* were followers of Henri de Saint Simon, Auguste Comte, John Stuart Mill and Francis Bacon; they believed that pubic opinion had to take second place to what reason, empirical data and scientific analysis dictated as the best basis to make good decisions in government.

The **Castillo de Chapultepec** in 1913, scene of the start of the *Marcha de la Libertad*, the march from the *Castillo* to the *Palacio Nacional* in Mexico city, escorted by students from the Colegio Militar. It was the beginning of the *Decena Trágica*; a view of Mexican troops loyal to Madero during the **defense of La Ciudadela**, a fortress full of war materials. Generals Félix Díaz and Manuel Mondtagón eventually took it over in an important step to secure the defeat of the constitutional forces of Madero.

the penitentiary was killed, Díaz was freed. The cadets and soldiers under the leadership of their officers, proceeded to the Santiago Tlatelolco military prison, where they demanded and secured the release of General Reyes. Reyes mounted a horse and led part of the cadets and a column of soldiers to the National Palace, arriving there at 7:30 am. He was sure he could have the palace delivered over to him; instead, he was fired on, and fell mortally wounded from his horse. The men behind him ran for their lives.

Many spectators were killed in the confusing shooting that followed; within three hours 400 people lay dead and over 1,000 were wounded. The citizens of Mexico City left the streets in panic. Madero was at the presidential residence in Chapultepec and was at the scene in Tlatelolco by 9:00 am. Minutes later Victoriano Huerta arrived by his side. Huerta was resentful at Madero for not having been made Madero's Minister of War. Madero, on his part, had reservations about Huerta, an efficient but brutal officer with serious drinking problems. It was then that Madero, not thinking of other better and safer choices to pacify the city, appointed Huerta as Commander of the Army of the Capital. With Huerta standing by his side, Madero stepped out on a balcony of the National Palace [71] and made a speech to the crowd. Close by, General Felix Diaz had retreated to the city Arsenal, *La Ciudadela*, a few blocks from where Madero was. He found himself in possession of a rock-solid fort, with the government's reserve of arms and ammunition at his disposal. Soon he would have to resist the bombardment by Madero's forces under the direction of Victoriano Huerta.

Indeed, at about 10:00 am on February 11, Victoriano Huerta began the bombardment of *La Ciudadela*. The action was met with a vigorous response, and the city was heavily damaged. In an

---

[71] **Mexico's National Palace** is situated at the Zócalo, in Mexico City. The first palace on this spot was built by Aztec emperor Moctezuma II in the early 16th century. Cortés destroyed the palace in 1521, rebuilding it as a fortress with three interior courtyards. In 1562 the crown purchased the building from Cortés' family to house the viceroys of *Nueva España*, a function it served until Mexican independence. The building includes several famous panoramic mural of Mexican history by Diego Rivera. As you face the palace, high above the center door hangs the *Campana de Dolores*, the bell rung in the town of Dolores Hidalgo by Padre Miguel Hidalgo in 1810 at the start of the War of Independence.

President Madero (center) and ***General Victoriano Huerta*** (first from left to right) at a balcony of the Palacio Nacional, hours before Huerta betrayed the constitutional government of Mexico and helped to overthrow the Madero government;
President Madero on his ***road to the National Palace*** on February 13, 1913.

unprecedented act of political foolhardiness the ambassadors of the US, England, Spain and Germany took the view that President Madero, by not surrendering instantly to the mutineers, was responsible for the bloodshed. The Austrian and Japanese legations, with many Latin American representatives, led by Brazil, Chile, and Cuba, took the opposite view that the constitutional government resistance was warranted in maintaining its authority, and that it was no business of foreign diplomats to interfere against the constitutional Mexican government in a domestic conflict. Incredibly, the foreign ambassadors retorted that ...

> «*Madero ought to resign. Public opinion, both Mexican and foreign, holds the Federal Government responsible for these conditions.*»

Paul von Hintze, the German ambassador was designated by his colleagues to visit the National Palace and inform the President of the unanimous opinion of the diplomatic corps, which was that he should resign. President Madero replied to them...

> «*I do not recognize the right of diplomatists accredited to a nation to interfere in its domestic affairs; let me call your attention to the fact, which I fear many of you have somehow overlooked, that I am the constitutional President of Mexico. My resignation would plunge the country into political chaos. I might be killed, but I would not resign.*»

Incredibly, the ambassador went immediately to the National Palace to confer with General Huerta.

«*Upon arrival,*» Paul von Hintze would later comment,

> «*much to our regret, we were taken to see President Madero. Huerta also attended the meeting and an armistice was agreed on to clear the cities of cadavers, bury the dead and relocate non-combatants out of the danger zone . I was sent to the arsenal to obtain, Diaz's consent, which he gave.*»

On Monday, February 17, 1913, Gustavo Madero, the president's brother, was told at *Bambrinus restaurant*, where he was having breakfast with Victoriano Huerta, that his brother would be arrested at the Palacio Nacional at noontime. After learning the news, Gustavo was himself taken prisoner to *La Ciudadela* under military escort. **Victoriano Huerta** never intended to defeat *General Felix Diaz* and remove him from *La Ciudadela*. His makebelieve attack was a farce orchestrated by both to facilitate a traitorous *Coup d'Etat* and seize the presidency for themselves. After the arrest of the Madero brothers, Felix Díaz pressed his claims for the presidential office on the grounds that he had fought a valiant battle. But Huerta's claims were stronger since, had he had not betrayed Madero, the revolt could not have succeeded. He also

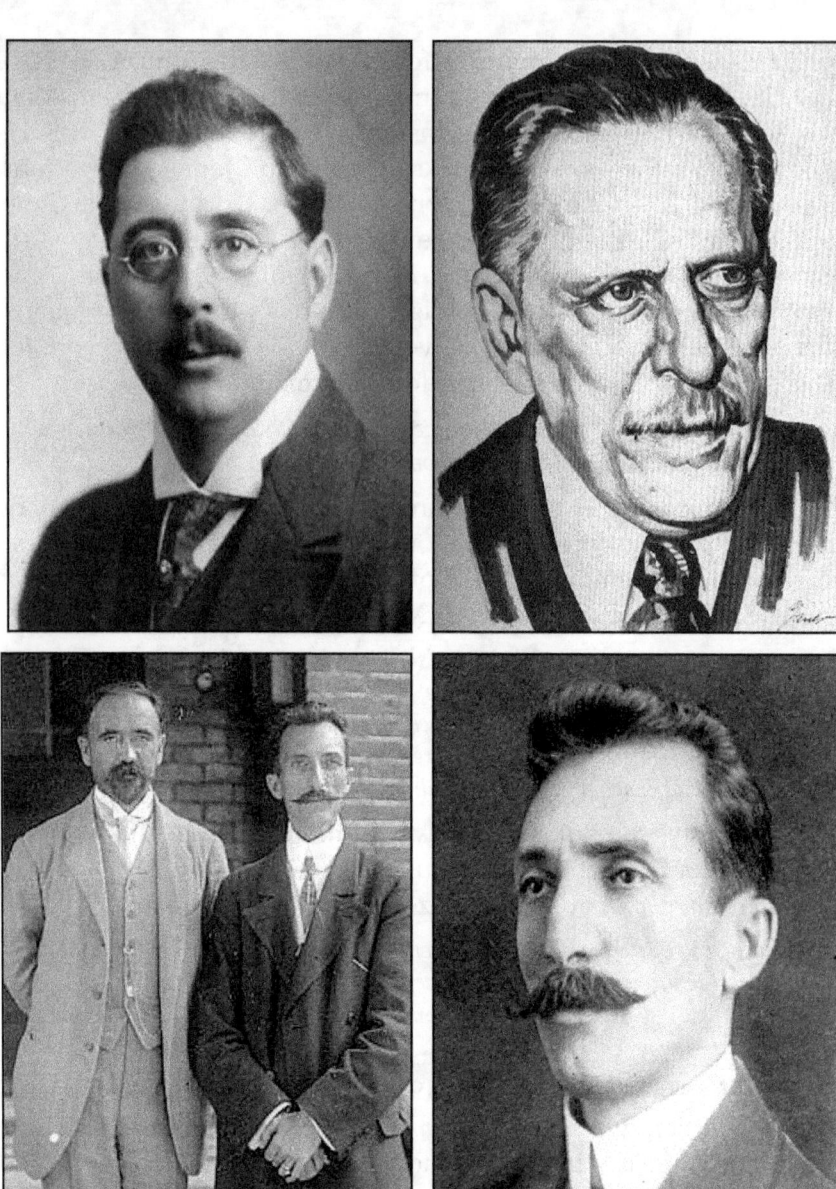

Portraits of four important personalities at the end of the *Decena Trágica*: ***Gustavo Madero*** (1875-1913), member of a wealthy Mexican family, brother of the president, tortured and killed in 1913 by orders of Victortiano Huerta; ***Manuel Marquez Sterling*** (1872-1934), Cuban ambassador to Mexico during the revolution and later ambassador to the US; ***President Madero and his VP José María Pino Suórez; Jose María Pino Suárez*** (1869-1913), Mexican statesman, jurist, poet, journalist and revolutionary who was assassinated with president Madero on February 22, 1913.

reminded Felix Diaz that he commanded more troops than him.

The *decena sangrienta* continued its insatiable search for victims. Now the removal of Madero would be seen as a viable end to the violence that was consuming Mexico. On February 18, 1913 Huerta arrested Madero and appointed himself as acting president of Mexico. That very night Gustavo Madero, the president's brother, was taken to an empty lot just outside *La Ciudadela*; his body was riddled with bullets and thrown into a makeshift tomb in the ground. Before killing him they had savagely tortured him and rendered him blind by emptying with a sword the eye socket of his one eye that had normal vision.

On the following day, Francisco I. Madero, in detention at an unknown place and threatened with death, upon hearing the pleading of his wife and mother, and to save their lives rather than his own, signed his resignation. Vice President Pino Suárez did the same.

Both resignations were placed in the hands of the Cuban minister, Manuel Márquez Sterling y Loret de Mola (1872-1934) [72] for delivery only after the two "retiring'" government executives and their families were safely out of the country.

Márquez Sterling was told on February 19 by a confidential source at the National Palace... «*A don Pancho lo truenan de un momento a otro.*» (Francisco Madero will soon be a dead man). He knew that to be a real possibility when he was told that Gustavo had already been killed the night before. He immediately went to the National Palace where he was assured that the life of Madero and his VP Pino Suárez were not in jeopardy.

The Cuban ambassador found out that Madero and Pino Suárez had been transferred to the Quartermaster area of the National Palace and he asked to visit them. Madero received him with joy and relief. He accepted the plan to be taken to Veracruz by Márquez Sterling and to go aboard a Cuban ship sent by President José Miguel Gómez to take him, Pino and both families into exile in Cuba under the protection of the Cuban government.

---

[72] ***Manuel Márquez Sterling y Loret de Mola*** had been born in Lima, Peru, at the legation of the Cuban Government in Arms in that city on August 28, 1872. His father had been a veteran in the War of Cuban Independence in 1868. His mother was Belén Loret de Mola, a distinguished Peruvian lady. After Peru recognized the independence of Cuba, Márquez Sterling was sent there as the Cuban representative. In 1902 he had been secretary to Gonzalo de Quesada in Washington; later he represented Cuba in the USA, Argentina and Mexico.

President Madero under arrest in 1913; on the left, ***Francisco Cárdenas***, assassin of Madero in February of 1913; on the right, ***Rafael Pimienta***, assassin of Pino Suárez; bottom, the back side of the *Penitenciaría del Palacio de Lecumberri*, on Northeast Mexico City (today's *General Mexican Archives*): on the ground, on the left, the cadaver of VP Pino Suárez, on the right the cadaver of Presidente Madero. Madero was 39 years old. Pino Suárez 34 years old.

Nothing seemed to foresee a catastrophe, yet Marquez Sterling was apprehensive because he had not received a safe passage document that Huerta had promised.[73] Word came out that the train trip to Veracruz would be starting at 5:00 am. Late that night, after Márquez Sterling had decided to stay with Madero until he could see him aboard the Cuban ship, Madero had a premonition and taking a picture from his suitcase he wrote on the back:

«*To my fine friend Manuel Márquez Sterling, as proof of my esteem and appreciation.*»

As he handed it to the ambassador he told him... «*Keep it in memory of this desolate night. There will never be any trains to Veracruz for me.*»

At 10:00 pm that night a guard came for Madero and Pino Suárez to take them by cars to the penitentiary of *Lecumberri* in ciudad Mexico. He told Márquez Sterling he had to take his own car and could not travel with them. A group of soldiers were waiting in front of the penitentiary building for the two cars where Madero and Pino Suárez were traveling. Madero was asked to dismount and as soon as he placed his foot on the ground a soldier shot him on the back of his head. Moments later Pino Suárez was murdered on the rear seat of his car. The soldiers at the entrance of the building fired more than 100 rounds all over the cars to set up a scenario of preventing a rescue attempt by the president's followers.

Márquez Sterling returned to Havana the following day with the families of Madero and Pino Suárez. The Cuban cruiser arrived in Havana at 10:00 pm on March 1, 1913. At the dock Manuel Sanguily, the Cuban Foreign Minister and the President's daughters were waiting for them. Márquez Sterling was received by president José Miguel Gómez within minutes of his arrival. His words were:

«*Your work in favor of the assassinated president went beyond the expectations from a diplomatic envoy. Ambassador, you have won for Cuba the hearts of every honest man.*»

---

[73] Days later **Márquez Sterling** wrote in his diary: «*To take the hat, quietly, and saying goodbye, au revoir, leaving them with a sentinel armed with a bayonet, would have been improper for a man in my situation, laden with my responsibility as the Cuban ambassador and the character of my chivalrous race. To protect with the flag of my country the president to whom a month before I had solemnly presented my credentials, was to meet with honor my sacred duty and to carry out my mission with all the intensity and respect that the circumstances were imposing on me.*»

Photos showing scenes from the **Decena Trágica** (February 9 to February 19, 1913), during which there was a *Coup d'État* against the constitutional government of Mexico (organized by Emiliano Zapata in Morelos, Pascual Orozco in Chihuahua, Bernardo Reyes in Nuevo León and Félix Díaz in Veracruz). The ten days culminated with the assassination of President Francisco I. Madero, and his Vice President, José María Pino Suárez, and the ascension of **Victoriano Huerta** to the presidency on February 20, 1913

Additional photos of the *Decena Trágica*.

Additional photos of the *Decena Trágica*

An American correspondent at the scene on the back side of the penitentiary of *Lecumberri* in ciudad Mexico, where the bodies of Madero and Pino Suárez laid on the ground a few feet apart, was told that a group of armed men had tried to rescue the president and the vice president and they were both accidentally shot in the crossfire; the story was that the two political leaders had leapt from the cars running towards their presumed rescuers. The account was greeted with general disbelief.

On that final day of the *decena trágica,* February 21, Madero's leadership came to end very fast. He had made several significant mistakes early in his presidency. His inaction alienated Zapata and the Constitutionalists who wanted to disband the haciendas and divide the lands among the nation's farmers. Madero, always the moderate, followed Mexican tradition of corruption and attempted to buy Zapata's complacence with a large piece of land and a hacienda of his own. This offer, his first mistake, only succeeded in turning Zapata against him.

Madero's second mistake was to try to please everyone, which resulted in severe indecision and total inaction. His hesitancy caused the revolutionaries from the North, Villa and Orozco, to join Zapata in denouncing him. The consequences were horrifying. Victoriano Huerta, and a small opposing faction led by Porfirio Diaz's nephew, Felix Diaz, fought recklessly in Mexico City in the *Decena Trágica;* it left the capital and the rest of the country exhausted.

The third and probably the worst mistake by Madero was to trust Victoriano Huerta, who eventually revolted against the president; his only defense was the army of his only true ally, General Felipe Angeles. In the process hundreds of civilians were brutally slaughtered in the worst carnage in the history of Mexico.

Huerta was a villain of the worst class, a drunkard and insatiable assassin who earned a permanent spot in Mexico's hall of infamy by deviously scheming the murder of president Francisco Madero. He was born in 1845 at Colotlán, in northern Jalisco, land of the Huichol tribe from which he derived. Since he was a youngster he was said to be distrusted and disliked in his native village. After graduating from the Military College, he distinguished himself in campaigns against the Yaqui Indians in Sinaloa and the Maya in Yucatan. The fact that he was an Indian himself did not prevent him from suppressing local indigenous uprisings with the utmost ruthlessness.

Victoriano Huerta embrazing one of his accompklices in the overthrow of Madero, General **Pascual Orozco Vázquez;** Victoriano Huerta with another co-conspirador, **Félix Díaz Velasco**, nephew of Porfirio Díaz. Félix Díaz in the end was betrayed by Huerta and had to take asylum in Havana; the US ambassador to Mexico in 1913, **Henry Lane Wilson** (1857-1932), whose role during the *Decena Trágica* was so devious that Presient Woodrow Wilson recalled and fired him; a Mexican newspepers of the times.

Huerta greatly admired Porfirio Diaz, another Indian who had succeeded in the outside world. When the *Porfiriato* came to an end, Huerta commanded the honor guard that accompanied him to Veracruz on his way into exile and it was said that he was moved to tears for the first and only time in his life.

When in 1912 Pascual Orozco went into rebellion against Madero (he believed Madero had slighted him by not appointing him Governor of Chihuahua), Madero reluctantly turned to Huerta to reduce Orozco to submission.[74] At first he had disapproved of Huerta's drinking; one of his advisers persuaded him to trust the man pointing out that General Ulysses Grant's fondness for the bottle never impaired his ability to command Lincoln's army. Huerta badly defeated Orozco but was infuriated when asked to account for funds he had received for the campaign, arrogantly replying that he was not a bookkeeper.

Madero was appalled by the murderous artillery duel all over Mexico city between Huerta's forces and those of Felix Diaz, the old dictator's nephew during the *decena trágica*. Madero knew this to be a sham battle staged between Huerta and Diaz in order to create a state of chaos that would pave the way for the removal of Madero. Huerta would then become president and name, with Diaz's approval, a new cabinet. After serving his term, Huerta would support Diaz as his successor.[75]

Huerta's rule over Mexico lasted between February 20, 1913 and July 15, 1914. At its end he failed to defeat a rebellion in the north mounted by Venustiano Carranza, Pancho Villa and Alvaro Obregón and was forced to resign and go into exile.[76] During those 30 months he spread fear and repression in Mexico while he was frequently seen in cafés and bordellos, heavily guarded, consuming his favorite bands of brandy.[77]

---

[74] Barely two years later, in 1913 and 1914, Orozco and Huerta reconciled and Orozco became chief of the **Colorados**, a paramilitary force that sowed terror in the countryside on behalf of Huerta. During WWI both Huerta and Orozco, attempted a failed *Coup d'État* in Mexico with the support of Germany.

[75] It has been amply confirmed that the American Ambassador to Mexico, **Henry Lane Wilson**, was instrumental in deposing Madero; he detested Madero as much as Madero detested him. From early in the *Decena Trágica* he clearly sympathized with the rebels and took it upon himself to steer the uprising as he thought best. Woodrow Wilson, however, elected president of the US on January 17, 1911, was a decided supporter of Francisco Madero.

[76] **Victoriano Huerta** died in exile on January 13, 1916 of cirrhosis of the liver.

[77] It was said art the time that his two best friends were **Hennessy** and **Martel**.

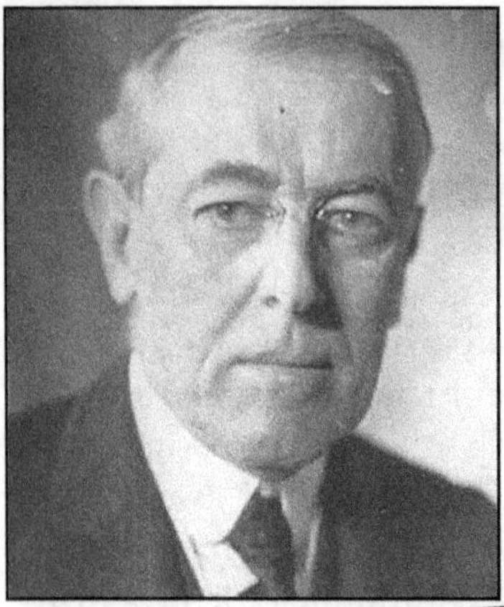

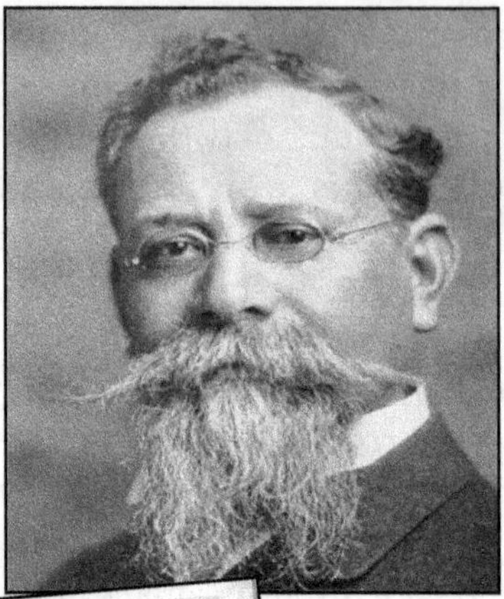

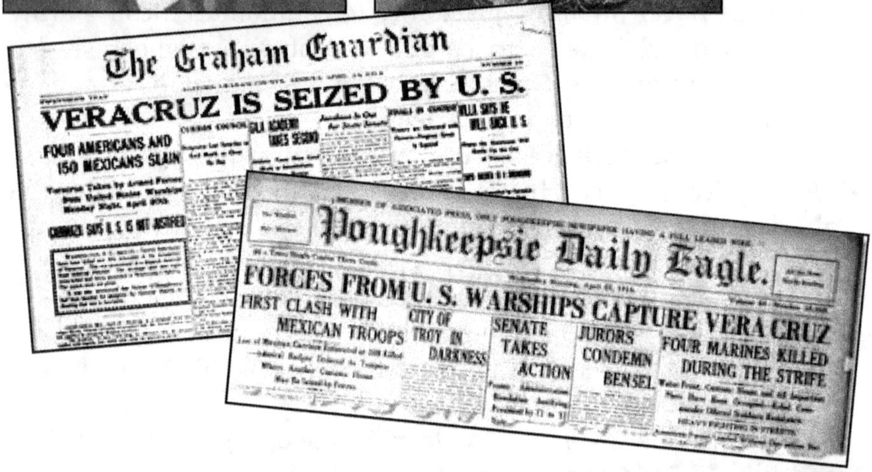

The Graham Guardian

VERACRUZ IS SEIZED BY U. S.

FOUR AMERICANS AND 150 MEXICANS SLAIN

Poughkeepsie Daily Eagle.

FORCES FROM U. S. WARSHIPS CAPTURE VERA CRUZ

FIRST CLASH WITH MEXICAN TROOPS

CITY OF TROY IN DARKNESS

SENATE TAKES ACTION

JURORS CONDEMN BENSEL

FOUR MARINES KILLED DURING THE STRIFE

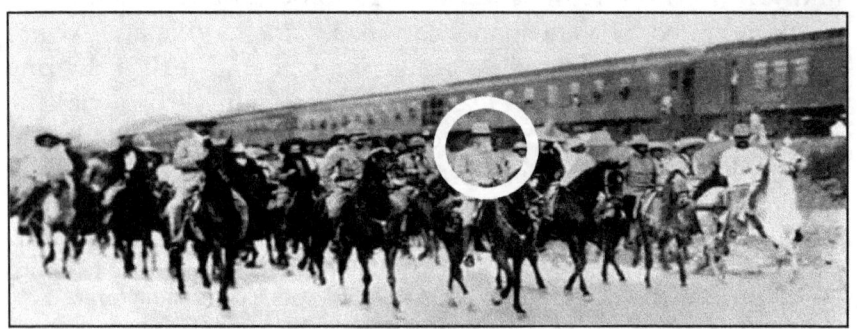

US President ***Woodrow Wilson*** (1856-1924), who refused to recognize the Huerta government after the overthrow of Madero; ***Venustiano Carranza*** (1859-1920), the Mexican constitutionalist leader who deposed Victoriano Huerta; newspapers reporting on the US bombing and occupation of ***Veracruz*** for seven months in an attempt to overthrow the Huerta government; forces by ***Venustiano Carranza*** at *La Cañada*, Queretaro, on January 22, 1916. At *La Cañada* Carranza and his allies formulated the bases for the ***Mexican Constitution of 1917***.

In the 1912 elections in the US, Woodrow Wilson (1856-1924) [78] won when William Howard Taft and Theodore Roosevelt split the Republican vote. His domestic policy included updating tariffs, revising of the banking system, checking of monopolies and fraudulent advertising and prohibiting unfair business practices. In terms of his foreign policy, he was somewhat aghast at the part the US ambassador had just played in Mexico, not only brokering a coup, which resulted in the overthrow of an elected president and his death, but also how he had handled the affair from the start.[79]

Woodrow Wilson decided early on not to recognize the government of Huerta. It was a great irony that Huerta had reached the presidency through his relation with US ambassador Henry Wilson and was later to lose it with another Wilson that was now the ambassador's boss. Wilson was decidedly favoring a *Maderista* General called Venustiano Carranza. On April 9, 1914, Mexican soldiers detained nine US soldiers in Tampico [80] and the US occupied the port city of Veracruz, causing the US and Mexico to brake diplomatic relations. Huerta resigned in July of that year. The new leader of Mexico as of July of 1914 was Venustiano Carranza (1859-1920).

Venustiano Carranza was a shrewd politician more than a military man. He supported Madero's challenge to Porfirio Díaz' regime in the 1910 elections and Madero's *Plan de San Luis Potosí* to nullify the elections and overthrow Díaz by force. Madero appointed him governor of Coahuila, his home state. When Madero was murdered in February 1913, Carranza drew up the *Plan de*

---

[78] ***Thomas Woodrow Wilson*** was the son of a Presbyterian minister, raised in a pious and academic houehold, an alumnus of Princeton University, the University of Virginia and Johns Hopkins University. He was enormously successful as a lecturer and very productive as a scholar. In 1902 he became president of Princeton University. He died of a cerebral hemorrage as an invalid, exhausted after his commitment to peace and the founding of the *League of Nations*.

[79] Wilson never doubted that ***Henry Lane Wilson*** had been the backbone and anchor of success for what evidently would have been a small, and unsuccessful revolt in Mexico. His actions had been taken without consultation, in direct opposition to what Washington preferred. He was dismissed by Woodrow Wilson shortly after the new US president took office.

[80] At the time ***Tampico***, north of Veracruz, was the second largest oil exporting port of the world with a substantial US investment and a large US expatriate community.

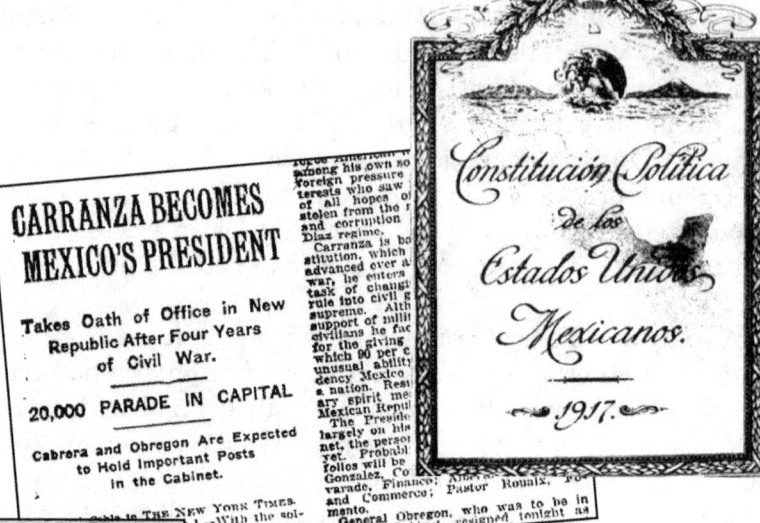

The enormously popular and durable *Constitución Política de los Estados Unidos Mexicanos*, the **Mexican Constitution of 1917**. It was praised as the model for the *Weimar Constitution of 1919* and the *Russian Conastitution of 1918*. It was approved on February 5, 1917, strongly based in *Benito Juárez' Constitution of 1857*. It imposed numerous anticlerical restrictions on the Catholic Church in Mexico; On the left Venustiano Carranza with Pancho Villa; on the right, a widely circulated photo of US Marines looking at several dead mexican fighters at the entrace of **Hotel Diligencias** in Veracruz on April of 1914. It was first published in Paris' *L'Illustration* in May, and is credited as having established photography as an important element of journalism.

Guadalupe, a political plan to oust Huerta. He was a tall and robust man, standing a full 6'4 and looked very impressive with his long white beard and glasses. He was intelligent and stubborn, but had very little charisma and no sense of humor. Although from a rich, northern landowning family he was concerned that Mexico's land property had not been fundamentally restructured by the Revolution. He was far more conservative than both Zapata and Villa.

Although Villa and Zapata had fought against the Huerta government, they never signed on to Carranza's *Plan of Guadalupe*. Once it became evident that Carranza was not going to introduce radical social reforms, Zapata broke with Carranza on September 5, 1914, at a time where there were tensions between Carranza and Villa over diplomatic incidents that Villa had provoked. When Huerta was overthrown, Villa defied Carranza's orders and rushed to capture Mexico's strategic silver-producing town of Zacatecas.[81] In addition, Carranza also distrusted Villa and did not wanted him to get to Mexico City. In August, Carranza refused to let Villa enter Mexico City with him, and refused to promote Villa to major-general. Villa formally disavowed Carranza on September 23, 1914.

Carranza and the victorious *Constitutionalists* disbanded what was left of the Huerta's Federal Army by August 13, 1914. The Army at the time included 10 Generals of Division, 61 Generals of Brigade, 1,006 *Jefes*, 2,446 Officers, 24,800 other ranks and 7,058 horses. There were also 21 regiments of *Rurales* with about 10,500 men. The Constitutional Army of Venustiano Carranza became the Army of Mexico. As a result, in subsequent fighting, they became known as the Federal Army or *Federales*. While they inherited the name of the Díaz/Huerta Army, Carranza's and Obregon's new Federal Army was a very different force.

Eventually Huerta attempted to return to Mexico by organizing a counter-revolution. He sought refuge in Spain and then moved on to the United States to be close to Mexico. He had met with German agents in an effort to secure the Kaiser's support for a *Coup d'État*. The Germans provided some funding, hoping that Huerta's return to the presidency would distract the United States and discourage American intervention in World War I. When Huerta attempted to enter Mexico. American authorities arrested

---

[81] Villa's successful capture of the town of **Zacatecas** was the last straw that broke the back of Huerta's regime.

On the left, Pancho Villa (right circle) and Emiliano Zapata (left circle) entering Mexico city on December 7, 1914.

Above is probably the most reproduced photo of the entire Mexican Revolution. Villa with his elite troops, and Zapata with his family, met at Xochimilco, 12 miles south of Mexico city, on December 6, 1914; there they decided to jointly occupy the capital. After they had taken the city, they threw a banquet at the *National Palace*, where this photo was taken.

Villa is on the presidential chair, and joked with Zapata insisting they take turns sitting in the presidential chair for a photograph. *«I didn't fight for that,»* Zapata allegedly said, *«We should burn that chair to end all ambitions.»*

In the photo *Villa* is (# 1), *Zapata* is (# 2), there are native Mexicans of dark complexion (#3), mestizos (#4), caucasians (#5), boys (#6 and #11), senior people (#7), aristocrats (#8) and foreigners (#9). Standing up on the extreme right (#10), is *Rodolfo Fierro*, Villa's personal bodyguard and his most ruthless murderer. On the right of Villa is *Tomás Urbina Reyes* (#12), Villa's best General.

him and Pascual Orozco near the Mexican border on June 27, 1915. Authorities charges them with conspiracy to violate U.S. neutrality laws. They were held in a U.S. Army prison at Fort Bliss, were released on bail, but later imprisoned again as they were considered a flight risk. Huerta's health deteriorated in prison and died of cirrhosis of the liver on January 13, 1916.

Carranza had become an important revolutionary figure in Mexico and he prevailed over other revolutionaries after Huerta's ouster. He would become the natural leader of Mexico from 1915 to 1917, and with the promulgation of a new revolutionary *Mexican Constitution* in 1917, he was elected president, serving from 1917 to 1920.

When Carranza assumed the presidency, both Villa and Zapata refused to recognize him. Villa with his Army of the North and Zapata with the Army of the South entered Mexico City. Carranza and Obregón with their Armies fled the capital and retreated to Veracruz, Mexico's major port. The Villistas and Zapatistas held raucous celebrations after reaching Mexico City. They did not, however, have the organizational skills to set up a real government. While in Veracruz Carranza and Obregón reorganized and resupplied and launched a new offensive to retake the capital.

In the fighting that ensued, Obregón largely destroyed Villa's cavalry at Celaya (1915);[82] Obregón lost there his right arm, but won the battle. He commanded a modern force with artillery and machine guns while Villa relied solely on his men with hand weapons and rifles on horse. Villa's role, from Celaya on, became simply a continuing pesty irritation in the North of Mexico and never again seriously threatened the government.

Celaya, followed by a well earned presidency, was an extraordinary major accomplishment for Venustiano Carranza. It finally

---

[82] The **Battle of Celaya** (present day *Guanajuato*) in April of 1915, was a long series of engagements which probably constitute the most massive battle ever fought anywhere in Latin America. The hero was Alvaro Obregón, a man loyal to Carranza who was without doubt his best general; 4,000 of Villa's soldiers were killed and 6,000 captured. Obregón had chosen the site of battle, arrived well in advance and waited for Villa to stage his typical blind cavalry charge. Villa's defeat was the result of his overconficence on his 2 to 1 advantage of men over Obregón's army. Villa was lured away from his supplies and communication lines into a field full of canals, trenches, barbed wire obstacles and hidden machine guns. Villa and his senior staff ended up escaping from the theater of action. 120 of his junior officers were captured and executed on the fields they had attacked.

Photos and press reports of the *death of Emiliano Zapata* in 1919. On April 10, 1919, rebel warlord Emiliano Zapata was double-crossed, ambushed and killed by federal forces working with Coronel Jesus Guajardo under direct orders from President Venustiano Carranza. Zapata was greatly loved by the impoverished people of Morelos and southern Mexico, but had proved to be a nuisance to every man who would try to lead Mexico during revolutionary times because of his stubborn insistence on land, freedom and justice for the poor of Mexico.

destroyed the primarily feudal system imposed on Mexico by the Spanish which had operated in Mexico for four centuries. The US recognized Carranza as President of Mexico in October 1915.

The Government finally dealt with Zapata, a man greatly loved by the impoverished people of Morelos and southern Mexico but an annoyance to every man who tried to lead Mexico because of his stubborn insistence on land, freedom and justice for the poor of Mexico. He clashed with dictator Porfirio Diaz, President Francisco I. Madero, usurper Victoriano Huerta and reformer Venustiano Carranza, always taking to the field with his army of ragged peasant soldiers every time his demands were ignored. In 1916, President Venustiano Carranza ordered his generals to get rid of Zapata by any means necessary. On April 10, 1919, after a vicious anti-guerrilla campaign weakened his forces, Zapata was lured into a trap by a government army colonel, betrayed, ambushed and killed.[83]

Once Villa and Zapata were out of the way, president Carranza appointed General Álvaro Obregón as Minister of War and of the Navy. Carranza and Obregón worked well together leading the more moderate elements within the Constitutionalists, although their aims were quite different; Carranza wanted a liberal, democratic government that would not get involved in social reforms; his focus was a narrow, legalistic reform. Obregón, on the other hand, knew that a comprehensive reform of the political life of Mexico was inevitable.[84]

As Carranza's presidential period was approaching its end, Carranza knew he was under a no-reelection promise and attempted to hold power by backing the election of a supportive *alter ego* in 1920. Obregón announced his candidacy for the presidency on June 1, 1919. Carranza was determined to continue his presidency directly or indirectly.

The people of Mexico had other designs; it soon became clear that Obregón would win the election by a landslide. Carranza attempted a preemptive *Coup d'État*, and Obregón was forced to

---

[83] ***Zapata's*** influence persisted long after his passing away; his agrarian reform movement, known as *zapatismo*, remains important to many Mexicans to this day. In 1994, for instance, a guerrilla group calling themselves the *Zapata Army of National Liberation* launched a successful peasant rebellion in the southern state of Chiapas.

[84] ***Alvaro Obregón*** did not concur, however, on the wide-spread reform advocated by Zapata in the *Plan de Ayala*.

On the top left, President **Plutarco Elías Calles** (1877-1945), powerful interior minister under President Álvaro Obregón, who chose Calles as his successor. His efforts to improve the lives of Mexicans was blurred by his rabid antri-clerical ideology. On the top right, the funeral of assassinated President **Venustiano Carranza** (most likely killed by Alvaro Obregón followers in May of 1920); at the center, the corpse of **Francisco (Pancho) Villa** (1878-1923), assassinated on July 20, 1923. Villa challenged Porfirio Díaz, disapproved Madero's trust in Venustiano Carranza, fought Huerta, had disputes with Zapata, joined Carranza, was friendly to US General John J. Pershing, pacted with Zapata against Carranza, attacked the US territory and retired to Chihuahua. On July 20, 1923, he was assassinated while driving in his black 1919 Dodge touring car with his bodyguards; on the bottom left, **Adolfo de la Huerta** (1881-1955), leader of the *Revolution of Agua Prieta* which put an end to the presidency of Venustiano Carranza and was Mexico's 38th President for 6 months in 1920. He was succeeded by Alvaro Obregón.

flee to safety in the state of Guerrero and from there organize a military campaign against his former mentor. He was supported by two leading generals, Plutarco Elías Calles (1877-1945) [85] and Adolfo de la Huerta (1881-1955).[86] As Obregón's forces were about to enter his final campaign against Carranza's army and approached the capital, Carranza panicked and fled, trying to reach the port of Veracruz from where he could leave the country; it was, once more, the time-honored escape route for battered Mexican presidents and generals. It failed him as it had failed Madero. Obregón's forces arrested and shot Carranza on May 21, 1920 and went on to serve as the next Mexican President from 1920 to 1924.

When General Alvaro Obregón assumed the presidency of Mexico the country was politically and socially unhinged; he was probably the only man that could rebuild it after the Revolution. He was the greatest general throughout the Mexican Revolution, committed to a full implementation of the Constitution of 1917; this made him one of the most radical presidents Mexico had seen. He used to say that the best compliment he had ever received was «he was both a true Mexican and a diplomat.»

Obregón was no full blooded aristocrat like Madero and Carranza but was more European than Indian. His family had a solid upper crust lineage, but he was a successful farmer and business man, sincere, friendly and humble. He had married in 1902, but his wife died in 1907, leaving him with two small children and

---

[85] *Plutarco Elías Calles* was a military and political Mexican leader who modernized the revolutionary armies and later became president of Mexico. He joined Madero against Porfirio Díaz and defeated Victoriano Huerta and Pancho Villa as Gweneral in the Mexican Army. Carranza appoointede him secretary of Commerce, Labor and Industry but he resigned to support the candidacy of Alvaro Obregón in 1919. As president after Obregón he took radical measures against the influence of the Catholic Church and the US. In 1934 he was forced to support Lázaro Cárdenas as candidate for the presidency and because of his mild endorsement he was forced into exile until 1941, when he was permitted to return to Mexico.

[86] *Adolfo de la Huerta* (no relation to Victoriano Huerta, the *Jackal*, who presided Mexico from 1913 to 1914), was a politician and Governor of the state of Sonora who led the revolt that put an end to the presidency and the life of Venustiano Carranza. He had presided over the surrender of Pancho Villa and started his own revolt against president Obregón in 1923, denouncing him as *incorregibly corrupt*. With his extraordinary organizing ability and popular support, Obregón crushed Huerta's rebellion and forced him into exile on March 7, 1924. On that day, as Huerta was flying to Los Angeles, Obregón ordered the execution of every officer in Huerta's army with a rank higher than a major.

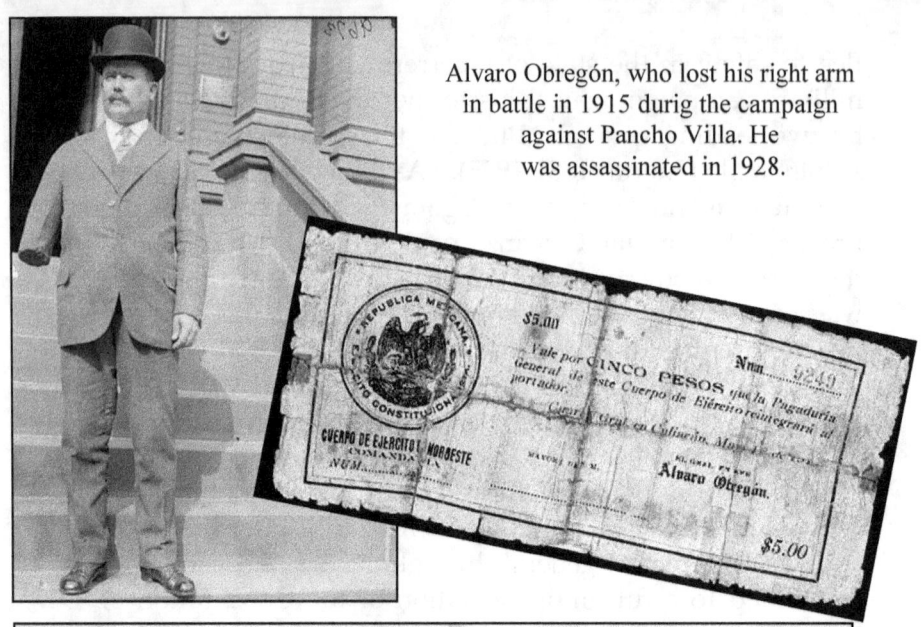

Alvaro Obregón, who lost his right arm in battle in 1915 durig the campaign against Pancho Villa. He was assassinated in 1928.

On top, *Álvaro Obregón* (1880-1928) in 1915. He opposed Orozco's rebellion and was a supporter of Carranza when he opposed Huerta in 1915.
Later he launched a revolt against Carranza in which Carranza was assassinated. His presidency was the first stable period since 1910. Below, the signers of the *Plan de Agua Prieta*, Sonora, who repudiated the government of Carranza and had him killed at an ambush on the early hours of May 21. 1920.

business problems with little time or interest in politics. Madero's revolutionary achievements changed all that.

Once he entered the military he displayed a natural talent for soldiering. He joined forces with Madero to defeat Orozco during the revolution; he joined Venustiano Carranza take up arms against Victoriano Huerta and his natural executive and fighting abilities gained him the leadership of the *Constitutionalist Army of the Northwest*. He became the most feared and respected military man in Mexico, having never lost a battle. It was Obregón who accepted the surrender of the Federal Army under Carranza's presidency; it was he who stopped Villa from taking control of the Revolution, and it was he who began to build a new *Mexican National Army*.

Once Carranza realized that Obregón qualities and popularity surpassed his own, he became apprehensive of the ambitions of his popular and powerful War Minister; looking for an excuse to dislike Obregón, he began to consider him too radical politically. Obregón resigned as War Minister and retired to civilian life; it only delayed the unavoidable clash between these two powerful revolutionary personalities. Carranza was a creature of militarism and maintained his power by befriending all of Mexico's triumphant military chiefs. Obregón was decidedly against militarism; he believed that the treason, brutality, corruption, and personal opportunism of the revolutionary leaders were damaging the good name of the Constitutionalist Army. Once Obregón resigned as War Minister, there was little implementation of his programs for military reforms. Carranza's leadership was very ineffective in military matters, however, and the *Constitutionalist Army* was soon demoralized and began to defect to Obregón in 1920.

Obregón declared his own presidential candidacy in 1920 with his *Plan de Agua Prieta*, where he pledged to clean the widespread corruption in the government. As a man who build coalitions, he was supported by Porfirian elites, foreign business interests, ruthless caudillos, and land-hungry peasants. As a patrician he was happy to receive the support of the *Casa del Obrero Mundial*,[87]

---

[87] The *Casa del Obrero Mundial* was a socialist and anarcho-syndicalist worker's organization located in the popular Tepito Barrio of Mexico City. It had been founded in 1912 during the presidency of Madero and functioned as the headquarters for many syndicates and unions on a mutual aid basis. Its aims were the abolition of capitalism and the active support of worker's syndicates for a confederated socialist economy.

On top: a meeting of the *Constitutional Assembly* in Querétaro in 1917. On the bottom right, Venustiano Carranza and Alvaro Obregón. Below left, Obregon had many retractors. In a book published in 1920, José María Martorena, a deadly enemy, stated that Obregón had the intention to «*consolidate his power by means of a dictatorship stronger than that of Porfirio Díaz.*» The book made the best seller list.

which supplied him with six battalions of workers to fight against Villa. At both the *1917 Constitutional Convention* and the 1919-1920 presidential campaign, the workers' support of Obregón's position contributed immensely to Carranza defeat.

After his successful 1920 rebellion, he became president over Carranza. The labor unions were rewarded with his respect of the guarantees in the *1917 Constitution* concerning right to organize, to strike, minimum wages and maximum hours. As president, his task was to organize a strong gubernatorial system that would generate a civilized political environment but also an economic atmosphere that would satisfy the powerful classes without betraying the ideals of the *1917 Constitution*. This created much unwanted turmoil during his first years as president. The development of mass support was a key feature of Obregón's plan to establish a strong national government. Under Diaz, the church, the business interests, the landholders and the army, under a broad umbrella, were able to maintain effective control of the country and its institutions. The Madero revolution had broken the coalition Diaz had formed and neither Madero, nor Huerta, or Carranza, could reestablish it.

Not counting with only traditional forces, Obregón included workers and peasants in his civilian base; like Diaz, he had developed a closely controlled and reliable army to support a powerful central government. He accomplished that task through a much desired agrarian reform; it redistributed land to peasants to appease the militant agrarian radicals and recruit them into his political coalition.

Unlike his predecessors Obregón did his very best to make friends with the US. He painstakingly established good relations and understood the political power United States. By developing close ties with the US and its important international financiers, he was able to make good use of Mexico's most important natural resource—oil. Oil was use to repay their international debt and present sound financial statements to investors.

It became clear by late 1922 that Obregón preferred Calles to succeed him for the 1924-28 presidential term instead of De la Huerta, who outranked Calles but had not been a good administrator as Secretary of Finance and Public Credit. Obregón's selection of Calles alienated his supporters and many of them started conspiring against the candidacy of Calles while denouncing Obregón as corrupt.

On top, ***Presidents Calles and Obregón*** in 1920; a woodcut showing the ***assassination of Obregón*** in Mexico at the hands of a man who held Obregón responsible for religious persecutions in 1928. On the right, ***the hand of Obregón***; he had lost the arm at the elbow during a battle on June 3, 1915. For over half a century, the limb was on display in a jar of formaldehyde at a large pink and black marble monument under the angel of Paseo La Reforma in Mexico city, surrounded by inscriptions praising the general as a military genius.

In December 1923, a rebellion by De la Huerta, Villa and others negated all Obregón's efforts to build a strong, principled and apolitical national army. He was faced with a military uprising which nearly destroyed his government.[88] When his term ended in December 1924, he had not finished his efforts to build a professional army. The work had to be continued by his handpicked successor, General Plutarco Elias Calles. Calles mandate enjoyed a great deal of political stability thanks to Obregón's previous efforts to stabilize Mexico. Obregón's reconstruction efforts resolved some of Mexico's debts problems and gained international diplomatic recognition through advanced negotiations with international banks. He was trusted and popular enough to earn a second presidential term [89] with programs that were basically those of 1920-24. Before taking office, however, he was assassinated by a fanatical Roman Catholic. He had done what no other Mexican leader had accomplished, restoring order to the chaotic and war exhausted Mexico. Unfortunately he had to pay the price of the rabid anti-Catholic sentiment nurtured by many of Calles decisions.

With the death of Obregón, Calles continued his decade of dominance of Mexican political life; to his 4 years as president he added 6 years as the *"power behind the throne."* His most important decisions were to implement and enforce constitutional provisions regarding religious matters and eradicate foreign ownership of petroleum resources. On the first topic he precipitated a conflict between the Church and the state in the form of an economic boycott, suspension of religious services, and the armed rebellion of the *Cristeros*. On the second, he launched a policy that became sacred for successive Mexican governments for almost a century.

The 1924 presidential campaign of Plutarco Elías Calles was the first populist presidential campaign in Mexico's history; he called for land redistribution, promised equal justice and more and better public education as well as additional labor rights and demo-

---

[88] The ***rebel generals***, as the main founders and masterminds of the revolution, felt entitled to political power. They were not happy to confine themselves to the role of supporters of the central government. They wanted to be "in charge" and felt like the president was overly attentive to agrarian complaints about land distribution. Obregón prevailed and eventually executed all of his activist political and military rivals.

[89] Calles could not be reelected but effected a constitutional amendment that allowed non-consecutive re-elections for president; it made possible Obregón's return to the presidency. Calles was also hoping it would allow his own return to power in 1928.

The rebellion of the Cristeros in 1927. On top, a ***secret Catholic mass*** in a secluded place; center, a ***sacrilegious mass*** performed by anti-cristeros to make fun of their religious liturgy; the original and post-*profanation look of a Catholic church* during the agressions against the Church in the late 1920s.

cratic governance. Calles indeed tried to fulfill his promises during his populist phase from 1924 to 1926. Unfortunately he moved later into an anti-clerical phase that lasted from 1926 to the end of his "formal" presidency in 1928. His influence persisted during 1928 to 1935, a period known as the *Maximato*.[90]

Calles was a staunch opponent of the clergy for several reasons including its real or alleged power and influence in Mexico's public and political life; during his term as president, he moved to enforce the anticlerical articles of the *1917 Constitution*, which led to a violent and lengthy conflict known as the *Cristero War*, during which the Mexican government violently persecuted the clergy, massacring suspected priests, lay followers, catholic educators and businessmen and their supporters.[91] On 14 June 1926, Calles enacted anticlerical legislation known formally as *The Law Reforming the Penal Code* and unofficially as the *Calles Law*. His anti-Catholic actions included outlawing religious orders, closing Catholic schools, depriving the Church of property rights and depriving the clergy of civil liberties, including their right to trial by jury in cases involving anti-clerical laws, and the right to vote. Catholic antipathy towards Calles was enhanced because of his vocal atheism.

People in strongly Catholic areas, especially the states of Jalisco, Zacatecas, Guanajuato, Colima and Michoacán, began to oppose him, and on 1 January 1927, a war cry went up from the faithful Catholics, "¡*Viva Cristo Rey!*"[92]

---

[90] The name has its roots in the name of Calles himself, who was popularly known as "**El Jefe Máximo**." During the *Maximato* there were three presidents in México: *Emilio Portes Gil* (1928–1930), was designated by Congress to replace the president-elect Álvaro Obregón, assassinated before taking office; *Pascual Ortiz Rubio* (1930–1932), who was elected to complete Obregón's term but resigned within months after there was an attempt on his life; and *Abel Mata Hernández* (1932–1934), who was designated by Congress to substitute for Ortiz Rubio.

[91] In May 1926, Calles was awarded a medal of merit from the head of Mexico's **Scottish Rite of Freemasonry** in recognition of his actions against the Catholic Church.

[92] On November 23, 1927, a Jesuit priest, **José Ramón Miguel Agustín Pro Juárez**, known among Catholics as *Padre Pro*, was sent to the firing squad without trial. President Calles gave orders to have Pro executed under the pretext of having participated in the assassination of president-elect *Álvaro Obregón*. In reality he was killed for defying the virtual outlawing of Catholicism. Calles ordered a careful photographed documentation of the execution, and most Mexican newspapers published the photos on their front page the following day. The photos strengthened the *Cristeros* resolve.

A cruel execution of Catholics gave rise to the ***Cristeros rebellion*** in the years 1926 to 1929. The rebellion was a widespread struggle in central Mexico against the secularist anti-clerical policies of the Mexican government. On top, the execution at age 36 of ***Father Miguel Pro*** (1891-1927) a Jesuit; bottom, the execution of ***Father Francisco Vera*** on May 21, 1927.

Almost 70,000 lay Catholics and 400 priests, nuns and religious brothers died in the war. By 1934 out of an initial register of 4,800 priests residing in Mexico prior to the rebellion, only 334 were allowed to stay, the rest were expelled from the country. At the time Mexico had 15 million Catholics. A truce was negotiated only when the *Cristeros* agreed to lay down their arms. Calles initially agreed but later, within a few weeks, reneged on the terms of the truce; he had approximately five hundred *Cristero* leaders and 5,000 other *Cristeros* shot on firing squads or, frequently, in their homes in front of their wives and children. After the truce was accepted by the Mexican government, it was particularly repulsive to Catholics to tolerate the stubborn Calles's determination to create a complete state monopoly on education, suppressing all Catholic education, at any and all levels, and introducing "*socialist*" education in its place, saying:

> «We must enter and take possession of the mind of childhood, the mind of youth.»

The end of the *Cristeros War* was made possible when world opinion turned aggressively against Calles;[93] the driving forces against the criminal abuses in Mexico were the US ambassador, the *US National Catholic Welfare Conference*, Mexican Archbishop Leopoldo Ruíz Flores, the *US and Mexican Councils of the Knights of Columbus*,[94] Los Angeles Archbishop John Joseph Cantwell, Pope Pius XI through his encyclical *Firmissimam Constantiam* on March 28, 1937 and the worldwide *Catholic Action* movement. [95]

---

[93] There were also organizations outside Mexico that publicly supported the persecution of Catholics in Mexico and even sent Calles funds to continue the fight against the Catholic Church, notably the ***American Ku Klus Klan***.

[94] The American ***Knights of Columbus*** collected more than $1 million to assist exiles from Mexico, to continue the education of expelled seminarians and to inform citizens of the US about oppression in Mexico. After the end of the *Cristeros War*, nine of the Catholic victims tortured and killed by Mexican government troops that were beatified or canonized were *Knights of Columbus*.

[95] *Catholic Action* was the name of worldwide groups of lay Catholics who were committed to increase Catholic influence on society. They were very active in the XIX and XX centuries in historically Catholic countries that fell under anti-clerical regimes such as Spain, Italy, Bavaria, France, Russia, Germany, Belgium and Mexico. Adolf Hitler, for instance, attacked the *Catholic Action* groups in Nazi Germany during and after the *Night of the Long Knives*. During the Cuban Revolution of 1959, the communists in power attacked and literally dispersed all the *Catholic Action* groups on the island.

Lázaro de Cardenas and the *Mexican ejidos*. On the left, President Cárdenas reads the decree of expropiation of land and the creation of ejidos on March 18, 1938.

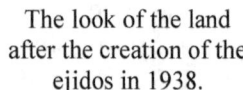

The look of the land after the creation of the ejidos in 1938.

Ejido land is not private property and cannot be bought and sold. A foreigner cannot buy Ejido land; it can only be sold to Mexicans. A Mexican citizen wishing to purchase Ejido land must have the agreement of the whole community that 'owns' the land and it is not often clear who the owners (or their ancestors) are. If an Ejido is sold without the agreement of all (potential) owners, the buyer can risk a legal battle after the purchase which, in the worst case scenario, can lead to a loss of the land. In 1920 the concept of the Ejido was adopted by Mexican President Álvaro Obregón, in the form of the "" (Ejido Act). The government ceded land to local inhabitants, as a community, mostly of Indian origin, for use as farmland. The Ejidos were then passed down from generation to generation and could not be sold to ensure that the local farmers would never be stripped of their land again.

In 1934 Lázaro Cárdenas (1895-1970) was elected president of México. He earned the respect of Pope Pius XI and befriended major figures in the Mexican Catholic Church, who in turn persuaded the faithful to obey the government's laws in a peaceful manner. Cárdenas was originally the hand-picked candidate of president Plutarco Elías Calles, who had founded the *Partido Nacional Revolucionario* in 1929 [96] and tried to remain the power behind the president after the election of his disciple. Cárdenas, however, out-maneuvered Calles politically and forced him into exile, establishing his legitimacy and power in his own right.

Cárdenas, if anything, was a very shrewd politician and crafty administrator. His government overhauled the agrarian reform that had been crudely initiated by the Mexican Revolution, and created *ejidos* [97] in the Mexican agricultural sector, which gave peasants access to land, but did not give individual titles to it. He granted asylum to exiles from the 1936-1939 Spanish Civil War, and strengthened the educational system.

Historians have debated when was it that the Mexican Revolution ended. The execution of Carranza and the 1920 election of Obregón were initially good dates marking the end of the Revolution. Many historians nowadays believe that the best end of the revolution was 1946, when Lázaro Cárdenas turned over the presidency to Manuel Ávila Camacho.

---

[96] The 1928 assassination of president-elect Álvaro Obregón led Plutarco Elías Calles in 1929 to launch the **Partido Nacional Revolucionario, PNR** (National Revolutionary Party).

Mexico's presidents from 1924 to 1928, Emilio Portes Gil, Pascual Ortiz Rubio and Abelardo L. Rodríguez, were all members of the PNR. When Lázaro Cárdenas became Mexico's president (most renowned for expropriating the oil interests of the United States and European petroleum companies in the run-up to World War II), he had the party renamed the **Partido de la Revolución Mexicana, PRM** (Party of the Mexican Revolution).

In 1946 Cárdenas's successor, Manuel Ávila Camacho, gave the party its present name, **Partido Revolucionario Institucional, PRI** (Institutional Revolutionary Party)

From 1929 to 1982, toward the end of his term, every incumbent president in consultation with party leaders, selected the PRI's candidate in the next election in a procedure known as *el dedazo* (the tap of the finger). The PRI won every presidential election in those years by well over 70 percent of the vote; margins that were usually obtained by massive electoral fraud.

[97] The *ejidos* were areas of communal lands used for agriculture, on which community members had individual control of designated parcels and collectively maintained communal holdings such as roads, equipment, tools and sheds.

♪♫♪♫...
...si Adelita se fuera con otro...
la seguiría por tierra y por mar ...
si por mar en un buque de guerra,
si por tierra en un tren militar
...♪♫♪♫

Mexican ***Armed Forces*** marching constantly through the cities during the times of the Mexican revolution; "***Adelita***" became one of the most popular Mexican corridos during revolutionary times. It was inspired by a *soldadera* from Durango. The balad honors all heroic women who dedicated their lives to the revolution by joining the war efforts in the battlefield.

The general world impression regarding the Mexican Revolution, not only abroad but also in Mexico, was that during 30 years Mexico was nothing but chaos. Abroad the impression also included the conclusion that the Mexican people had an incorrigible tendency towards disorder and war. Between 1910 and 1940 all possible forms of government tried to rule Mexico, from brutal military movements without organization of any kind, such as those of Zapata and Villa, to governments of apparent democratic principles but headless, such as the factions taking turns after the *Convención de Aguascalientes*.[98] The press headlines of the time told foreigners of bloody deeds, battles, assaults, executions, betrayals, trains that were blown, massacres, thousands of men in armies that moved from one place to another, incursions on US territory, shootings in front of children, incarcerations, thousands of people going into exile and the like.

A closer look to Mexico during those years showed a multiracial population that included hundreds of indigenous people that spoke different languages and dialects, *mestizos*, Spaniards remaining in Mexico after the *Conquista*, North Americans and many other Europeans attracted by the climate and the business opportunities in Mexico. So diverse was the Mexican population that it made no sense to speak of a Mexican race or ethnicity. In addition, Mexico had an educational problem: a large percentage of the population was uneducated. On the religious front, the Spanish system of patronage extended to the Catholic Church by the Spanish kings gave a considerable power to the clergy, which lasted well into the times of the revolution. In terms of land cultivation, Mexico had a centuries old condition of serfdom of its rural classes while large tracks of affluent estates escaped the obligation of paying taxes.

Initially in 1910, the Mexican Revolution did not begin as a revolt of the lower classes asking for their rights to share in the direction and the wealth of the country. It began as a struggle bet-

---

[98] The ***Convention of Aguascalientes*** had the intention of settling the differences between the four great leaders, Pancho Villa, Emiliano Zapata, Venustiano Carranza and Alvaro Obregón. Its formal title was *La Gran Convención de Jefes militares con mando de fuerzas y gobernadores de los Estados*. From the onset on October 10, 1914, it was clear that nothing could be accomplished. Zapata and Villa went to Mexico City on December 6 with 60,000 men, celebrated their luck and got drunk. Carranza retreated to Veracruz. Obregón left the grounds in support of Carranza. A new president, General Eulalio Gutiérrez Ortiz, was appointed; his term lasted 20 days.

A woodcut shoring **Emiliano Zapata** (1879-1919) with his slogan *Tierra y Libertad* (Land and Freedom); a group of Mexican revolution rebels during a lunch pause eating tortillas; City troops in formation on a city in Mexico during the times of the revolution.

ween two sections of Mexico's capitalist class: the oligarchy of old wealth that was thriving around Porfirio Díaz[99] on the one hand, and, on the other hand, a new modernizing bourgeois class of people, of which Francisco Indalecio Madero was a prime example; this was particularly true and strong in the Northern Mexico area that had close contact with the North American experience. The development of capitalism during the prosperous years 1880-1910 fostered the formation of this emergent bourgeois middle and professional class that found itself systematically shut out of the nation's political life by the Porfirian oligarchy.

Those prosperous years resulted in an increase in land concentration and many other forms of rural oppression, which resulted in growing landlessness, poverty, hunger, and destitution among the rural majority. As a result, Mexico was witness to a political revolt from above and a social revolution from below. When Madero and Orozco launched their political bourgeois revolt against Díaz in 1910, it opened an opportunity for the rural poor (90% of the population) to vent their accumulated grievances, mostly the return of the lands that had been taken from them in the *Porfiriato* and the exaction of retribution against abusive local landowners. These were the origins of the revolution's popular, agrarian impulse, epitomized in the figure of Emiliano Zapata and his slogan "*Land and Liberty*."

Zapata, and later Villa, created a new narrative of Mexican history that put natives and *mestizos* rather than the middle class at the center of the nation's future (as shown graphically in the murals of Diego Rivera), while seriously eroding the long-established bonds of domination-subordination that were indelibly engraved in Mexico's past history. It unfortunately failed to deliver on the promise of agrarian reform for quite a long time.

A reality that the revolutionaries could not predict was that when the politically disenfranchised rising middle class competed with the impoverished agrarian masses, the former decidedly triumphed; witness the dominance and the entrenchment in power of the *Sonorans*, the increasingly conservative policies after 1920 and the formation in 1929 of the predecessor to the *PRI* (Institutional Revolutionary Party), the notorious oxymoron of a political

---

[99] Contemporary historians have defined the ***Porfiriato***, the thirty-five year dictatorship that preceded the Revolution, as the consolidation of bourgeois capitalism, rather than a period of semi-feudalism, as was suggested by historians of the 1930s generation.

A mural showing **Venustiano Carranza** on Feruary 5, 1917 during the proclamation of the *Mexican Constitution*; **Lázaro Cárdenas** (1895-1970), a general in the Mexican revolution and a statesman who served as President of Mexico between 1934 and 1940. A former follower of his mentor Plutarco Calles, he out-maneuvered him politically and sent him into exile; a ggantic **stone head of Cárdenas** in Guerrero, Mexico.

party that was (and remains) "*revolutionary*" in name only, that dominated the country's politics in a "*one-party democracy*" for most of the 20th century. It would not be until the presidency of Lázaro Cárdenas (1934–40) that popular demands for agrarian reform were finally met.[100]

Scholars have tried to make sense of the Mexican Revolution, a movement that ended as a series of regional battles where factions with contrasting agendas fought each other in a struggle for land, power, and autonomy. Many have interpreted the Mexican Revolution as encompassing "*varias revoluciones*" occurring simultaneously in the various regions of Mexico.

In the opinion of many historians, the Mexican Revolution failed to produce any significant revolutionary changes; Mexico had developed capitalism well before the Revolution; the Mexican Revolution was a disorganized rebellion which pitted factions of one rebel family against another. The *1917 Constitution*, for instance, fell short of revolutionary because it stressed continuity rather than radical reform. The guaranteed redistribution of peasant lands that it ordered was merely an affirmation and continuation of the *1857 Liberal Constitution*, promulgated after the fall of Santa Ana in 1855. In fact, some historians claim that Madero's bourgeois supporters, Villa's workers army, and Zapata's peasant insurgents all rebelled against the Porfirian dictatorship, but none of these factions had the capacity to hold political power. Mexico therefore needed a strong man to achieve political consolidation. That man was Lázaro Cárdenas, under whose *Institutional Revolutionary Party* government Mexico would fully install capitalism.

Not finding solace in the accomplishments of its 30 years of Revolution, Mexicans faced the sad truth that when the revolution began in 1910, Mexico was home to an estimated 15 million people; 30 years later that number had dropped to 12 million. Between one and two million Mexicans died unspeakable and horrendous deaths during this "*age of violence*," while an additional one million or more migrated north to the United States, which were the origins of many Mexican-American communities in ma-

---

[100] The **Sonorans** were a true dynasty, a group of leaders from the northwestern state of Sonora who, as liberal, populist, businesslike, centralizing and anticlerical state-builders, set their stamp on the new order until 1940. Its chief leader was Plutarco Elías Calles, president from 1924 to 1928, and "*jefe máximo*," from 1928 to 1934. Other notable Sonorans were Obregón and Adolfo de la Huerta

On March 18, 1938, all oil reserves, facilities, and foreign oil companies in Mexico were expropriated by **President** and General ***Lázaro Cárdenas***, who declared that «*all mineral and oil reserves found within Mexico* [mostly owned by US and Anglo-Dutch operating companies] *belong to the government,*» in accordance with article 27 of the *Mexican Constitution of 1917*.

jor U.S. cities like Detroit, Chicago, Los Angeles, Albuquerque, El Paso, San Diego, Phoenix and others.

On the top, all sides during the Mexican Revolution committed numerous atrocities and *executed their opponents without due process*. On the bottom, Carranza presiding the *1917 Constitutional Convention*.

On top, ***President Carranza*** (circled) with General Obregón and members of his top staff. In the middle, the outstanding mural **"Effective Sufrrage, No Re-Election"** by Juan O'Gorman (1905-1982), at Chapultepec Castle. On the bottom, the ubiquitous ***use of railroads*** by Mexican revolutionaries of all sides.

The revolution condemned Mexico to 30 years of crimes and instability, with a loss of 3 million citizens, and culminated in an additional quarter of a century of corruption, poverty and a one-party autocracy.

The Russian Revolution
1917 - 1923

«One does not establish a dictatorship in order to safeguard a revolution; one makes a revolution in order to establish a dictatorship.»
ERIC ARTHUR BLAIR, BETTER KNOWN AS GEORGE ORWELL (1903-1950)
ENGLISH NOVELIST, OUTSPOKEN ENEMY OF TOTALITARIAN AUTHORITY

The Russian Revolution: a condensed timeline

1905
- January — *Bloody Sunday* - Tsarist troops open fire on a peaceful demonstration of workers in St Petersburg.
- October — General Strike sweeps Russia which ends when the Tsar promises a constitution.

1906
- March — The promised parliament, the *Duma*, is dissolved when it produces an anti government majority.

1914
- October — A new wave of workers unrest ends with the outbreak of the First World War.

1917
- March — Bending to riots by women, striking workers and defecting soldiers, tsar Nicholas II abdicates, thereby ending the Romanov dynasty.
- March — The Petrograd Soviet of Workers' Deputies is formed.
- April — Vladimir Lenin, leader of the *Bolshevik* party in exile, returns to Petrograd.
- May — Leon Trotsky returns to Petrograd from exile.
- June — The Bolsheviks win the majority in the Petrograd soviet.
- July — Alexander Kerensky is appointed by the *Duma* as prime minister of the provisional government.
- September — The *Bolsheviks* win the majority in the Petrograd soviet and Trotsky is appointed chairman of the Petrograd Soviet.
- November — *Bolsheviks* overthrow the Kerensky government and install Lenin as leader of Russia ("*October Revolution*") against the will of the *Mensheviks* and of the Left Socialist-Revolutionaries
- December — Lenin creates the secret police *Cheka* under the command of Feliks Dzerzinisky.

1918
- January — Lenin dissolves the *Constituent Assembly* and declares the separation of state and church.
- March — *Menshevik* leader Julius Martov publishes an article exposing the *Bolsheviks* as ordinary criminals.
- March — Lenin changes the name of the *Bolshevik Party* to *Russian Communist Party*.
- March — Russia moves the capital from Petrograd (St. Petersburg) to Moscow.
- March — The *Bolshevik* government signs a peace treaty (Brest-Litovsk treaty) with Germany and accepts territorial losses.
- March — Trotsky is appointed head of the "Red Army"

June	The *Bolshevik* government introduces a policy of food requisition and peasant revolts break out throughout Russia
July	Nicholas II, his wife and their children are killed by the secret police of the Bolsheviks
November	World War I ends with the defeat of Germany

1919

March .	The Comintern (or "*Third International*") is founded in Moscow with the aim of spreading the revolution all over the world.
May .	The *Bolshevik* government orders the creation of a concentration camp in each province
December .	The *Cheka* has arrested 500,000 deserters in 1919.

1920

September .	Martov flees to Germany.
December .	The Soviet army finishes off the White Army in the Crimea (50,000 are killed).
December .	The ruble has lost 96% of its pre-war value.
December .	The *Cheka* has arrested 800,000 deserters in 1919. It is now 15 times bigger than the Tsarist secret police arrested in 1920 (250,000 people) and has already administered 50,000 death sentences.

1921

January	The civil war ends with Lenin's victory (millions have died of starvation, the population of Petrograd has dropped from 2.5 million in 1917 to 0.6 in 1920) .
February .	Lavrenti Beria is appointed in charge of the Cheka to suppress the nationalists
March.	Lenin enacts the New Economic Policy (NEP)
July .	While the famine is killing millions, Lenin orders to bolster food requisitions
September	70,000 people are held in concentration camps.

1922

February	The *Cheka* is abolished and replaced by the *GPU* (*State Political Administration*).
April	Stalin is appointed general secretary of the Central Committee of the Communist Party
May	Lenin suffers the first of three strokes
December	The Soviet Union is created by uniting Russia, Ukraine, Belarus and Transcaucasia (Armenia, Georgia, Azerbaijan).
December	Five million people have died during two years of famine, mostly in the lower Volga
December	The anti-religious campaign has killed 2691 priests, 1962 monks and 3447 nuns in 1922.

1923

March	Lenin suffers a third stroke and is de facto removed from power, opening a power struggle.

1924

January	Lenin dies and is succeeded by the triumvirate of Stalin, Kamenev and Zinoviev.
January	The Communist Party denounces Trotsky and his ideology.
February	Petrograd is renamed Leningrad.

1925

January	Volgograd is renamed Stalingrad.
January	Trotsky is forced to resign as head of the Red Army.
April	Nikolai Bukharin introduces the thesis of *Socialism in One Country* that is adopted by Stalin against Trotsky's *Permanent Revolution*.
December	Kamenev demands that Stalin be fired from the position of General Secretary.

1927

September	The Soviet Union launches a campaign of eradication of Islam.
November	Trotsky is expelled from the Communist Party.
December	Kamenev is expelled from the Communist Party.

1928

January	Trotsky is exiled to Alma Aty.

1929

April	The government begins an anti-religious campaign.
December	1,778,000 people are convicted of crimes in 1929.
December	Stalin orders the persecution of "*kulaks*" (capitalist farmers), 15 million peasants are deported to the Arctic; 6.5 million die.

1930

April	The GPU establishes the "GULAG" (*Chief Administration of Corrective Labor Camps and Colonies*) to handle prisoners in labor camps.
July	The *Gulag* manages 140,000 prisoners.1930:
August	More than 20,000 people are sentenced to death.

1933

June	At least 203,000 people are held in labor camps in Siberia.
November	The USA recognizes the Soviet Union.

1934

July	The GPU is renamed NKVD and the *Gulag* is reorganized.
October	The Soviet Union joins the League of Nations.
December	Stalin's collaborator Sergey Kirov is assassinated and blame is placed on Trotsky. Stalin begins the "*Great Terror*" to annihilate the Communist Party's left and right wings, led respectively by Leon Trotsky and Nikolai Bukharin
December	More than 500,000 people are held in the Gulag.

1935
　December　The Gulag has 800,000 prisoners in camps and 300,000 in colonies.
1936
　April　　　Only 17,000 thousand priests are left of the 112,000 in 1914.
　August　　Accused of a conspiracy led by Leon Trotsky against the Soviet government, Lev Kamenev and Grigory Zinoviev are executed
　　　　　　The GPU hands down 274,000 convictions in 1936
1937
　January　　Trotsky moves to Mexico.
　May　　　 Stalin begins the purge of the Red Army (in 18 months 3 out of 5 marshals, 13 out of 15 army generals, 8 out of 9 admirals and a total of 35,000 officers are liquidated).
1938
　March　　 Bukharin and Rykov are tried, forced to confess and executed in a show trial.
　　　　　　More than 90,000 people die in labor camps that now count 1,360,000 prisoners.
　November　Lavrenti Beria replaces Nikolai Ezhov as head of the secret police (NKVD), (1.5 million people have been arrested in two years, 680 thousand have been executed, and more than 100 thousand have died in camps).
1939
　September　Germany invades Poland and starts World War II.
　September　The Soviet Union invades Poland a few days after Germany and annexes the territories lost in 1921 (12 million Belarussians, Ukrainians and Poles)
　December　The *Gulag* has 1.3 million prisoners in camps and 350,000 in colonies.
1940
　January　　The Gulag contains 1,670,000 prisoners distributed in 53 camps and 425 colonies.
　August　　Trotsky is assassinated in Mexico and Stalin is the only survivor of the six members of the original Politburo of the October Revolution (the other five having been executed or assassinated).
1941
　May　　　 The *Comintern* is dissolved.
　November　Joseph Stalin, Franklin Roosevelt and Winston Churchill meet at the Tehran Conference
　December　167 thousand prisoners have died in 1941 in prison camps
1945
　February　Roosevelt, Churchill and Stalin hold a conference in Yalta
　May　　　 Germany surrenders after 30 million people have died on the "Eastern Front"

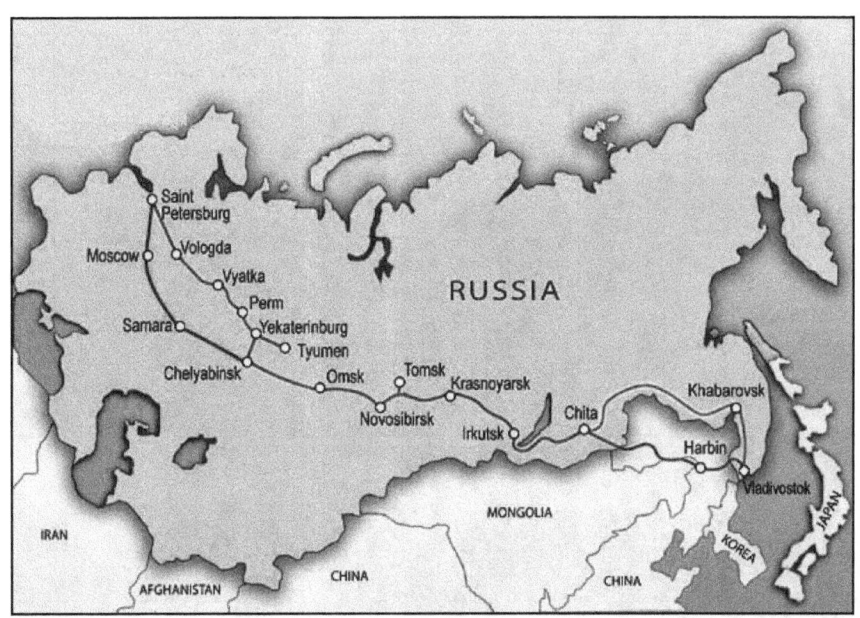

A *map of Russia in 1905*, showing the Tsar's Trans-Siberian railroad; a painting showing the *emancipation of the Serfs*. The serfdom that tied the Russian peasants irrevocably to their landlords was abolished by Tsar Alexander II, father of Nicolas I, in 1861, four years before the slavery was declared unlawful in the US.

Petrograd before the 1917 Revolution; The demonstration in Petrograd on ***June 18, 1917***. The banner reads "*All power to the Soviets, Down with Capitalist ministers;*" Petrograd, the famous ***Nevsy Prospekt*** (street) ***demonstrations of July 4, 1917***, attacked by troops of the Provisional Government which opened fire with machine guns.

The Russian Revolution
1917 - 1923

Russia at the beginning of the Twentieth century was a enormous empire stretching from the eastern frontier of Poland to the Pacific Ocean; it was home in 1914 to 165 million people, a full three quarters of which were peasants who lived and farmed in small villages with numerous languages, cultures and religions. Ruling such a gigantic state was difficult, and it was not a surprise for historians that Russia would sooner or later have a revolution that would convulse the empire and sweep away the old system. Many predicted that World War I, when it exploded all around Russia, could be the short term trigger that would precipitate the fall of the empire, as indeed it was.

It was clear that peasant life in Russia had improved in 1861, when serfs ceased to be owned and traded by their landowners. On that year the serfs were freed and granted a small track of land; it was not to be free of charge, however, since they had to pay a "fair" price to the government, and as a result a large number of small farmers fell deeply in debt. The state of agriculture in central Russia was very rudimentary, using techniques dating from feudal times, extremely out of date; there was little anticipation that things could improve because of the widespread general illiteracy of small farmers and their lack of capital to invest.

Peasant families lived just above the subsistence level, and more than a few had a father or son who had left the village to find work in the towns. As the central Russian population boomed, the problem was compounded when arable land became scarce.

Life in the countryside was in sharp contrast to the way the rich landowners lived in the cities; they held more than 20% of the land in large estates and were often members of the Russian bourgeois class. On the West and South of the Empire, things were slightly less difficult. A large number of better off peasants made a better living in large commercial farms. In central Russia, masses of disaffected peasants were increasingly irritated at large landholders that were effectively controlling them through unfair competition

Russia was a land of contrasts in 1905. In the picture on top, living conditions in *Odessa in 1905*; below, workers in *Kulotino flax factory*. They were provided with houses, good equipment and machines from abroad.

and less than subsistence prices for their crops; these were people who profited from the land without directly working it.

What most competed with farmers at the beginning of the XX century, however, were middle class urban people, the beneficiaries of the the industrial revolution that arrived in Russia in the 1890s, for which the tools were not farm instruments but steam powered machinery installed in ironworks, factories and other workplaces of the new industrial society. While the development of industries was neither as advanced or as hasty as in Britain, France or Germany, cities in Russia began to expand and entice large numbers of peasants to move to urban centers to take up better jobs. By the turn of the century, millions of former peasants were in Russia's tightly packed and expanding urban areas, experiencing problems like poor and cramped housing, meager hygiene, bad wages, and a lack of rights in their jobs. The Russian government was fearful of this developing urban class, but did not wish to scare foreign investment away by supporting better wages; hence there was no public will to reform the working system. Most of the workforce in the cities often remained closely linked to the peasant countryside, since a good part of the family usually remained in the villages.

Anti-Tsarist ideology among urban workers and their peasant families swiftly began to develop into a fertile ground for "socialist revolutionaries" who moved between cities and countryside listening to complaints and supporting demonstrations. In order to try and counter the spread of protests and hundreds of limited but annoying revolts, the Tsarist government authorized the formation of legal but neutered trade unions to take the place of the banned "socialist" and heavy politicized contingents that were sprouting in many cities and towns. By 1917, these heavily politicized socialist worker factions were ready to play a major role under the umbrella of "redeeming socialism".

At the time, Russia was ruled by an unelected aristocrat Tsar, Nicholas II; for three centuries this position had been held by the Romanov family. They ruled alone, with no true competing or supervisory representative body. By 1905 the *Duma*, an elected body, could be completely ignored by the Tsar when he wished to, and he did. Freedom of expression was almost non-existing, books and newspapers were permanently censored, a secret police operated to crush dissent, frequently resorting to either executing people or sending them to exile in Siberia. The result was an auto-

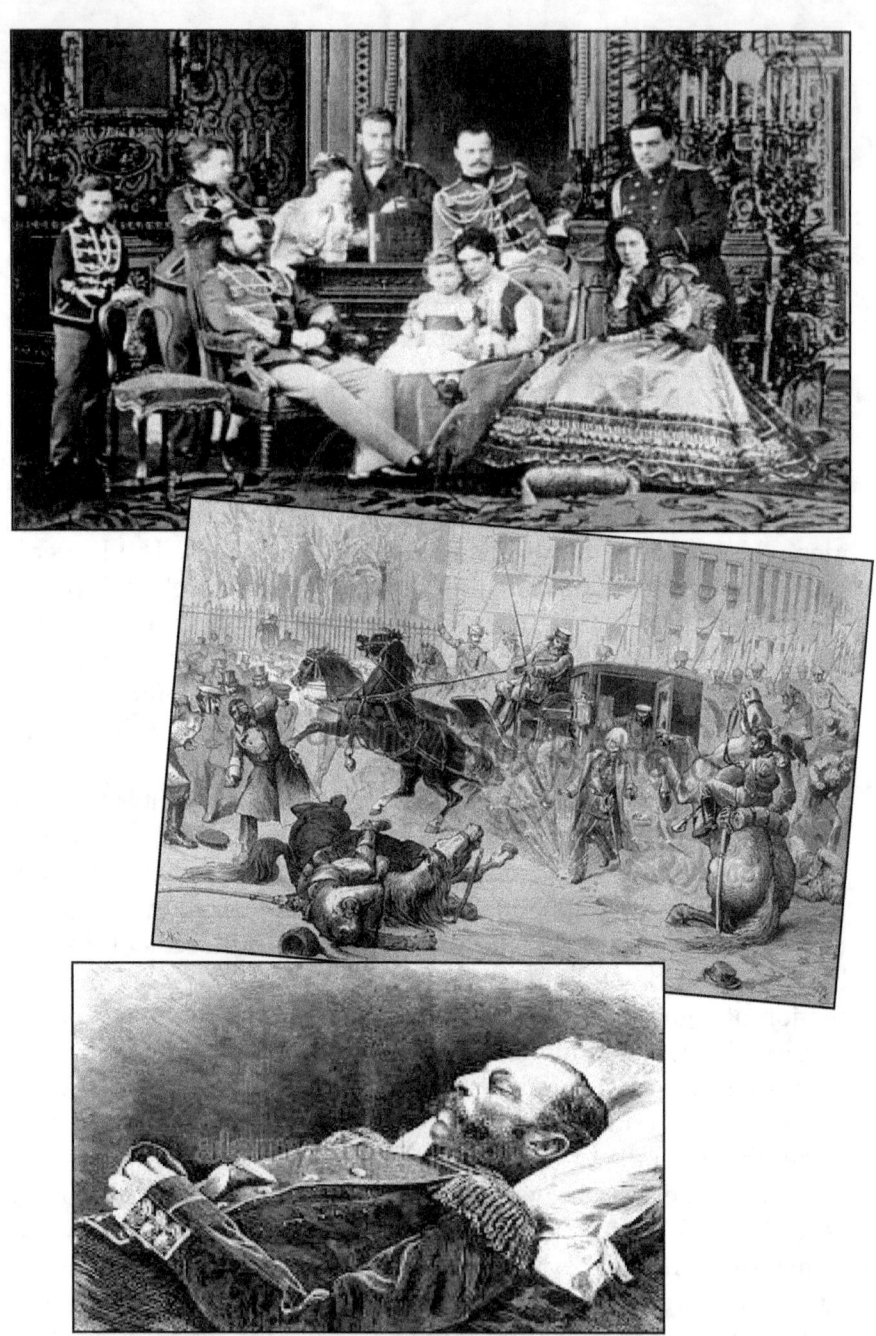

Family portrait of emperor *Alexander II*. He was Tsar of Russia, King of Poland and Grand Duke of Finland; a painting showing the *assassination of Tsar Alexander II* on March 13, 1881 on the grounds of the Winter Palace in St. Petesburg; *the Tsar in his deathbed*.
Alexander II was Nicolas II grandfather.

cratic regime under which republicans, democrats, revolutionaries, socialists and others, all disagreed with the crown and were increasingly desperate for reform. Some wanted violent change, others preferred peaceful amends, but opposition to the Tsar was almost if not totally unanimous. Opponents were banned and were increasingly driven to extreme measures.

Tsar Nicholas II, in the opinion of some historians, has been accused of lacking the strength of character to govern. Other historians have concluded that Nicholas was no fool and was determined to govern but had no idea or ability about how to run as an autocrat. His answer to the crises facing the Russian regime was to look back to the XVII century and resurrect medieval schemes that had served his antecessors instead of reforming and modernizing XX century Russia. His shortness of imagination and resolve, his lack of modern, good and trusted advisors, were the major cause that made a revolution inevitable.

There had been a strong reforming movement in Russia during the reign of Nicholas's II grandfather Alexander II. A constitution was being written when Alexander II was assassinated in 1881. From there on, the elites split between reform and entrenchment. Nicholas II, when his turn came, sided against the reform, not only halting whatever had been accomplished under his father Alexander III, but starting a risky counter-reform towards a centralized, autocratic government.

The government of Tsar Nicholas II was worse than just autocratic, it simply wasn't any good. There was confusion in the strategies of governing; rulings and government decisions seemed entirely arbitrary, random, or reliant on patronage. Russia was chaotically governed, the masses of peasant villages had no contact with the upper reaches of the imperial government and there were no room for local decisions anywhere. The government lost the support of even the landholders, the bedrock of previous Tsarist regimes, which began to turn against the Nicholas II, demanding reform. The rulers had little idea of the peasant view, and the mass of peasants had no regular rendezvous with government; all citizens in Russia had no worries about the wiping away the whole Tsarist regime in 1917. Nicholas II was probably the last one who accepted the news.

The backward Russian military, on the other hand, consisted of soldiers who had been treated inhumanely and with less consideration than even common Russian citizens; they yearned for

The **Kremlin fortifications** in 1905, surrounded by houseworkers that were part of the staff of the compound; ***Tsar Alexander III and wife Maria Fyodorovna*** in 1893, paents of Nicholas II; ***The Tsar's family***. Nicholas II is behind Alexander III, who was a corpulent man.

some shred of dignity and better conditions. They began to believe that the *Bolsheviks* would offer them the security, self-esteem and comforts they craved. In addition, the officers were also at odds with the Tsar and his court over the urgent need to modernize. In became clear to the officers that the perils and pressures on Russia were increasing, but the army was stalled in the past. The officers saw no better approach than to turn to the *Duma* for solutions. The Duma did not acknowledge their misery.

By the turn of the XX century, however, Russia had developed an educated, small political class among a group of people, between the aristocracy and the peasants and urban workers, who were ready to earn the moniker of *Middle Class*. This group was part of a developing civil society which read newspapers, send their kids to school and identified more with "Russia" than with the Tsar. The severe famines at the end of the XIX century politicized and radicalized this potential *Middle Class*, as they contemplated how ineffective the Tsar's government was, and how much they could gain if they were free to choose a chief executive for Russia. The Tsar ignored them and refused to look at the state of their жалоба (grievances, *doléances, quejas*). Soon they would be turning against the Romanovs and their blind and deaf government.

In order to fully comprehend the totality of the Russian Revolution historians look back into 1887. On March 1 of that year, the sixth anniversary of Alexander II's murder,[101] three suspects were arrested in the *Nevsky Prospekt*, the main street in the city of St. Petersburg; they were accused of attempting to throw several bombs into the carriage of Alexander III of Russia, who always visited churches that day to pay tribute to his assassinated father. One of the men, called Aleksandr Ilyich Ulyanov, who was both the main ideologist of the group and the chemist preparing the bombs, was one of the arrested. In court, Ulyanov gave a political

---

[101] ***Alexander II*** succeeded to the throne of Russia upon the death of his father Alexander I in 1855, and was Emperor until his assassination in 1881. On March 13, 1881, he fell victim to a conspiracy in Saint Petersburg. A young member of the *Narodnaya Volya*, (the People's Will movement), waiting on the side of the road, raised both arms and threw something at the emperor's feet who was traveling in a heavy armored carriage. Alexander was carried by sleigh to his study in the Winter Palace, where almost the same day twenty years earlier he had signed the *Emancipation Edict* freeing the serfs. He was bleeding to death, with his legs torn away, his stomach ripped open, and his face mutilated. He died at 3:30 pm on that day.

Alexander Ilyich Ulyanov (1866-1887), Lenin's revoltionary elder brother. In 1887 he attempted the assassination of Alexander III, on the sixth anniversary of the assassination of Alexander II. On May 8 he was executed, an event that radicalized his younger brother Lenin, already involved in student protests and revolutionary propaganda. On the right, the *Ulyanov family* with Lenin sitting on the right; on the bottom, Tsar *Alexander III lying in state*.

speech to justify his actions. All the conspirators were sentenced to death and were hanged at Shlisselburg.[102] Aleksandr Ilyich Ulyanov was the older brother of Vladimir Ilyich Ulyanov, alias *Lenin* (1870- 1924). Both were born to a wealthy middle-class family in Simbirsk.[103] It is said that Vladimir first became attracted to revolutionary socialist politics following his brother's execution in 1887.

The man that Aleksandr Ilyich Ulyanov attempted to assassinate was formally called *Alexander Alexandrovich Romanov* (1845- 1894), Emperor of Russia, King of Poland, and Grand Prince of Finland. He was highly conservative and reversed some of the liberal reforms of his father, Alexander II. Throughout his reign Russia fought no major wars, for which he was called "*The Peacemaker*." He was more than six feet tall and famous for his colossal physical strength; but he was also an enthusiastic amateur musician and an passionate patron of ballet. People nevertheless saw him as lacking sophistication and class. He was cumbersome and heavy set and relished the fantasy of being of the same rough texture as most of his subjects. Having a sebaceous cyst on the left side of his nose, he was always close-up photographed with his head turned to the left. As he ascended the throne upon the death of his father he made clear to everyone that his autocracy would not have any limitations.

In 1894 Alexander III, the Tsar known also as *the robust emperor*, became ill with nephritis and on October 21, while resting in the island of Corfu in Northwestern Greece, weak and feverish, he received his eldest son and heir, the Tsarevich Nicholas as well as his fiancée, Princess Alix, who had come from her native Darmstadt to receive the Tsar's blessing. Despite being exceedingly frail, Alexander insisted on receiving his future daughter in law Alix in full dress uniform, an event that left him exhausted Soon after, his health began to rapidly deteriorate and he eventually died on the afternoon of November 1, 1894 at the age of forty-nine. He was succeeded by the Tsarevich, who took the throne as Nicholas II.

---

[102] *Shlisselburg* (originally Schlüsselburg or Nöteborg) was one of the most important medieval fortresses in northwest Russia.

[103] *Simbirskthe* was also the birthplace of *Alexander Kerensky* (1881-1970), the future revolutionary minister of the Russian Gobernment, *Alexander Pushkin* (1799-1837), the famous author, playwriter and romantic poet and *Andrey Sakharov* (1921-1989), the nuclear physicist that achived fame as a dissident and human rights activist.

Top photo, *Alexandra and Nicholas II* in their officialpicture; on the right, *Lenin's first arrest record*; on the bottom, the *Russian Social Democratic Labor Party* in 1895, with Lenin presiding.

Fifteen days later, on November 14, 1894, Czar Nicholas II married Alexandra Fedorovna (1872-1918), who became the new Empress Consort of the Russian Empire. She had been born *Alix of Hesse and by Rhine*, granddaughter of Queen Victoria of the United Kingdom. She was the last and most famous royal carrier of the *hemophilia* disease that stroke Victoria's descendants. Although Queen Victoria had intended for Alix to be Britain's future queen, she relented to Alix' wishes and objections, an indication of her strength of character. Alix had met and fallen in love with Grand Duke Nicholas, heir to the throne of Russia, whose mother, Empress Maria Feodorovna (Dagmar of Denmark), was a sister of the then Princess of Wales, and whose uncle Grand Duke Sergei Alexandrovich[104] was married to Alix's sister Elisabeth.[105]

On December 8 of the year following the Russian royal family wedding, 1895, the young drop out of Kazan Imperial University [106] in Tatarstan named *Vladimir Lenin*, was arrested, kept in solitary confinement for 13 months, and then exiled to Siberia for three years. After his exile, he moved to Western Europe, where he became a prominent party theorist through his newspaper articles. In 1903, he took a key role in an ideological split of the *Russian Social Democratic Labor Party (RSDLP)*, leading the *Bolshevik* faction against Julius Martov's *Mensheviks*.[107]

Lenin was the major moving force for an insurrection throughout Russia's in 1905; he later campaigned for the First World War to be transformed into a Europe-wide proletarian revolution, which as a Marxist he believed would cause the overthrow of capitalism and its replacement with a socialist world.

---

[104] **Sergei Alexandrovich**, was the uncle of Nicholas II but also his brother in law because he was married to Elisabeth, the sister of Tsarina Alexandra. He was assassinated by a terrorist at the Kremlin on February 17, 1905, at age 47.

[105] **Alix and Nicholas** were related to each other via several different lines of European royalty: the most notable was their shared great-grandmother Princess Wilhelmina of Baden, mother of Alix's paternal grandfather Louis III, Grand Duke of Hesse, and Nicholas's paternal grandmother, Empress Maria Alexandrovna of Russia, making them second cousins via this line; and King Frederick William II of Prussia, who was simultaneously the great-great-grandfather of Alix and the great-great-great-grandfather of Nicholas, which in that line made them third cousins once removed.

[106] **Kazan Imperial University** was the second oldest institution of higher education in Russia, founded by Alexande I in 1804.

[107] The **Bolsheviks** were the majority faction after the split of the party, the **Mensheviks** the minority.

Kazan University in 1832. Lenin (1870-1924), was expelled from this school as a distracting element in 1888; a photo of the January 22, 1905 ***Bloody Sunday***, in St. Petesburg when demonstrators led by a *Father Georgy Gapon* were fired upon by soldiers of the imperial guard; right, a photo of ***Father Gapon*** at the *Narva Gate* of the Winter Palace in S. Petesburg.

On January 22, 1905, as had become the tradition, peaceful protesters approached the Winter Palace grounds in an attempt to bring petitions to the Tsar. Alarmed by the unusual size of the crowd, Nicholas II ordered his guards to put down the protest, even if they had to fire on the protesters. The resulting melee became known as *Bloody Sunday*; it increased tensions throughout Russia and a general strike threatened to cripple the Empire. By the end of January over 400,000 workers were on strike. On January 26, over 100 strikers were shot and killed on the streets. By March all higher academic institutions closed their doors for the rest of the year. In St. Petersburg a *Soviet* [108] of workers, *Bolsheviks* and *Mensheviks*, was controlling the strikes. By May there were almost no active railways in all of Russia.

During the rest of 1905 the Empire was convulsed by the wave of mass political and social revolts that had spread all across its territory; worker strikes, peasant rebellions, factory slowdowns, military mutinies, crime and arson in the cities, boycotts in transportation, closing of roads, warehouse fires, and the like.[109] Thousands of people refused to go to work in the cities, and in the countryside peasants began to burn their master's manors houses.

Nicholas II was forced to act before all his power was lost. He soon agreed to issue pledges and concessions, which included a *Constitutional Reform* that would establish fundamental civil liberties, the establishment of a legislative assembly with oversight powers, the *State Duma*,[110] the recognition of a multi-party political system, and the formulation and approval of a *Russian Constitution* by 1906. On August 6, Nicholas II issued a convocation for the Duma that a few weeks later became known as the *October Manifesto*, a document that was to serve as preliminary to the new

---

[108] A *Soviet*, in the terminology of the times, was a local council, originally elected only by manual workers, with certain powers of local administration.

[109] The **great unrests of 1905** were due to the rapid industrial growth of urban industry, which was not accompanied by political reforms. As a result, the expanding working class in cities and towns became disconented. Despite the emancipation of the Serfs, on the other hand, the agrarian problems of poor crops, lack of capital and zero instruction persisted on the countryside.

[110] The **Duma** was to function as a lower house of parliament while a *State Council* would be the upper house. The State Council was the supreme advisory body to the Tsar, dealing mostly with external affairs. Peter I, Catherine I and Peter III, all had Councils at their times, with roles changing according to the needs of the empire.

On top, the 1905 **Battle of Port Arthur,** February 8 and 9, 1904. The surprise attack of Japanese destroyers decimated the Russian fleet archored there. When Japan and Russia signed the Treaty of Portsmouth ending the war, Japan retained its captured territories and forced Russia out of Manchuria and Korea. The Japanese victory made the Russian people lose confidence on its military under the Tsarist regime, leading indirectly to the Russian revolution of 1905;   below, crowds gathered to hear the **Imperial Manifesto** of June 3, 1907, granting rights and liberties (too late) to the Russian people.

Constitution and was announced as the response of Nicholas to the unrests of 1905. Nicholas II intimate advisors knew from the beginning that he would be forever opposed to any reforms that involved limiting his authority. He felt it was not his place to limit a system created by his ancestors and he was even quoted as saying «*I cannot squander a legacy that is not mine to squander.*»

The *October Manifesto* was a fairly good compendium of pledges that addressed the unrest throughout the Russian Empire by granting basic civil liberties such as:

- Genuine inviolability of the person, freedom of conscience, speech, assembly and association.
- Admission to participation in the Duma to all classes of the population that were completely deprived of voting rights.
- An unbreakable rule that no law shall take effect without confirmation by the State Duma.
- Universal male suffrage in Russia, which was common in Western countries at the time.

The document did not guarantee that the Russian Empire would function in democratic terms; it just stated some people's rights and gave them a voice in legislation. There were no ways to check if its pledges were followed to the letter, therefore it was considered by many as a flawed document, more so since it was implied that the Tsar could disband the Duma at his will.

The *Manifesto*, however, ended much of the violence as soon as it was published; the Empire was swept with enthusiasm as people believed they had freedom and representation in the government. But its immediate success was followed by a return to the cycle of strikes and violence. Nicholas II began to reaffirm his power once again and within months the executions of dissenters began again. The Government decided to suppress political parties and by the start of 1906 Russia was under martial law. Instead of being a true reform, the *Manifesto* became just a short term ploy by Nicholas II to regain order in Russia.

To further complicate things, Nicholas II had been fighting a war between the Russian Empire and the Empire of Japan from February of 1904 to September of 1905. Russia had been seeking a warm-water port on the Pacific Ocean for its navy and for maritime trade. Vladivostok was operational only during the summer, whereas Port Arthur, a naval base leased to Russia by China in Liaodong Province, was operational all year. The war had started when Japan, perceiving Russia as a threat to its strategic interests,

On top left, ***Japanese troops charging a Russian position*** in Manchuria during the Russo-Japanese War; on the right, ***President Theodore Roosevelt*** shown mediating between Russian and Japan in 1905; below, the ***Caucasus Campaign*** in World War I.

opened fire on the *Russian Eastern Fleet* at Port Arthur in a surprise attack. The war only concluded on September 5, 1905, with the *Treaty of Portsmouth,* mediated by US President Theodore Roosevelt. [111] The agreements of the Treaty were lopsided in favor of Japan and were not well received in Russia, particularly since they provided the Japanese the status of the pre-eminent power in East Asia and forced Russia to abandon any possibilities of expansion in the Pacific.[112]

By the end of the war, the Japanese Army had suffered 47,000 dead, 27,000 casualties from disease, and 12,000 wounded. The Russian Army suffered 170,000 dead. China had 20,000 civilian deaths, and a financial loss of over 120 million ounces worth of silver.[113] Russia lost two of its three fleets and only its *Black Sea Fleet* survived. Japan became the sixth-most powerful naval force.[114] The hefty costs of the war sank the Russian economy and the external balance of payments into deficit.

In Russia there was unanimous popular support for the war after the 1904 Japanese attack on Port Arthur; things changed after the continued defeats of the Imperial Navy at the hands of Japan. The shock and humiliation of the Tsar became a prelude to the fall of the Romanov dynasty and added fuel to the simmering *Russian Revolution of 1905,* an event Nicholas II knew would be devastating to the old Empire. Twelve years later, that discontent boiled over into the February Revolution of 1917.

With the Russo-Japanese War (February 8, 1904 to September 5, 1905) out of the way, Nicholas II could concentrate on credible attempts to save his regime; the road to do it was to offer reforms similar to what most rulers would when pressured by a revolutionary movement. The *October Manifesto,* the creation of the *Impe-*

---

[111] It earned **Roosevelt** the *Nobel Peace Price* for these efforts in December of 1906.

[112] The **Treaty of Portsmouth** included an immediate cease fire, the recognition of Japan's claims to Korea, the evacuation of Russian forces from Manchuria, the return of its leases in southern Manchuria to China (**Port Arthur and Talien**), and the turn over of the *South Manchuria Railway* and and its mining concessions to Japan. Russia was only allowed to retain the much smaller *Chinese Eastern Railway* in northern Manchuria.

[113] *120 million ounces worth of silver* are US $2.1 billion in 2016 money.

[114] Following the victory of Japan, the British presented a lock of Admiral Nelson's hair to the **Imperial Japanese Navy**, judging its performance on a par with Britain's victory at Trafalgar in 1805. It is still on display at Kyouiku Sankoukan, the *Naval History Museum* in Etajima City, Japan.

The *Tauride Palace*, built by Prince Gregory Potemkin in 1783, home of the Duma in 1906; *Count Vladimir Kokovtsov* (1853-1943), Prime Minister of Russia from 1911 to 1914, presenting a speech **before** the Russian Imperial Duma in 1905; the *royal family of the Romanovs* in 1908.

rial *Duma* and the *1906 Russian Constitution* that created a multi-party system and a limited constitutional monarchy, were a good part of these reforms.

The Russian aristocratic classes, not conformed with the Tsar's veto powers prescribed by the new Constitution, kept insisting on more restrictions to the Duma's legislative powers. A decree in February 20, 1906, transformed the *State Council*, the advisory body, into a second chamber with legislative powers «*equal to those of the Duma.*» Not only did this transformation violate the *Manifesto*, but the Council became a buffer zone between the Tsar and Duma, slowing whatever progress the latter could achieve. The decree also limited the Assembly's powers by proclaiming the Tsar as the sole authority to appoint/dismiss ministers, as well as various other facets of Russia's political life. Defeated and frustrated, the majority of the *Duma* voted *net nikakoy uverennosti v tom* (no confidence) and handed in their resignations on May 13, a few weeks after its first meeting.

The Russian government was evidently returning to Pre-Manifesto levels of suppression; the *Duma* and *Manifesto* solutions began to lose the indispensable crucial support from the populace. Nicholas II remained too cautious about having to share power with reform-minded elected members of the *Duma* and decided to order its dissolution just after 73 days of meetings. As the 1905 Revolution subsided, Nicholas was able to bring economic growth back to Russia's industries, a period which lasted until 1914; his efforts did nothing to prevent, however, the collapse of the *House of Romanoff*, nor seemed to satisfy the conservatives and the aristocrats. He was literally placed between a rock and a hard place, but continued to think of himself as the «*father and protector of the Russian people.*» Heavy on his mind was also the illness of his son, whose struggle with *hemophilia* was already been overseen by the charismatic monk Rasputin, as championed by Alexandra Feodorovna, Nicholas' wife.

The ubiquitous presence of a revolutionary climate continued for several years, well into the start of World War I. Political terrorism became an epidemic that shook the aristocrats, the civil servants and the police. Between 1906 and 1910, 7,500 people were killed by revolutionaries; of the dead, more than 2,500 were close to the upper echelons of the Russian government, including *Dmitry Sipyagin*, Minister of Interior, *Victor Sakharov*, War Minister, *Admiral Chukhnin*, Commander of the Black Sea Fleet, *Nikolai*

The **Congress of Vienna** (1814-1815) under the leadership of *Prince Klemens von Matternich* (1773-1859), gave Russia most of the Duchy of Warsaw (Poland) and was allowed to keep Finland (which it had annexed from Sweden in 1809 and held until 1917). It ignored national and liberal impulses, and by imposing a stifling reaction on the Continent (setting the extent of Austria-Hungary, for instance) contributed to the start of World War I; a map of *Austria-Hungary* in 1914.

Bobrikov, Governor-General of Finland and Nicholas' uncle, the *Grand Duke Sergei Alexandrovich of Russia*. Those years, of course, were marked by a rising number of death sentences and executions,[115] which no one knew if they were a good palliative or a reinforce of violence. Unbeknownst to the royal *House of Romanoff*, however, destiny was reserving for them a much serious surprise than the relatively gentle and easy to control revolts and violence of the 1905 Revolution.

Back in November of 1814, the European states had met at the *Congress of Vienna* and established an international order and a balance of power that would hopefully last forever. By 1914, however, a multitude of interests threatened to tear that order apart. The Balkan Peninsula, in southeastern Europe, was a particularly hot spot; formerly under the control of the Ottoman Empire, its status was uncertain at the end of the 1800s, as the weakened Turks continued their slow withdrawal from Europe. The region's peace depended on the cooperation of two competing powers, Russia and Austria-Hungary. The decaying Austria-Hungarian Empire, populated by two incompatible peoples (Germans in Austria, Magyars in Hungary) attempted to control large populations of restless Slavs, worried for its own future as a great power. In 1908 the Austro-Hungarians annexed the twin Balkan provinces of Bosnia-Herzegovina.[116] This grab for territory and control angered the independent Balkan nation of Serbia, who considered Bosnia a Serb homeland. Serbia, until then almost a non-entity, doubled its territory in back-to-back Balkan wars (1912 and 1913), further threatening Austro-Hungarian supremacy in the region.

Meanwhile, Russia, protecting itself from a growing German hazard, entered into an alliance with the two western powers that were also distrustful of German intentions: France, which was angry over Germany's annexation of French territory in the aftermath of the Franco-Prussian War in 1870-71, and Great Britain, whose legendary naval dominance was now threatened by Ger

---

[115] Historians claim the **number of "official" executions** as follows: 2,628 between 1905 and 1908; 4,664 between 1909 and 1917; these do not include summary executions by punitive army detachments and executions of military mutinees. By 1917 there were more than 16,500 prisoners all across Russia, particularly in Siberia, the Caucasus and the Baltic provinces.

[116] **Bosnia-Herzegovina** was at the time a province of the Ottoman Empire. The Serbs believed that if these two territories were no longer part of the Orttoman Empire they should belong to Serbia.

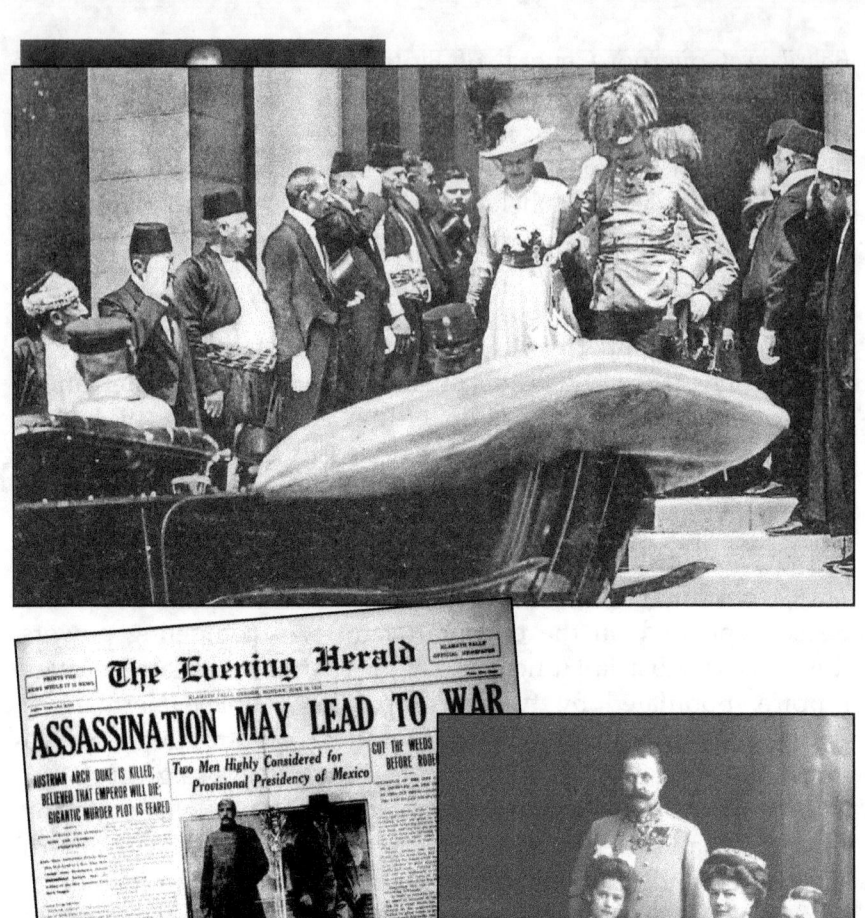

The archduke *Frank Ferdinand* (1863-1914), heir to the Austro-Hundary empire, as he approach the car where he were shot to death along with his wife Sophie, Duchess of Hohenberg (1868-1914) by a Serbian nationalist in Sarajevo on June 28, 1914; the *Evening Herald* newspaper the following day; the *family of Frank Ferdinand and Sophie*: Princess Sophie, Maximilian and Ernst.

many's growing navy. This *Triple Entente*, Russia-France-England, ready to confront the German-Austro-Hungarian alliance, meant that any regional conflict in the area could develop into a general European war, if not a worldwide war.

The fragile situation in the Balkans was a serious concern for Austrian Archduke Franz Ferdinand and his friend Kaiser Wilhelm of Germany. They met on June 13, 1913 at the hunting lodge of the Austrian Archduke in Konopischt, Bohemia. At the insistence of Franz Ferdinand, Wilhelm reluctantly agreed that Germany would back Austria unconditionally in case of a confrontation with Serbia.[117] Two weeks later, however, on June 28, Franz Ferdinand and his wife Sophie were killed by *Gavrilo Princip*, a young Serbian nationalist during a diplomatic visit to Bosnia. Vienna, along with most of the world's capitals, blamed Serbia. Kaiser Wilhelm was shocked, distraught and irritated. Barely a month later, Europe was witness to the *Great War of 1914*, ending a long stretch of unparalleled peace and prosperity. Some historians argued that if Franz Ferdinand and Kaiser Wilhelm had continued to work together to pursue their common aims, World War I might never have happened.

The Austro-Hungarians needed to enforce their authority in the face of such an insolent crime, in spite of the complete unpreparedness of its army and Russian possible intervention. On July 6 Austria confirmed that Vienna had Kaiser Wilhelm and Germany's full support. Serbia appealed to Russia for help and the czar's government began a fast mobilization of its army. Austria-Hungary declared war on Serbia on July 28. On August 1, after hearing news of Russia's general mobilization, Germany also declared war on Russia. The German army then launched its attack on Russia's ally, France, through Belgium, violating Belgian neutrality and bringing Great Britain into the war as well. The entire continent had fallen into war.

---

[117] The **Austro-Hungarian Empire** was not a cohesive national entity. Franz Ferdinand, a rock-hard Austrian aristocrat, the eldest son of Archduke Karl Ludwig of Austria (younger brother of Maximilian, the assassinated would be Emperor of Mexico) and his second wife, Princess Maria Annunciata of Bourbon-Two Sicilies, detested the *Magyars* (Hungary's majority population), and resented the weakness that forced Austria to partner with Hungary in the government of the empire.

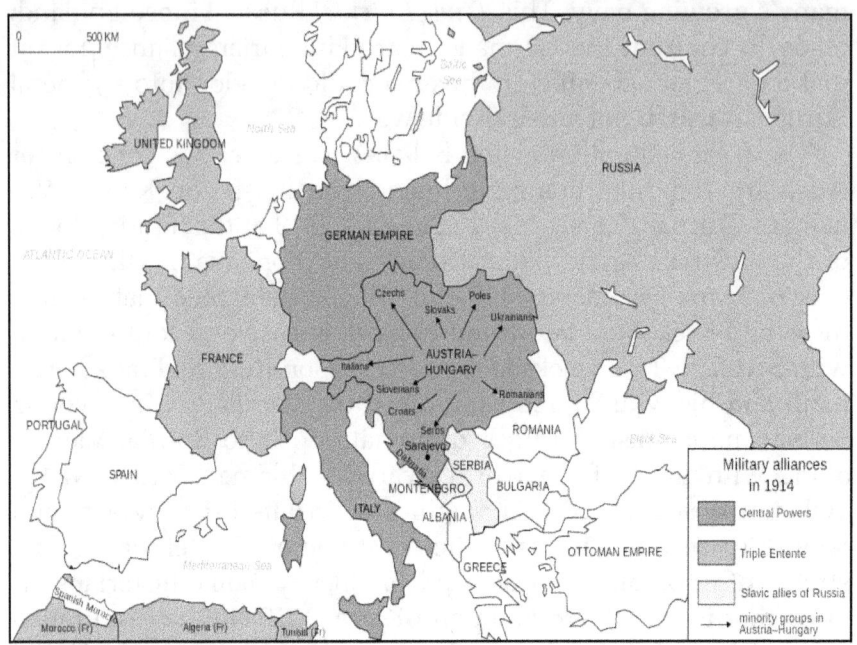

Map on the top side: the ***European alliances in 1914***, the central powers of the *Austria-Hungary empire*, which included Germany and Italy, and the *Triple Entente* countries, France, England, Russia and Northern Africa; Maps below, ***Alsace and Loraine***, the two departments of France that were in German hands after their quick victory in the 1870 Franco-Prussian War.

In 1914 the Russian Empire included Poland, Finland and large parts of Transcaucasia. The majority of the 166 million population were Slavs but there were also Jews and Turks and thousands of Russians with other ethnic origins. Several of these groups wanted regional autonomy and this threatened to tear apart the fabric of Russian nationality.

Tsar Nicholas II ruled the Russian Empire as an absolute monarchy, but following the loss of the war with Japan in 1905, serious disturbances had taken place in St. Petersburg and the Emperor was persuaded to accept a lessening of his power. His plans to create the *Duma* as a Russian Parliament did not go far enough in the minds of his people and since then the country entered a period of permanent instability. In 1907 Russia joined Britain and France to form the *Triple Entente* in response to Germany, Austria-Hungary and Italy having formed the *Triple Alliance*. It was evident that the European nations were all ready to go to war with each other at the first provocation.

Russia was specially well prepared for war. Industrial unrest in Russia was troublesome, however; in 1912 hundreds of striking miners were massacred at the Lena goldfields and during the first six months of 1914, almost half of the total industrial workforce in Russia took part in strikes.

On the positive side, in 1914 the *Russian Army* was the largest army in the world, a fabulous resource that was only hindered by the condition of Russia's poor roads and railways, which made the effective deployment of these soldiers difficult. The *Russian Army Air Service (RAAS)*, established in 1912, owned 360 aircraft and 16 airships. It was the largest air force in the world. The *Russian Navy* had 4 battleships, 10 cruisers, 21 destroyers, 11 submarines and over 50 torpedo boats.

As the world watched in horror, the French broke hostilities; their initial plans were to attack Germany to get them out of Alsace and Loraine. The British were to join at once and operate as France's left flank. The Russians, with more than 95 divisions, were to engage the armies of Austria-Hungary in the south and turn quickly to invade German East Prussia. The plans began to be delayed by several problems: the Russian railway network was single tracked, [118] far behind Western European and the deployment of troops quickly went behind schedule. The Russians had

---

[118] *Trains* travelling in both directions shared the same track.

The **Battle of Tannenberg** in a photo from the *Manchester Guardian* of August 1, 1914. The Russia-German conflict in the first month of WWI resulted in almost complete destruction of Russia's Second Army and the suicide of its Commanding General Alexander Samsonov. Although the battle actually took place in Polish territory, Hindenburg named it after *Tannenberg*, 30 km to the west, to avenge the defeat of the Teutonic Knights after an earlier Battle of Tannenberg in 1410. The lower photo shows **hundreds of Russian soldiers** taken prisoners at Tannenberg (today's Stebark in Poland.

decided to deploy large numbers of cavalry and Cossacks; every day each horse needed ten times the resources that a man required. Finally, the Russian supply of cable was insufficient to run telephone or telegraph connections from the rear; therefore, they relied on mobile wirelesses stations, even though the Russians were aware that the Germans had broken their ciphers.

The German plan was to defeat swiftly the French while the Russians were mobilizing and then rush to confront the Russians in the eastern front. They counted with 173,000 troops to defeat two Russian armies consisting of 485,000 men. On August 30, 1914, the armies of Germany and Russia met at the *Battle of Tannenberg*. The battle resulted in the almost complete destruction of the *Russian Second Army* and the suicide of its commanding general, Alexander Samsonov. A series of follow-up battles destroyed most of the *Russian First Army* and kept the Russians off balance until the spring of 1915. [119] By the end of the week Russia had lost two entire armies, over 250,000 men. *Tannenberg* signaled the beginning of an unrelenting Russian retreat on the northern sector of the Eastern Front. By the middle of 1915 all of Russian Poland and Lithuania, and most of Latvia, were overrun by the German army.

Fortunately for the Russians, they began to do better in 1916. The supply of rifles and artillery shells to the Eastern Front was vastly improved, and in an offensive in June 1916, Russia achieved significant victories over the Austrians - capturing Galicia and the Bukovina - and the Russian army was also more than holding its own in Transcaucasia, against Turkey.

However, the country's political and economic problems were greatly exacerbated by the war. Many factors - including the militarization of industry and crises in food supply - threatened disaster on the home front. Added to this the rumors that the Tsarina Alexandra, and the infamous Rasputin, were German spies. The rumors were unfounded, but by November 1916 influential critics of the regime were asking whether Russia's misfortunes, 1,700,000 military dead and 5,000,000 wounded, were a consequence of stupidity or treason. The outdated strategies of Russia's

---

[119] The battle was particularly notable for fast rail movements by the Germans, enabling them to concentrate against each of the two Russian armies in turn, and also for the failure of the Russians to encode their radio messages. It brought high prestige to **Field Marshal Paul von Hindenburg**.

Soldier workers and deputies gathering for an *election of Soviets*; the leaders of the *Menshevik* party in May 1917, Pavel, Axelrod, Martov aand Martinov; the leaders of the *Bolsheviks* in 1917, under the presidency of Lenin.

General Staff had cost hundreds of thousands of lives, while the regime seemed careless of such appalling losses.

In February of 1917, food riots, demonstrations and mutinies forced Nicholas II to abdicate. A *Provisional Government* led by liberals and moderate socialists was proclaimed; real power in Russia, however, became clearly in the hands of the Petrograd socialist leaders of the *Soviet of Workers' and Soldiers' Deputies*, who had successfully extended his jurisdiction nationwide as a rival power of the *Provisional Government*.[120] Unlike the ministers of the later, the Petrograd socialist leaders had been elected by popular mandate.

The leaders of the *Soviet of Workers' and Soldiers' Deputies* were half-heartedly supporting a defensive war, but were more committed to an unrealistic program of ending the conflict through a general peace without annexations or indemnities, a formula that neither the Allies nor Germany were likely to accept. To prevail over the *Provisional Government* they had to act swiftly. Or so they thought.

On January 27, 1917 their entire leadership (mostly Menshevik deputies) was taken by surprise, arrested and carried away to the *Peter and Paul Fortress* on the orders of Alexander Protopopov, Imperial Russia's Minister of the Interior. They were freed by a crowd of disaffected soldiers on the morning of February 27; it was unequivocally the beginning of the February Revolution.

That very night a meeting was held at the *Tauride Palace*. *Izvestia* was chosen as the official newspaper of the group and the moderates launched an appeal to representatives from factories and the military to join the *Soviet*, which grew to over 3,000 deputies, mostly soldiers, in the next two weeks.

The *Soviet* began to undermine the *Provisional Government* by issuing its own orders. Its first order instructed soldiers and sailors to obey their officers and the *Provisional Government* only if their orders did not contradict the decrees of the *Petrograd Soviet*. Other orders included the election of army officers by their subordinates, the blacklisting of undesirable officers from the army, all weapons to be taken from the officers that had not pledged loyalty to the *Soviet*, dispensation of soldiers from standing to attention

---

[120] In the Soviet historiography the rivalry of the Petrograd *Soviet of Workers' and Soldiers' Deputies* and the *Provisional Government* is known as the *Dvoyevlastiye* (**Dual power**).

The ***Provisional Government*** of the Duna. Inside a circle, ***Alexander Kerensky*** (1881-1970), shown also on the left, Minister of War between July and November of 1917; ***Vladimir Lenin and his wife Nadezhda Krupskaya*** in 1917.

and saluting their officers when off duty and elimination of the ritual of addressing officers as "*your Excellency.*"

Soon thereafter a *Menshevik* turned *Bolshevik* theorist revolutionary and prominent *Soviet* politician was appointed *Chairman of the Soviet*; his name was Leon Trotsky. Alongside some unknown deputies called Lenin, Zinoviev, Kamenev, Stalin, Sokolnikov and Bubnov, he was one of the seven members of the just founded first *Politburo*, in charge of managing the brand new *Bolshevik Revolution*.

The *Soviet's* orders were highly controversial to all except the *Bolshevik* delegates; *Mensheviks* saw them as an effort to prevent continuation of Russia's war effort by crippling the government's control of the military, as well as part of a plot by the *Bolsheviks* to undermine the *Provisional Government*. [121]

As the *Bolsheviks* campaigned for a retreat from World War I, Alexander Kerensky (1881-1970), War Minister of the *Provisional Government*, was moving to strengthen Russia's military offensive on the Eastern Front. It became a lost cause; by then the ability of Russia's officers to encourage their men to abide by the rules had been totally negated. The hope of social and political revolution together with an end to the war had unleashed in the trenches a large support for what became known as the *Trench Bolshevik Revolution*. The German General Staff, on the other hand, had spent over 30 million marks trying to foment disorder in Russia's army; in April 1917 they gave a *Coup de Grâce* by ferrying Vladimir Lenin (1870-1924) from his exile in Switzerland to Moscow.

The 1917 summer offensive was a disaster. Peasant soldiers deserted en masse to join the revolution, and fraternization with the enemy became common. Several important Russian generals attempted a failed military *Coup* in combination with Kerensky. The *Provisional Government* and Keen ski's reputations plummeted. The *Bolsheviks*, with Lenin at their head, toppled Kerensky without any resistance from either the *Provisional Government* or the Russian Army. The stage was set for the Russian Revolution.

The *Bolsheviks* promised to deliver «*peace, bread and land*» to the besieged people of Russia. On October 26 they issued a broad appeal, the Декрет о мире (Decree on Peace) calling upon all Euro-

---

[121] **Leon Trotsky** referred to them as «*the only worthy document of the February Revolution.*» Historians today agree that they struck at the very heart of the Russian army discipline and contributed powerfully to the breakdown of the armed forces.

Richard von Külmann, Germany's Foreign Secretary and Count Ottokar Czernin, Austro-Hungary's Foreign Minister, signing the **Brest-Litovsk Treaty** on March 3, 1918. Russia ended his participation in World War I and **lost all territories shown in the map at right**. On the left. *Leon Trotsky* (1879-1940) at the end of the war.

pean belligerents to end the slaughter of World War I. Lenin, of course, was far from being a pacifist. His hope was to transform the war into a stronger conflict when the "imperialistic forces" refused the call for a cease fire. Unfortunately for him, the Central Powers responded to the *Bolsheviks'* appeal by agreeing to an armistice on the Eastern Front, and Lenin's lieutenant, Trotsky, found himself in the uncomfortable position, during the winter of 1917-18, of negotiating a separate peace treaty with Imperial Germany and her allies at the Polish town of Brest-Litovsk.

When Trotsky had his bluff called and tried to delay matters, Germany resumed its fight on Russia's Easter Front. To Lenin's consternation Russia was forced to sign the *Treaty of Brest-Litovsk* on March 3, 1918. The treaty ended the participation of Russia in World War I but was devastating for the Russians: They agreed to hand over Finland, Poland, the Baltic provinces, Ukraine and Transcaucasia to the German-Austro-Hungarian-Italian coalition, together with one-third of the old Russian empire's population, one-third of its agricultural land and three-quarters of its industries. Outraged, the *anti-Bolshevik* Russians, actively assisted by German forces in Russia, took up arms against the *Bolsheviks*. Among others, the Bolsheviks had to face the *Czechoslovak Legion*, a 40,000-strong army made who in 1918 seized the entire Trans-Siberian Railway, from the Volga to Vladivostok.

A civil war was unleashed in Russia. The *Reds*, as the *Bolsheviks* were called, controlled Petrograd, Moscow and the central Russian heartland. The *Whites*, conservative elements in Russia, surrounded them in a series of campaigns that threatened to crush the revolution. The *Reds*, however, counting with almost 5,000,000 soldiers, rebuffed these attacks, and survived, and by late 1920 had driven the *Whites* back into the Black Sea, the Baltic and the Pacific, causing hundreds of thousands of *White* soldiers and civilians to emigrate. The Whites never understood the *Bolsheviks* capacity to resist, had less than 250,000 men under arms, their armies were separated by huge distances from each other and were based around the less developed peripheries of Russia.[122]

---

[122] It was surprising that Trotsky could organize a **Red Army** more effective than what the *White* generals assembled against him. He introduced a revolutionary innovation, the network of *Political Commissars*. They were devout *Bolsheviks* who were supposed to offer political guidance to the Red Army but in practice were *snitches* who watched over the loyalty of the 50,000 imperial army officers the Reds employed to help command their forces. He also used terror ruthlessly against deserters, complainers and the unmotivated.

Soldiers from the **Russian White Army** in 1917;
Leon Trotsky and the **Russian Red Army** at the time.

It must be acknowledged, however, that the White Army also exhibited cruelty, venality, disarray and an uncomforting lack of political and military direction. Even the *Cossacks*, their most valuable fighters, were more attracted to booty and the autonomy and prosperity of their own regional areas than in driving Lenin and his *Bolsheviks* from the Kremlin.

More than the *Reds*, the *Whites* were internationally isolated. Lloyd George, Prime Minister of the *Wartime Coalition Government* and England's leader of the Liberal party, Clemenceau, the French prime minister and Woodrow Wilson, the American president, did not sympathize with Lenin, but neither were they particularly happy with the *White* generals that had supported the Tsar for so long. As a result, only a few thousand British, French and American troops ever set foot in Russia, and fewer of them saw action to contain the Red Army. Altogether, 10 million lives perished in the war that brought the Reds to the control of Russia.

Once the Bolsheviks seized Petrograd on October 25, 1917 and overthrew the *Provisional Government*, [123] what had been known as the *February Revolution* became the *October Revolution*; all government buildings were seized, including the *Winter Palace*.

On March 8, 1918, the *Bolsheviks* changed the name of their party to *The Communist Party* and on March 11 changed the capital of Russia from Petrograd (St. Petersburg) to Moscow. The final blow of the *Bolsheviks* to the White Army took place in Crimea, where hundreds of White Army soldiers had gathered and made their position very protected and tenable. The Red Army continued to fight them and once their fight elsewhere in Russia ended, various divisions of the Red Army reinforced their comrades in Crimea.

---

[123] The **control of Petrograd and the Winter Palace** by the *Bolsheviks* was practically a bloodless *Coup d'État*. The palace was defended by 3,000 cadets, officers, cossacks and female soldiers. Cadets and Cossacks were allowed to leave and return to their barracs. While the *Provisional Government* was busy debating what actions to take, all communication lines to the city were cut off and dozens of *Bolsheviks* began to infiltrate the palace. Late at night the cruiser *Aurora* fired a blank shot from the harbor; the streets became crowded with insurgents and the *Provisional Government* surrendered. All accounts of fierce fighting and a heroic resistance were part of a well planned communist propaganda; it was dramatically depicted on a film,*The Storming of the Winter Palace*, which was staged in 1920, showing Lenin as risking his life against the firepower of the Cossacs. In reality, the practically unoccupied *Winter Palace* fell not because of acts of courage or a military barrage, but because the back door was left open by a complicit *camarade*, allowing the Red Guard to enter. The actual engagement produced 18 arrests and the loss of two horses in the melee.

The ***Romanovs of Russia*** in one of their last photos on July 17, 1918; the ***Ipatjew House in Yekaterinburg***, where they were held prisoner and assassinated; the ***children having a picnic*** at *Tsarskoe Selo*, one of the royal residences, in the spring of 1917. Left to right Grand Duchesses Maria, Olga, Anastasia and Tatiana.

In March of 1917 the Romanovs, Nicholas II, his wife Alexandra and their children Olga, Tatiana, Anastasia, Maria and Alexei, were under house arrest by orders of the *Provisional Government* at the *Alexander Palace*, a countryside residence they frequently used, located 15 miles from St. Petersburg. There they were addressed with contempt by the sentries, who also scrawled lewd drawings on the building to embarrass and offend the girls. They were on soldiers rations, without butter, coffee and sweets and with no service from their staff. As the White Army gathered strength, they were moved under the same conditions to a small palace called the *Ipatiev House*, in *Yekaterinburg*, a large city in the Ural mountains, on the border of Europe and Asia, where they were under the custody of the Red Army. The city was under the threat of falling to the White Army, which had the mission of surrounding and capturing *Yekaterinburg* to protect the nearby path of the Trans-Siberian Railway which was in their hands.

At 1:00 am on July 17, 1918, under the belief that the approaching White Armies were making a move to rescue the Romanovs, the commandant of the *Ipatiev House* ordered the Imperial family to get dressed and be taken to a 20' x 15' feet semi-basement room. There he read an order given to him by the high command of the Red Army:

> «*Nikolai Alexandrovich, in view of the fact that your relatives are continuing their attack on Soviet Russia, the Red Army authorities have decided to execute you and your entire family.*»

An execution squad of secret police was brought in and the weapons were raised. The executioners then began shooting chaotically until all the intended victims had fallen. Nicholas died instantly and so did Empress Alexandra, Grand Duchess Olga and the Tsarevich Alexei. Tatiana, Anastasia, and Maria were carrying a few pounds of diamonds sewn into their clothing which gave them some protection from the firing, and initially were only wounded. The soldiers stabbed them with bayonets until they died. To eliminate witnesses Alexandra's maid was stabbed to death.

The bodies of the Romanovs were transported to a mineshaft in a nearby forest, stripped of their clothing and valuables, piled up carelessly and burned. They were then lowered into a shallow pit and their bodies sprinkled with sulphuric acid, their faces smashed with rifle butts and finally covered with quicklime. To prevent future recognition of the remains and to confuse people searching for the corpses, Alexei and Olga were partially burned, their bodies pounded to fragments and tossed into a different grave.

Alexander Kerensky in his days at *Stanford University*; soldiers of the *Russian White Army* in 1917; one of the last photos of *Kerensky* before his death in 1970; Lenin in 1918, addressing the *Congress of Soviets*, the supreme governing body of Russia from 1917 to 1922, .

This action defeated the White Army in November 1920. The civilian toll of the Russian Civil War was heavy: it is estimated that 8 million people died due to food shortages, hunger, and epidemics.

Russia was exhausted and disintegrated after the Civil War. The central government had completely disappeared during the war. Kerensky had seen the progress of the Red Army and declared a policy of *"no enemies on the left"* for the *Provisional Government*, and positioned himself neutral in the fight between Reds and Whites. The *Bolsheviks*, however, did not forgive his neutrality and went after him. He narrowly escaped his *Bolshevik* persecutors and fled the country, taking refuge in Paris, where he lived until 1940, busy with the endless splits and quarrels of the exiled Russian politicians. When Germany invaded France in 1940, he emigrated to the United States, where he stayed until his death in 1970. [124]

When the fall of the *Winter Palace* was announced, the Congress of Soviets[125] adopted a decree transferring power to the *Soviet of the Deputies of Workers, Soldiers and Peasants*, thus ratifying the legitimacy of the Russian Revolution.

The economic loss of Russia during the Civil War was immense, as noted by the quotations on the value of Russia's ruble. In 1914, a US dollar could be bought with 2 rubles. In 1920, one had to give 1,200 rubles to buy one US dollar. The war probably cost the Soviet economy around 50 billion rubles or $35 billion in today's money. Production of industrial goods fell to very low levels. Compared to 1913, the Soviet Union was producing only 5% of the cotton, and only 2% of the iron ore. In general industrial

---

[124] **Kerensky** decided to settle himself and his family in New York City, but spent much of his time at the *Hoover Institution* at *Stanford University* in California, where he taught graduate courses and contributed to the University's huge archive on Russian history. He wrote and broadcast extensively on Russian politics and history and died at his home in New York City in 1970, probably the last surviving major participant in the turbulent events of 1917. The local *Russian Orthodox Church* in Manhattan refused to grant a religious burial because it saw him as largely responsible for Russia falling to the *Bolsheviks*. A *Serbian Orthodox Church* also refused interment and his body was flown to London where he was buried at a non-denominational cemetery.

[125] The **Congress of Soviets** was an assembly of representatives of local councils that assumed power after the October Revolution of 1917. In theory, it was the supreme power of the State. No bourgeois, no noble, no aristocrat, no priest could vote, only working people.

In December, 1917, Felix Dzerzhinsky was appointed as Commissar for Internal Affairs and head of the All-Russian Extraordinary Commission for Combating Counter-Revolution and Sabotage (Cheka).

«*Do not look in materials you have gathered for evidence that a suspect acted or spoke against the Soviet authorities. The first question you should ask him is what class he belongs to, what is his origin, education, profession. These questions should determine his fate. This is the essence of the Red Terror.*»
Martin Latsis, Checha commisar in 1922.

The **CHEKA** was the Bolshevik security force or secret police. It was formed by Vladimir Lenin in a December 1917 decree and charged with identifying and dealing with potential counter-revolutionaries.

production fell to 20% of the production of 1913. The results were equally dismal for agriculture. Farms produced only 37% of the normal production, the number of horses fell from 35 million in 1916 to 24 million in 1920. Cattle heads declined from 58 million to 37 million.

The social cost of the Russian Civil War was even greater. The total number of men killed in action in the Civil War was estimated to be over 300,000; 125,000 in the Red Army, 175,500 in the White armies, and the total number of military personnel dead from disease, on both sides, as 450,000. During the Red Terror the *Cheka*[126] carried out at least 250,000 summary executions of *"enemies of the people"* with estimates reaching above a million.

To compound things, the droughts of 1920 and 1921, as well as the 1921 food shortage, worsened the adversity still further. Disease reached pandemic proportions in 1920 with 3,000,000 dying of *typhus* alone. Millions more died of pervasive starvation, wholesale massacres by both sides and *pogroms* against Jews, particularly but not exclusively in Ukraine and southern Russia. By 1922 there were at least 7,000,000 homeless children living on the streets as the result of nearly ten years of devastation from World War I and the Civil War. In addition, two million or more White émigrés[127] fled Russia towards Europe, the Far East and the Baltic countries.

---

[126] The ***Cheka*** was the first of a succession of Soviet State security organizations, created on December 20, 1917, after a decree issued by Vladimir Lenin. By late 1918, hundreds of *Cheka Committees* had been created in many cities and towns. Dissidents, deserters, and other undesirable people were arrested, tortured or executed by various *Cheka* groups. After 1922, *Cheka* groups underwent a series of reorganizations, among which was the integration with the *NKVD* (the *People's Commissariat of Internal Affairs*). Members of the *NKVD* and other repressive bodies continued to be referred to as "*Chekisty*" or "Chekists" into the late 1980. Vladimir Putin, for instance, is often referred to as "*the Great Chekisty.*"

[127] The 900,000 to 2 million **White Russian émigrés** after the Civil War were considered at the time as the largest loss of human talent ever occurring in the civilized world. They were mostly *Mensheviks* and social revolutionaries who were opposed to the *Bolsheviks*. They included all classes; military soldiers and officers, Cossacks, intellectuals of various professions, dispossessed businessmen and landowners, as well as officials of the Russian Imperial government and various anti-*Bolshevik* governments of the Russian Civil War period. They were not only ethnic Russians but belonged to other ethnic groups as well. The white émigrés started from scratch or reinforced the existing Russian Orthodox Churches outside Russia in the 1920s. They continue their heritage to this day, acting as both the spiritual and cultural center of the Russian Orthodox communities abroad.

The first two pictures show the ***exraordinary famine*** in Russia starting in 1920 after the Bolsheviks took over; on the bottom, a ***relief truck*** loaded with food and medical supplies, sent by the *American Relief Association*.

The years 1921 and 1922 became an unparalleled and unprecedented period of *The Great Russian Famine*. Nothing similar to it had ever happened in Russia's history; it was as devastating as the events that caused it. To a certain extent, the conditions created by war and by revolution account for the some of the famine and scarcity; they cannot explain, however, the continuing disintegration of agriculture after four years of the *Bolshevik* regime. The gradual catastrophic decline of the areas under cultivation, down to two fifths of the normal surface, was the product and result of the *Bolshevist* policies. The import of agricultural implements was practically stopped by the *Bolsheviks*, although they knew that local manufactures were unable to supply the needs. An exceptional decrease in the number of livestock, due to the lack of fodder and to the Soviet authorities policy of requisitions and assessments for military consumption. Grain was confiscated with exceptional severity in the producing regions, and the Central Committee congratulated itself for collecting 170% of the amount assessed. It was a real orgy. The farming areas looked like a conquered country delivering its products as booty to victorious soldiers. Violence, looting, bribery, orgies of drunken commissaries, night visits to private houses, arrests and shots and what not were daily occurrences.

Although it had not officially recognized the Soviet regime, the United States government was pressed to intervene and help; in August 1920 President Warren Harding approved an informal agreement to start a famine relief program. In 1921 he appointed Herbert Hoover, then Secretary of Commerce, to organize the relief effort. Congress authorized $20 million, and Hoover proceeded to organize the *American Relief Administration (ARA)* to do the job. Under Hoover's terms, the ARA was to be a completely American-run relief program for the transport, storage, and delivery of relief supplies, mainly food and seed grain, to those in the famine region. After Soviet officials agreed, hundreds of American volunteers were dispatched to provide manpower to plan, work and oversee the program.

What the Americans found as they arrived were wells and lakes that had dried up because poor land management, fields and meadows transformed into continuous sunburn yellow steppes where whole herds of cattle had died or were dying. The streets and squares of many towns and cities were packed by starving crowds. The police could not disperse them, and actually there was no place where they could go. Starving and famelic men

Newspapers the world over published accounts of the ***great famine in Russia***, characterizing it as **genocide**, as well as denouncing the persecution of churches of all denominations.

and women were literally lying everywhere with their children and their sick: they had let the authorities know that they would rather be shot that agree to move. They lay prostrate, begging for alms and food, for weeks. After having eaten the little food they had brought with them from their ruined farms, and sold out everything they possessed, they besieged the *Bolshevik* institutions, begging for food and shelter. Many of them died right where they were begging, some on sidewalks, others on the streets. Over the months, little by little they began to gradually disappear; nobody knew where they were going. It was certainly not the places where they had come from. New beggars took their place in towns and cities, taking their spaces in the streets, lying down, or dying, or going away when their turn came. Human corpses on the streets became a familiar sight and it no longer frightened any one. Russia was crumbling under the arrogant, pompous and deranged minds of the *Bolsheviks*. The *Bolshevik* government was successful in its struggle against foreign intervention and internal revolt, but it was far less victorious in its attempts to set up a new social order based upon communist ideas in Russia.

The great success of the *Bolsheviks* in those years was purging the intellectuals in Russia. On August 17, 1922, very early in the morning, Soviet security operatives fanned across the country on orders of the Politburo shaking hundreds of intellectuals and their families awake. The *Cheks* rifled through their possessions looking for evidence of disloyalty to the government; convoys of police cars were whisking the dazed scholars to state prisons. Some of the most educated scientists, physicians, musicians, physicists, lawyers, professors and writers were imprisoned, dumped into shared cells. They were told they had two alternatives: support the *Bolshevik* revolution or leave the country. Bewildered, most of them hurried home, gathered their families and some belongings and departed Russia forever.[128]

---

[128] Many of these intellectuals are today unknown to the general public. They included figures such as Nikolai Berdayev, N.O. Lossky, and Fyodor Stepun - three of Russia's greatest philosophers, and the brilliant sociologist Pitirim Sorokin, who helped found Harvard's sociology department. They were sent abroad on two German liners, the *Oberbrgermeister Hacken* and the *Preussen,* which sailed Sept. 28 and Nov. 16 from St. Petersburg to Stettin, Germany. The vessels came to be known as the "*Philosophers' Ships*." In total, 228 writers, academics and students, leading representatives of the Russian intelligentsia, were involved. They carried away the nation's intellectual elite and, with it, the very notion of free intellectual pursuit.

Massive expulsions were also a milestone on Russia's way to totalitarianism. Politically loyal but intellectually free people who constituted the basis of what came to be known as civil society were no longer to be tolerated.

Photo on top, intelectuals and their *families emigrating from Russia* after the takeover by the Communist regime;
Bottom, left: ***Mark Twain having dinner with Maxim Gorky*** (1868-1936), a five time nominee for the Nobel Prize in Litereature. On April 11, 1906. Gorky had come to the US to recruit followers and monetary support for the Russian revolutionaries. Mark Twain received him saying «*I am most emphatically in sympathy with the movement now on foot in Russia to make that country free... I am a revolutionist by birth, breeding, and principle*» Twain recanted these words after knowing about the massacre of Russian Jews in Bialystok. He died on April 21, 1910 and did not live long enough to see any major political changes in Russia in spite of all of his personal and public writings supporting the revolution. One can only speculate about his reaction had he lived to know of the actual murders of the Romanov family. One of the greatest humorists in American literary history ***had been fooled*** by the romance of the Russian revolution. On the bottom tight, the seal of the Russian Socialist Federal Republic.

The 1922 forced exile of the intellectuals signaled to the world that the emerging Soviet Union would be a ruthless totalitarian regime that would not tolerate dissent. The purged intellectuals had to sign statements promising never to return to the *Russian Socialist Federal Socialist Republic* (the *USSR's* predecessor). If they did, they were subject to the infamous Article 71 of the new *Russian Criminal Code*, which provided for them to be executed immediately.[129] According to the documents, each deportee was allowed to take ...

> «*one winter coat and one summer coat, one suit and change of clothes, two shirts, two nightshirts, two pairs of socks, two sets of underwear, and 20 dollars in foreign currency.*»[130]

The paradox of the expulsions was that the existential, personal and family tragedy for these people, and for philosophy, the sciences and education in Russia, in the end saved them from almost certain death in the Stalin purges of the 1930s.

The year 1922 also saw a bloody campaign to kill church officials and confiscate church property and valuables. Lenin wrote in a now-famous note...

> «*The more representatives of the reactionary bourgeoisie and reactionary clergy we manage to shoot in this case, the better. It is now that we should teach the public such a lesson that it doesn't dare to think of any resistance for several decades. We will free this land, forever, of priests and monks.*»

---

[129] **Deportation of dissenters** became a Soviet practice through generation of literary giants such as novelist Alexander Solzhenitsyn, who was deported in 1974. The 1922 forced exile scattered some of the greatest talent of Russian intellectuals and artists, one of the best known was Vladimir Nabokov (1899-1977), the son of a leader of the pre-Revolutionary *Liberal Constitutional Democratic Party* and secretary of the *Russian Provisional Government* led by Kerenski.

[130] Allegedly, **Lenin** considered himself an important philosopher and his war on intellectual foes, whom he had described in letters as "*lackeys of capital,*" gained force on June 1, 1922, when he signed a new penal code into law. It effectively gave the government the right to kill anyone who threatened to destabilize the new power won by Soviet workers and peasants, i.e., the one-party system. The *Bolshevik* government tightened prepublication censorship as Lenin ordered all members of the Politburo to spend two or three hours each week reading books and magazines to identify enemies. He wrote to Joseph Stalin «*officials must draw up lists, and several hundred such gentlemen ought to be exiled abroad without mercy. We'll clean up Russia for a long time to come. All of them... thrown out of Russia. This must be done at once.*» Lenin ended his tirade with maniacal detail, a blunt statement saying «*This is all of supreme importance.*»

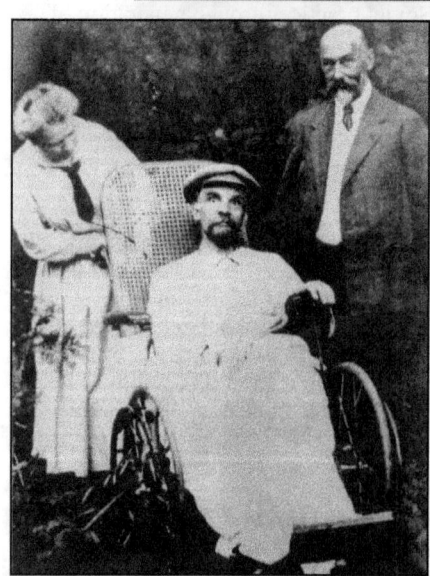

Vladimir Lenin (1870-1924) and Joseph Stalin (1878-1953), comrades but not necessarily buddies.
Lenin making a speech in Moscow in 1917.
Lenin's last photo, after three strokes he was unable to stand up or talk by 1923.

From the 1920s until the early 1950s, Joseph Stalin (1878-1953) was the *de facto* leader of the *Russian Socialist Federal Republic*, and later the leader of its institutional successor, the *Soviet Union*. Vladimir Lenin continued expanding his authority and eliminating his enemies, both as leader of the *Bolshevik* party and as Premier of the *Russia's Socialist Republic* and the *Soviet Union*; Stalin, however, was his right arm and as the Secretary General of the Communist Party's Central Committee was an individual more prone to enter into details and act with the rude and unforgiving manners of a wild beast.

After growing up in Georgia, Stalin became an activist in the *Bolshevik* party even before the Russian Revolution of 1917. After twelve years of militancy, he took leadership positions in the Russian Civil War and the Soviet-Polish War. He was one of the *Bolsheviks'* chief operatives in the Caucasus and grew very close to Lenin, who saw him as a competent and dependable follower.

History goes that Stalin proved to be too eager to succeed Lenin and both his master as well as many other comrades began to distrust him. In 1922, however, a stroke forced Lenin into semi-retirement at his dacha in Gorki, just after he had recommended Stalin's depuration dismissal or perhaps even death. Fortunally for Stalin, Lenin's death occurred in 1924 after two more strokes; Stalin suppressed all documentation of Lenin's recommendation in his testament and proceeded to politically isolate his major enemies, most of all his arch-rival Leon Trotsky.[131] Stalin had him dismissed from government altogether. This eventually led him to be the sole uncontested leader of the Party and the Soviet Union.

At that time the seven member Politburo[132] was split in two factions: the *radicals* wanted world revolution; their leader was Lev Borisovich Kamenev (1883-1936), whom Stalin saw as a source of discontent and a strong opponent to his own leadership; Kamenev

---

[131] Everyone thought Leon Trotsky, the brilliant chief of the Red Army would become the government leader, especially after Lenin's testament had severely condemned Stalin as dangerous and too ambitious. Lenin was explicit asking with his own hand that Stalin be dismissed. Trotsky, however, was briliant but very unpopular. His staff thought he was too big-headed and resented him for not attending Lenin's funeral (Stalin told him the wrong date and Trotsky missed the ceremonies). Trotsky was also commited to support not just a Russian but a world revolution; many Russians feared that this would ruin Russia.

[132] The seven members of the Politburo were Lenin, Zinoviev, Kamenev, Trotsky, Stalin, Sokolnikov and Bubnov.

"All the News That's Fit to Print."

The New York Times.

THE WEATHER

NEW YORK, WEDNESDAY, JANUARY 23, 1924. TWO CENTS

LENIN DIES OF CEREBRAL HEMORRHAGE; MOSCOW THRONGS OVERCOME WITH GRIEF; TROTSKY DEPARTS ILL, RADEK IN DISFAVOR

SOVIET CONGRESS IN TEARS

Mass Hysteria Only Averted by a Leader's Brusque Intervention.

BODY WILL LIE IN STATE

Is to Be Taken to Moscow Today From Village Where Premier Passed Away.

KREMLIN WALL HIS TOMB

Washington Expects No Immediate Change in the Policy of the Russian Government.

NIKOLAI LENIN (VLADIMIR ILYITCH ULIANOV). A sketch made from life for The New York Times by Oscar Cesare in Moscow, November, 1922, and autographed by Lenin.

Captain of Tacoma and Two Radio Men Lose Their Lives in Vera Cruz Storm

COOLIDGE SENDS WATCHER TO OIL HEARING; DAUGHERTY IS ALREADY INVESTIGATING; ASK SINCLAIR TO RETURN, FALL RECALLED

Sinclair Declares Oil Inquiry Is 'Politics'; Denies Paying Fall for Teapot Dome Lease

PRESIDENT READY TO ACT

Spokesman Indicates Coolidge Has His Eyes on Developments.

INQUIRY TO BE PRESSED

Senate Committee Wants Fall to Explain Archie Roosevelt's Story.

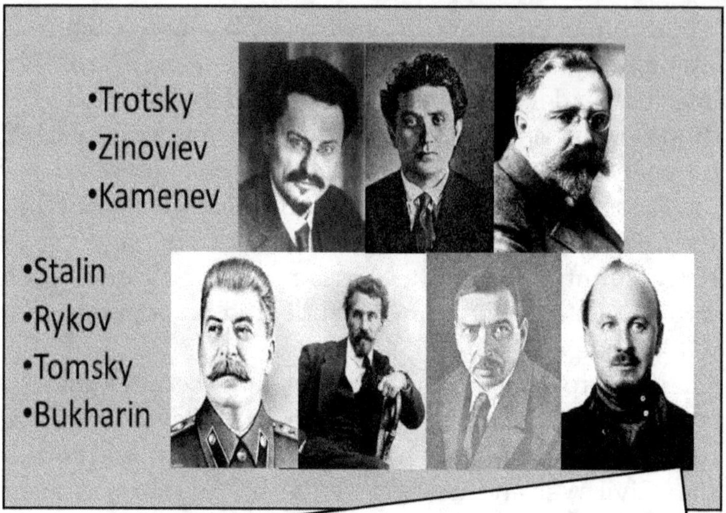

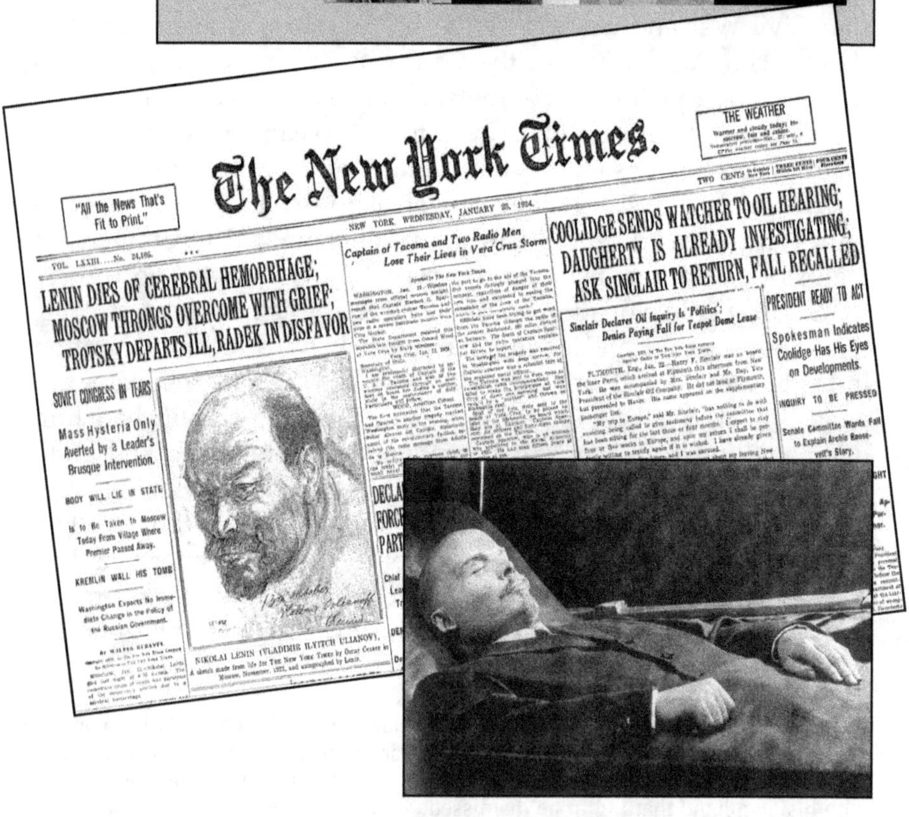

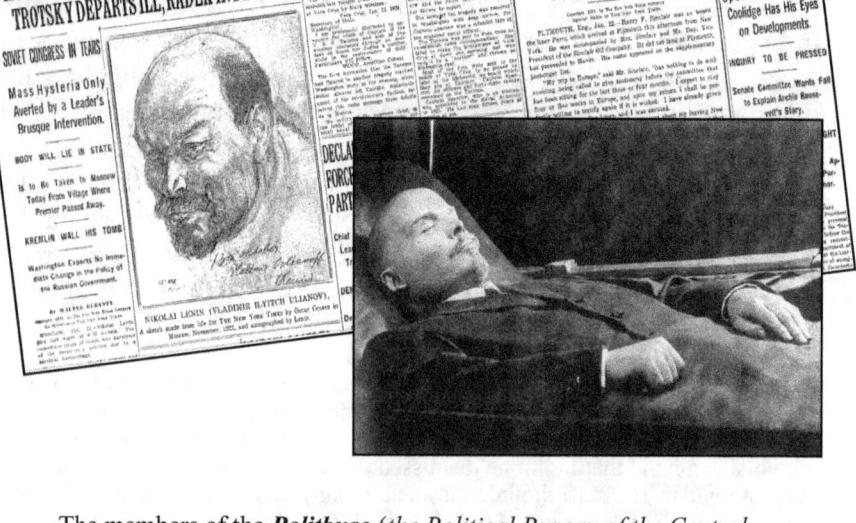

The members of the ***Politburo*** (*the Political Bureau of the Central Committee of the Communist Party of the Soviet Union*) in October of 1917. After 1952 it was known as the *Presidium*. Of all the members shown in the picture, only Stalin survived as a member in a few years. The Politburo met weekly, the Central Committee once a month and the Congresses annually. Bottom photos, newspapers and the deathbed of Lenin on January 27, 1924.

fell out of favor and was executed on 25 August 1936, aged 53, after a brief show trial. The *moderates* wanted to continue with the *New Economic Policy (NEP)* until the Russian experience were more solid and mature. Its leader was Nicholas Ivanovich Bukharin (1888-1938), a solid confidant to Lenin whom he had commissioned to infiltrate the media in New York city in 1917 through a newspaper called *Novy Mir*, the New World. After the success of the October Revolution, Bukharin became the chief editor of *Pravda* and after Lenin death he replaced him in the Politburo. In 1937 Stalin purged him and had him executed for being a "*Trotskyite*."

Using his position as General Secretary of the party, Joseph Stalin played one side against the other in his quest for the control of the Politburo after Lenin's death. He first made an alliance with Zinoviev and Kamenev in 1925 to prevent Lenin's Testament to be revealed to the XII Party Congress in April 1923; in exchange for this service Stalin got Trotsky dismissed.[133] He ended up going into exile in 1928. In 1927, Stalin advocated the line *Socialism in one Country*, proclaiming that the USSR should first become strong, then try to bring world revolution. Allied with the *moderates*, he succeeded to get Zinoviev and Kamenev dismissed; in their positions in the Politburo he appointed his own supporters. In 1929, his third maneuver was to argue that the *New Economic Policy* was "non-communist;" that proposition got Bukharin, Rykov and Tomsky dismissed. Trotsky lived in exile in *Alma-ata*, the largest city in Kazakhstan for a while, and was finally exiled from the Soviet Union itself in January 1929. He took refuge in Mexico.

---

[133] After **Lenin's death**, Trotsky and Stalin were ambitious about who was going to be the next successor. Trotsky and Lenin had more of a personal relationship and Lenin and Stalin had more of a political relationship. Stalin visited Lenin often, acting as his intermediary with the outside world. During this time, the two quarreled over economic policy and how to consolidate the Soviet republics. Lenin and Stalin were agreeing on more political ideas than disagreeing, which was creating a closer relationship. One day, Stalin verbally swore at Lenin's wife for breaching **Politburo** orders by helping Lenin communicate with **Trotsky** and others about politics; this greatly offended Lenin. As their relationship deteriorated, Lenin dictated increasingly disparaging notes on Stalin in what would become **his Will and Testament**. Trotsky criticised Stalin's rude manners, the excessive power he was seeking, his political ambitions and suggested that Stalin should be removed from the position of **General Secretary** of the party. One of Lenin's secretaries showed Stalin her notes; the contents shocked him. Before Stalin could mend any bridges, Lenin suffered a second heart attack on March 10, 1923 which left him completely incapacitated. A third attack caused him to die.

The ***Lenin Mausoleum***, situated in Red Square in the center of Moscow, an architectural design based on the 529 BC tomb of Cyrus the Great in ancient Persia. Over the years, it has been said that certain black spots appearing in the face and hands were cleared with Vodka. On the left, ***Leon Trotsky***. On the right, ***US troops feeding Russian soldiers*** in 1919, following a request from Lenin during the serious Russian famine.

A big boost to Stalin's ambition to control the *Politburo* in 1924 was his selection to be in charge of Lenin's funeral. It meant he was officially accepted as Lenin's successor, the leader of the ruling *Communist Party* and the highest political personality of the Soviet Union. Against Lenin's wishes, Stalin gave him a lavish funeral; his body was embalmed and put on display on *Red Square*. Stalin's enemies were ejected from the *Central Committee*.[134] By the 1930s private or open criticism of Stalin within the Party was virtually non-existent. Fear silenced all his adversaries.

Starting in 1927, Stalin began to push for rapid industrialization and central control of the economy, a position shared by many Party members. This policy was opposed to Lenin's strategies who had advanced and supported the concept of *New Economic Policy*.[135] At the end of 1927, a critical shortfall in grain supplies prompted Stalin to push for collectivization of agriculture. In January 1928, he personally travelled to Siberia where he oversaw the seizure of grain hoards from *kulak* farmers.

If anyone in 1927 deserved to lead Russia it was, in the opinion of contemporaries and historians, no other than Lev Davidovich Bronshtein, a true born revolutionary who in 1902 had changed his name to Leon Trotsky (1879-1940). His parents were Jewish and owned a farm in the Ukraine. When he was eight years old his father sent him to Odessa to be educated. In 1899 he met Alexandra Sokolovskya, an important revolutionary who became his

---

[134] Joseph Stalin was **Secretary General** of the *Central Committee of the Communist Party*; the *Committee* was *de jure* the highest body of the *Communist Party of the Soviet Union (CPSU)* between *Party Congresses*, which in the 1920s were annual events. According to Party rules, the *Central Committee* directed all Party and government activities between each *Party Congress*. Members of the committee were elected at the *Party Congresses*. The *Politburo* was a political bureau responsible to the Central Committee (dealing with urgent issues) which was created at the *8th Party Congress*. Stalin took control of the *Politburo* earlier than the control he exercised later in the *Central Committee* and turned it into a small clique of his friends. His best friend and close ally and *protégé* was a young communist named Vyacheslav Molotov. The last name Molotov was given to him by Stalin; it derives from the word *молот molot*, meaning *hammer*.

[135] Lenin called **The New Economic Policy** a temporary strategic retreat from his initial policy of extreme centralization and doctrinaire socialism, which had brought the national economy to the point of total breakdown . *The New Economic Policy* was put in effect in 1918 as the means to maintain the Party's hold on power. It consisted of the return of most agriculture, retail trade, and small-scale light industry to private ownership and management while the state retained control of heavy industry, transport, banking, and foreign trade.

Top photo, the leadership of the *League for Struggle for the Liberation of the Working Class* at a meeting in St. Petersburg in 1905. In the center Vladimir I. Lenin, on the right, in a circle, on the right *Julius Martov* (1873-1923), the first leader of the *Mensheviks*. On the bottom left, young *Leon Trotsky*; on the bottom right, Leon Trotsky and his wife *Natalia Sedova* in Mexico city.

wife. He divorced her and married Natalia Sedova and fled to Paris to escape arrest for his revolutionary activities. There he met Lenin, who was about to initiate the *Bolshevik* party. He became a member before Stalin, Kamenev and Bogdanov did but changed his affiliation to the *Mensheviks* in 1903 when he began to work with Julius Martov (1873-xxx).[136] Martov, according to Trotsky,

> «*was a gifted writer, an ingenious politician and a profound thinker, but lacked courage and his insight was devoid of will. My friendship and devotion to him did not survive the test of the first important events precipitated by the approaching revolution.*»

Trotsky and his wife travelled to St. Petersburg to take part in the 1905 Russian Revolution. She was arrested; he escaped to Finland. After the Potemkin battleship protests, Trotsky returned to St. Petersburg. Natalia was released and both joined the St. Petersburg Soviet. Trotsky, in spite of his youth, became the intellectual leader of the incipient revolution, far above Lenin and Martov. In December of 1905, however, the St. Petersburg Soviet was crushed after he October Manifesto and Trotsky was arrested and imprisoned. He escaped from Siberia in 1907 and moved to Vienna with Natalia and their son; at the outbreak of World War I they were forced out of Vienna and moved first to Zurich, then to Paris, followed by Madrid and New York, where he began to publish the revolutionary newspaper *Novy Mir*.

When Lenin returned to Russia in 1917 and was about to break with the *Bolsheviks*, Trotsky convinced Lenin to stay in the party with the promise he would join it himself, which he did in July of that year.[137] Kerensky became fearful of Trotsky's activities and had him arrested. Trotsky was released on September 23 and was elected Chairman of the Petrograd Soviet as the October Revolution exploded. He was closer to Lenin than Stalin at that time. I

---

[136] At the 1903 **Second Congress of the Russian Social Democratic Party**, *Julius Martov*, a close friend of *Vladimir Lenin*, argued for the creation of a large party of communist activists, while Lenin argued for a small party of professional revolutionaries with a large fringe of non-party sympathizers and supporters. Martov's view prevailed over Lenin's and it produced a split in the party. That resulted in the emergence of *Mensheviks* (idealists disinclined to violence, followers of Markov) and *Bolsheviks* (the more radical followers of Lenin, preaching the urgency to forcefully seize factories from the industrialists and land from the landlords). All considered, the difference between *Mensheviks* and *Bolsheviks* was more temperamental than doctrinal.

[137] Trotsky disapproved the support that the *Mensheviks* were giving to the *Provisional Government* and to the war effort.

Dora Kaplan, the 28 year old would-be assassin of Vladimir Lenin in 1918. On August 30, Lenin was speaking at the *Hammer and Sickle factory* in Moscow. When he was ready to leave, Kaplan called him and as he turned she fired three shots with a Browning pistol. Lenin never really recovered. Kaplan was interrogated by the ***Cheka***, who put a bullet to the back of her head. The foto on the right was taken days after Lenin's recuperation. The *Bolsheviks* reacted by intensifying the scope of the Red Terror.

fact, if Lenin was the brains, the planner and the driving force behind the Bolshevik Party, Trotsky became its voice; he was the orator and the rabble-rouser. He was the only one that could rouse the Congress delegates' excitement when they became listless after long hours of diatribes, tongue lashing, boring political tirades, satirical criticism and bitter verbal attacks. He was the man who could say the right thing at the right moment. Joseph Stalin at that time was simply a man who attended the meetings. Trotsky was the main figure arguing for an insurrection when others, including Stalin, were hesitant because «*an early action could result in the Bolsheviks being destroyed as a political force.*»

It was Trotsky who wrote a letter that Lenin sent to the members of the *Central Committee* on October 24, 1917:[138]

> «*The situation is utterly critical. It is clearer than clear that now, already, putting off the insurrection is equivalent to its death. With all my strength I wish to convince my comrades that now everything is hanging by a hair, that on the agenda now are questions that are decided not by conferences, not by congresses (not even congresses of soviets), but exclusively by populations, by the mass, by the struggle of armed masses... No matter what may happen, this very evening, this very night, the government must be arrested, the junior officers guarding them must be disarmed, and so on... History will not forgive revolutionaries for delay, when they can win today (and probably will win today), but risk losing a great deal tomorrow, risk losing everything.*»

---

[138] In 1917 Lenin was a very sick man. He would die in 1924 at age 54. According to his autopsy, «*his cerebral arteries were narrowed to tiny slits and were so calcified that when tapped with tweezers they sounded like stone.*»

As a baby, Lenin had a head so large that he often fell over. He used to bang his head on the floor, making his mother worry that he might be mentally disabled. As an adult, Lenin suffered diseases that were common at the time: *typhoid, toothaches, influenza* and a painful skin infection called *erysipelas*. He was under intense stress, of course, which led to *insomnia, migraines* and *abdominal pain.*

He had been shot twice by a socialist revolutionary woman named Dora Kaplan in an assassination attempt in 1918. One bullet lodged in his collarbone after puncturing his lung. Another got caught in the base of his neck. Both bullets remained in place for the rest of his life. In the two years before he died, Lenin had three debilitating *strokes*. His doctors diagnosed nervous exhaustion, chronic lead intoxication from the two bullets lodged in his body, cerebral *arteriosclerosis* and *endarteritis luetica* or *meningovascular syphilis*, for which he had been treated with injections of a solution containing arsenic, the prevailing *syphilis* remedy.

In his last hours and days of his life, he experienced severe *seizures*, which were quite unusual in a stroke patient..

On the right, young Stalin in 1905.
Below: Joseph Stalin (1878 - 1953)
with his son, Vasily (1921 - 1962)
and daughter Svetlana (1926 - 2011)
at one of Stalin's dachas. June 1933.
After she defected to the US in 1967
and got married Stevlana became
Lana Peters.

The ***Politburo*** (Political Bureau), the highest policy-making authority under the
Communist Party after the 8th Party Congress in 1919.
Left to right, top to bottom:
LENIN (died in 1924); TROTSKY (murdered in 1940); KAMENEV (shot in 1936);
ZINOVIEV (shot in 1936); BUKHARIN (shot in 1938); RYKOV (shot in 1938);
TOMSKY (suicide in 1936);
STALIN (only survivor, directed the elimination of all others).

On the evening of that day, Lenin issued orders for the *Bolsheviks* to occupy the railway stations, the telephone exchange and the State Bank. The following day the *Red Guards* surrounded the *Winter Palace*. Inside was most of the country's Cabinet, although Alexander Kerensky had managed to escape from the city.

In November, 1917, Lenin appointed Trotsky as the People's Commissar for Foreign Affairs. Running a government was a new task and often puzzling to these successful revolutionaries. They had a certain awe of Lenin, so they left him undisturbed; every little difficulty that came up was brought to Trotsky.

After the October Revolution Lenin decided that the old Russian Army would have to be turned into an instrument of the Communist Party. Trotsky and not Stalin, was given that task and began recruiting a large number of officers from the old army; Lenin approved of this tactic saying «*Show me another man who could have practically created a model army in a year and won respect of the military specialist as well.*»

In April, 1922, Lenin suggested that a new post of *General Secretary* should be created. Lenin's choice for the post was Joseph Stalin, a loyal supporter of his policies. Stalin's main opponents for the future leadership of the party, Trotsky included, failed to see the importance of this position and actually supported his nomination. They initially saw the post of General Secretary as being no more than *Lenin's mouthpiece*. Soon after Stalin's appointment as *General Secretary*, Lenin went into hospital to have a bullet removed from his body. The operation did not restore his health and soon afterwards a blood vessel broke in Lenin's brain. This left him paralyzed and unable to speak. As *Lenin's mouthpiece*, Stalin first became an important man; he made full use of his powers as *General Secretary*.[139]

When Lenin finally died on January 21, 1924, Stalin took over. He appointed himself as pallbearer with Lev Kamenev, Gregory Zinoviev, Nickolai Bukharin, Vyacheslav Molotov, Felix Dzerzhinsky and Maihail Tomsky. Conspicuously absent: Leon Trotsky, Lenin's most trusted man.

---

[139] At the Party Congress Stalin had been granted permission to expel "*unsatisfactory*" party members. This enabled him to remove dozens of supporters of Trotsky, his main rival for the leadership of the party. As General Secretary, Stalin also had the power to appoint and expell people from important positions in the government. The new holders of these posts were fully aware that they owed their promotion to Stalin. They also knew that if their behaviour did not please Stalin they would be replaced.They all became anti-Trotsky lackeys.

One simple way by which *Bolsheviks* forever eliminated their enemies from the pages of History. On the top, **Leon Trotsky** is edited out of one picture taken in Petrograd in 1921. By 1927, Troysky had never been there.

In the photo on the bottom, **Nikolai Yezkov**, one time a very powerful head of the *NKVD* (*People's Commisariat for Internal Affairs*), was erased from a 1926 photo with Stalin and Molotov, by apparently throwing him out of the boat.

Finally, in January 1925, Stalin was able to arrange for Trotsky to be removed from the government. Some of Trotsky's supporters pleaded with him to organize a military coup. As the former commissar of war Trotsky was in a good position to arrange this. However, Trotsky rejected the idea and instead resigned his post. His biographers all agree that...

> «He left office without the slightest attempt at rallying in his defense the army he had created and led for seven years. He still regarded the party, no matter how or by whom it was led, as the legitimate spokesman of the working-class.»

In 1929 Trotsky was ordered to leave the Soviet Union. As Trotsky was still advocating world revolution, most countries refused to take him in. Trotsky, his wife, Natalia Sedova, and his son, Lev Sedov, eventually were allowed to settle in France, where they published *Bulletin of the Opposition*. His younger son, Sergei Sedov, decided to stay in Moscow to continue his academic career. Joseph Stalin was furious with the Trotsky family and ordered Sergei's arrest. In December of 1934 he was assassinated. When the case came to court to sentence his murderer, all sixteen witnesses were first deposed and then put to death. Stalin could not afford any witnesses to what it was obviously a conspiracy to destroy Trotsky's links to Russia.

The French government came under pressure from Fascists and Stalinists to expel Trotsky from the country. In April, 1934, the French government issued a decree ordering Trotsky's deportation. No country would accept him and it was not until June, 1935, that Norway agreed to grant him the status of political exile. The Norwegians were soon encouraged to expel him. Under pressure from Joseph Stalin, the government placed him under house arrest before being deported to Mexico on December, 1936.[140]

---

[140] In 1940 Joseph Stalin ordered his NKVD agents to eliminate Trotsky. Ramon Mercader, a mercenary in the employ of the Russian government, became a regular visitor at the Trotsky's while the family was living in Mexico City. Trotsky's wife, Natalia Sedova, recalled that he visited them on 20th August, 1940:

> «Mercader knocked at our door and we received him at Lev's (Trotsky's) study; the door closed, and I walked into the adjoining room. Not more than three or four minutes had elapsed when I heard a terrible, soul-shaking cry and without so much as realizing who it was I rushed in the direction from which it came. On the threshold of the dining room, beside the door post stood Lev. His face was covered with blood, his eyes, without glasses, were sharp blue, his hands were hanging along his body. Next to him, still wielding on his right hand an ice-ax buried in Lev' head, was Ramon Mercader.»

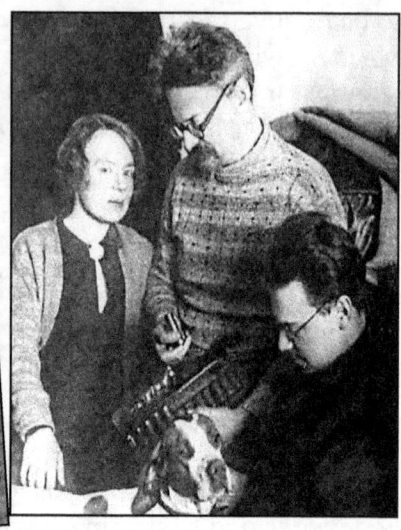
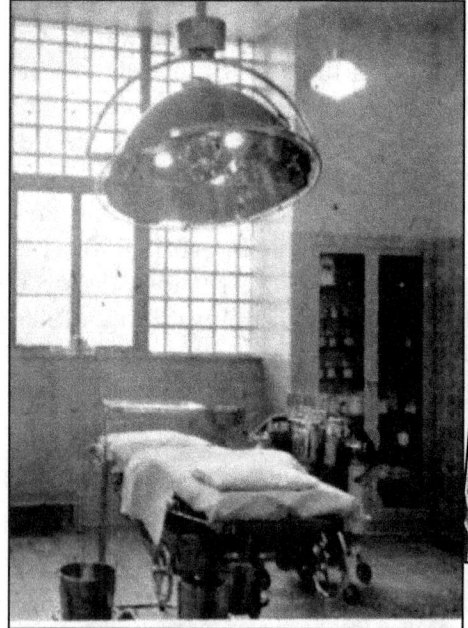
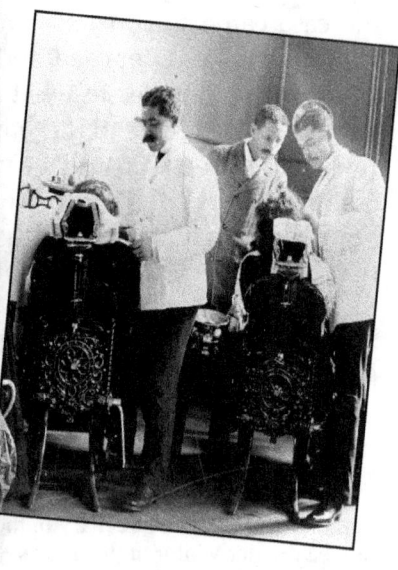

Top left photo, **Lev Sedov**, son of Leon Trotsky, in Paris. On the right, **Natalia Sevoda**, his wife, with his son Lev Sedov. On the bottom two photos, the **Russian Free Clinic** in Paris in 1923. It was opened to all Russian émigrés but its main purpose was to medically treat Russian diplomats. It was there that the Moscow government disposed of enemies that were intoxicated and given a one-way trip to the clinic.

Joseph Stalin, after the assassination of Trotsky's younger son Serge Sedov, continued seeking to destroy the family. Lev Sedov, Trotsky's oldest son became editor of the *Bulletin of the Opposition*, the magazine published in Paris by the "Old Bolsheviks" that were trying to keep the October Revolution in the course devised by Lenin. By all accounts Lev Sedov was an extremely energetic young man that worked long hours doing the work that his father was no longer able to undertake. Suddenly, in February of 1938 Lev had severe stomach pains and had to be taken to the *Beregere Clinic* in Paris, a small establishment run by Russian émigrés. He was operated the following morning but within 24 hours he began to feel critically ill. He died on February 16, under suspicion of murder. It was know later that the *Beregere Clinic* was the one hospital in Paris where the KGB took high ranking Russian officials for medical check-ups. A man who investigated the incident, Rudolf Klement, a trusted friend and secretary of Trotsky, compiled solid evidence of the murder of Lev. On July 14 his headless body was found floating in the Seine. Alexander Orlov, an FBI agent and former NKVD operative in Paris, confirmed to Trotsky that the KGV was responsible for the death of Lev Sedov and the kidnapping and assassination of Rudolf Klement.

The October Revolution final brutal and atrocious events occurred between 1936 and 1939 under the direction and command of Joseph Stalin. He mercilessly repressed and prosecuted all people considered *counter-revolutionaries* and enemies of the leadership of the Soviet Union. These "purges" were motivated by his desire to remove dissenters from the Communist Party and to consolidate his personal authority. They were carried out against government bureaucrats, leaders of the armed forces, members of the intelligentsia of the party and the country, peasants and especially those branded as *"too rich for a peasant"* (affluent landlords, independent farmers and peasants who resisted handing over their grain to detachments of Red Army soldiers, collectively known as the *kulaks*), and all kinds of free thinking professionals.

Hundreds of thousands of victims were accused of various political crimes: espionage, wrecking, sabotage, anti-Soviet agitation, conspiracies to prepare uprisings and coups. They were quickly executed by shooting, or sent to the *Gulag* labor camps. Many died at the penal labor camps of starvation, disease, exposure, and overwork. Other methods of dispatching victims were used on an

Lavrentiy Beria (1899-1953), a Soviet politician of Georgian ethnicity, Marshall of the Soviet Union and Chief of Soviet Security and the Secret Police, also Stalin's main executioner. On the left, his photo on *Time Magazine* front page as "enemy of the people." On the top right, a picture of Beria with **Stevlana Alliluyeva Stalin** (1926-2011), Joseph's daughter, also known as *Lana Peters* after seeking asylum in the US. On the bottom, a photo of Stalin's slave labor camps in 1833.

experimental basis. Secret policemen, for instance, gassed people to death in batches in the back of specially adapted airtight vans. During those days of Stalin's Great Purge, over 400,000 members of the Communist Party were "expelled." The term "expelled" became a cloaked word for «arrest, imprisonment, and often execution.» It has been estimated that about one million people perished during Stalin's Great Purge. From the *October Revolution* onward, Lenin had used repression against perceived enemies of the *Bolsheviks* as a systematic method of instilling fear and facilitating social control, especially during the campaign commonly referred to as the *Red Terror*. It paled in comparison to what Stalin organized and accomplished in the 1930s.

A final word:

The greatest myth of Marxism is the notion that the Russian Revolution failed solely due to the impact of objective factors, such as weather created famines, international economic recessions and conspiracies and corruption induced by capitalist nations. Moreover, down to the XXI century, for modern Marxists, Leninists and Stalinists, the failure of the 1917 revolution was the product of such things as civil war, foreign intervention, economic collapse and the isolation and backwardness of Russia, not the *Bolshevik* ideology. Never mind the authoritarianism under Lenin, Trotsky and Stalin, the genocides in the 1920s, the purges in the 1930s, the atrocities during World War II in the early 1940s, the failed implantation of Stalinism in the late 1940s and 1950s, and the failures of Marxist-Leninist ideologies in the modern world in Western Europe, Africa and South America, Cuba, Nicaragua, and other vulnerable regions of the world. Marxism-Leninism proved to be a historical fantasy since the days when the rebels of 1917 failed to turn themselves into a good and fair ruling class in 1918.

Deep down the problem with Communism was that it not only created social and political structures like centralized economic impositions, official snitching organizations, single party politics, state control of education and the press and single person management of the state, but also did away with social, political and economic incentives, private property, family autonomy and codified justice, which not only disempowered the masses but also made much worse any normal outside or internal challenge that needed to be faced.

The claim that the 1917 Bolshevik Revolution was unique in its proletarian aims has always been a fantasy. In every bourgeois

Three propaganda posters extolling the **Dictatorship of the Proletariat**, the **Worldwide Inspiration of Marxism** and the Slogan **Workers of the World, Unite!**

revolution in which workers participated, proletarian objectives were considered and achieved. There was no better example than the American Revolution; it raised simultaneously the living standards of patricians and also those of the common working classes.

The Russian Revolution, as well as many other Marxist-Leninist revolutions, created a dictatorship of one party and its premises were not logically consistent with the term "*dictatorship of the proletariat.*" Either the proletariat rules or it is ruled. The party is driven to rule in its own interests to secure its own permanence. The proletariat is a much larger social entity than the party and its needs were not the same and need not be subordinate to those of the small minority which is the party.

At any rate, the Bolshevik Revolution was not led by the workers but by the middle class, the bourgeoisie, who, if and when the need arose, stepped over the proletariat, took its production, sacrificed their leaders, and left them stranded in a quack mire.

More people died over a century due to the excesses of the *Bolshevik* revolution that started in St. Petersburg in 1917, than in all wars, famines and natural disasters in the entire history of the world.

More workers lost their rights in 1917 than at any period in the history of the working classes. The state took over all enterprises employing more than ten workers; labor was compulsory and strikes were outlawed. Internal trade was made illegal; only the government food commissary could buy and sell. Money became useless as the state took over distribution and production. All opposition parties were liquidated.

More peasants became poor during the *Bolshevik* revolution than during the oppressive days of feudalism. The government subjected the countryside to severe requisitioning, taking crops, grains and farm animals without compensation. It mobilized the poorer peasants against the *kulaks* (wealthy peasants). Famine was rampart after that.

Even Lenin became frightened about the future of his communist experiment. So was Stalin, who tried in vain to control the uncontrollable and to suppress the unrestrainable dissidence. He became the worst *matarife* in human history, but he remorselessly continued to experiment with his revolution from above. Was it worth the decimation of close to 100 million humans?

On the top photo, *23 of 24 members of the staff of Vladimir Lenin* were disposed of by murder, sentences to Siberia, fear for life or sequestration of their families by Joseph Stalin. On the bottom, two photos of the long lasting criminality of the Russian revolution: the anihilation of the leaders of the *Czechoslovakia uprising in 1868* and the similar elimination of leaders during the defeat of the *Hungarian insurgency in 1956*.

Russian revolutionary mobs burning down portraits and **symbols of old Russian history** in 1917. In 1921 and 1922, as a result of the famine **deliberately caused by Lenin,** 29 million people within the borders of the Soviet Union were caught in the grips of starvation.

Expulsion and persecution of **Kulaks** (middle class farmers) during the agricultural collectivization of 1928. In the bottom photo, the savage massacre of 8,000 gendarmes, landowners, freedom fighters, factory owners, lawyers, officials, and priests, all Polish nationals, carried out by Lavrentiy Beria's NKVD in April and May of 1940 in and around the **Katyn Forest** in Russia.

In spite of Stalin's criminal record, hundreds of Europeans, particularly Frenchmen and Italians, rendered homage to him after his death. Such was the case at the Parisian papers *L'Humanité* and *Les Letres Françaises* (showing a portrait of Stalin by Picasso) and *L'Unità* in Rome («*Eternal glory to the man that has done so much good for humanity...*»)

The Cuban 1959 Revolution
1959 to present

«I propose the immediate launching of a nuclear strike on the United States.»
FIDEL CASTRO QUOTED IN *THE NEW YORK TIMES*
ON OCTOBER 23, 1992

The 1959 Cuban Revolution: a condensed timeline

1959
>January 1. Fulgencio Batista and his collaborators escape in the early hours of the morning towards the Dominican Republic.
>Insurgents begin to descend from the mountains with rosaries on their necks. Castro seeks the blessings of Manuel Pérez Serantes, Archbishop of Santiago de Cuba.
>January 2. Raúl Castro sends to the firing squad over 70 military men, policemen and civilians in Santiago de Cuba.
>January 4. Insurgents from the *July 26 Movement* (Castro's J26M) clash with those of the *Directorio Estudiantil* at the Presidential Palace in Havana.
>January 5. President Urrutia takes the Oath of Office from José Miró Cardona, Prime Minister, Manuel Ray, Minister of Public Works, Rufo López Fresquet, Minister of the Treasury, Roberto Agramonte, Foreign Minister and others, as well as Felipe Pazos as President of the National Bank.
>January 7. The US recognizes the new government of Cuba.
>January 8. Fidel Castro and his troops enter the city of Havana. At the Columbia Military Camp he delivers a speech asking ¿*Armas para qué?* (Why do you need weapons?), criticizing the leadership of the *Directorio Estudiantil*.
>January 10. The death penalty applied retroactively is approved as an amendment to the *1940 Constitution*, as well as the government right to confiscate property.
>January 16. Castro visits the tomb of Eduardo Chibás and declares that he is not a Communist.
>January 22. On a visit to Venezuela Castro confirms that he will organize national elections within two years.
>January 30. The right of *Habeas Corpus* is suspended. The total number of enemies taken to the firing squads reaches 500.
>February 7. The Council of Ministers approves a *Ley Fundamental* that replaces the 1940 Constitution.
>February 16. Prime Minister Miró resigns and Castro takes his place. Raúl Castro is promoted to Minister of the Armed Forces.
>March 1. At a trial in Santiago de Cuba several Air Force pilots are found innocent of the crime of dropping bombs on civilians during the war. Castro declares the judgment not valid. The pilots are tried a second time and found guilty. They are condemned to 30 years in prison.
>April 5. The CTC, the *Confederación de Trabajadores de Cuba*, rejects the right to strike adducing that the government will take care of justice with the working classes.
>April 15. Castro visits New York and Washington. Eisenhower does not grant him an audience but Nixon does. Castro visits Argentina, Brazil, Uruguay and Canada the following weeks.
>May 17. The *Council of Ministers* sets up an *Institute for Agrarian Reform (INRA)*. Castro appoints himself as President of the Institute.
>June 4. The *INRA* expropriates farms larger than 30 Caballerías (1000 acres).
>June 15. Multiple bombs explode in Havana.
>June 30. The CIA declares that Castro is a Communist.

July 13. President Urrutia declares his opposition to the Communists in Cuba. Castro forces his resignation. Osvaldo Dorticós Torrado, a known Communist from Cienfuegos, replaces Urrutia as president of Cuba.

September 8. Rolando Cubela is imposed by Castro as President of the *Federación de Estudiantes Universitarios (FEU)* in opposition to Pedro Luis Boitel, a Catholic candidate who had a plurality of the student vote.

October 20. Hubert Matos, military chief in Camagüey, protests about the communist penetration in the Armed Forces. He is forced to resign and is arrested.

October 25. Camilo Cienfuegos, one of the leaders of the insurrection in Sierra Maestra, disappears as his plane was traveling from Camagüey to Havana. There are rumors that he was purged from the government.

October 26. A second round of revolutionary tribunals is announced.

November 26. Manuel Ray, Minister of Public Works, and Faustino Pérez, Minister of Recovery of Public Funds, resign their cabinet positions. Ernesto (Ché) Guevara is appointed as head of the *National Bank* replacing Felipe Pazos, who had originally supported Castro.

November 28. More than one million Catholics assemble in Havana at the *Congreso Católico Nacional*. The Castros attend the public mass.

December 13. Aleksandr Aleseiev, a soviet agent, arrives in Havana under the guise of being a reporter for the TASS news agency.

December 27. The government passes a law giving anyone who disagrees with any article in the newspapers the right to reply to such article right after the objected article. It is called "*La Coletilla*."

December 31. The total number of executions during 1959 tops 560 persons.

1960

January 21. During a Castro press conference on TV, the Spanish Ambassador, Juan Pablo de Lojendio interrupts his diatribe against Spain. The ambassador is expelled from Cuba.

February 4. Anastas Mikoyan, USSR's First Minister, visits Havana to open an exposition. He attempts to deposit flowers at the Martí statue in Havana's Central Park and is rebuffed by students from the University of Havana, which are beaten by the police.

March 31. All private Radio and TV stations are confiscated by the government.

May 1. Paraphrasing his slogan of January 8 (*¿Armas para qué?*) Castro now cynically declared *¿Elecciones para qué?* (Why do you need elections?).

May 11. The government confiscates all newspapers and magazines published in the island three days after establishing diplomatic relations with the USSR.

May 28. David Salvador resigns as president of the CTC (*Confederación de Trabajadores de Cuba*) due to the total imposed control by communists.

June 12. All large hotels in Cuba are confiscated, including the *Hilton* and the historical *Hotel Nacional*.

June 29. All petroleum refineries (*Texaco, Esso* and *Shell*) are confiscated when they refuse on technical grounds to refine Russian petroleum.

July 6. All US businesses are threatened with confiscation. On August 6 they are all confiscated.

September 8. The Cuban government sends 3,000 soldiers and 100,000 volunteers to suffocate an insurrection in the *Sierra del Escambray* in central Cuba.

September 13. The US starts a commercial embargo against Cuba.
September 15. Castro denounces the US government at the UN.
September 17. All US banks in Cuba are confiscated.
September 28. The Cuban government establishes a universal spying system called the *Comités de Defensa de la Revolución (CDRs)* in every block, every work place and every office.
October 12. First executions of student insurgents from the Escambray mountains. Eventually over 350 would be executed.
October 13. Every private business is Cuba is confiscated, including 105 Sugar Mills and more than 380 drugstores, breweries, department stores, railroad companies, banks and rum distilleries.
October 15. The government expropriates every house, apartment, warehouse and empty lot in Cuba. People that were renting would pay rent to the government. Nobody would be entitled to free maintenance.
October 30. So far, more than 1350 Cubans have been executed by the government. More than 120 union leaders have been condemned an average of 22 years in prison.

1961

January 2. Start of the alphabetization campaign organized by the Cuban government. The Cuban government asks the US to retire all but 11 members of its diplomatic delegation. The US breaks relations with Cuba.
March 4. The government declares its hostility against Catholic education. To date more than 100,000 Cubans have taken political refuge in the US.
April 5. The city of Havana suffers from sabotage; the *El Encanto*, the best department store in Hispanic America, is completely destroyed by fire.
April 15. B-26 Planes from Guatemala bombard several military airports in Cuba. Castro proclaims the irrevocable socialist character of his revolution.
April 17. The Bay of Pigs invasion starts. Thousands of people are arrested all over Cuba. Priests and lay Catholics are taken to cells in secret police headquarters. Dozens of suspects are shot at La Cabaña fortress. By April 20, after President Kennedy retracts his promise of help and retires the support to the exiles' Air Force, the invasion is defeated.
June 6. Schools across Cuba are prohibited to teach anything having to do with religion, whether history, dogma, practices or statistics.
June 16. Thousands of Cuban students are sent to the USSR.
July 26. The number of CDRs in Cuba exceeds 100,000.
August 5. All currency in Cuba is declared null and only 400 pesos would be accepted for exchange with new paper money printed in Czechoslovakia. Thousands of business go bankrupt and thousands of people and entire families go hungry.
September 6. Castro announces that any professional that has left the island will be considered as resigning his/her Cuban citizenship. They would not be allowed to ever set foot on the island again.
September 17. Over 130 priests and nuns are taken from their residences,

forced aboard the Spanish ship *Covadonga* and expelled from the island.

November 6. The government closes *Lunes de Revolución*, a leftist propaganda publication that turned against the oppression of the communist government.

December 15. The total number of opponents to the communist regime that have been taken to the firing squads up to the end of the year is above 4,000.

1962

January 3. Internal conflicts between the Communist Party and the 26 de Julio Movement. Castro takes the side of the Communist Party, which is now in his hands and not in those of its founders.

January 6. Rumors continued to spread in Cuba about the government seizing the *Patria Potestad* (rights of protection and custody) for all children between 5 and 16 years of age. Cuban bishops and volunteers intensified the transfer of children out of Cuba in what had become known as *Operación Pedro Pan*, which lasted from December 1960 to October 1962.

January 25. Cuba is expelled from the *Organization of American States* (OEA). Brazil, Mexico, Chile, Bolivia and Ecuador abstained from this vote.

February 11. The government of Cuba begins to establish a rationing system for medicines and foodstuffs. The CDRs would manage the rationing. Consumption would be limited to less than half of what it was in 1958.

July 3. The Cuban government begins a process of relocating people against their will if it serves the national interest. Hundreds of families are the first to be relocated from Las Villas to Pinar del Rio.

July 27. The CIA detects six Soviet ships discharging weapons and war materials in Cuba. Other ships are unloaded in *El Mariel*, Pinar del Rio.

October 14. A US U-2 plane takes pictures of Russian missiles and surface to air missiles (SAMs) in Pinar del Rio, Cuba. The CIA estimates that the range of these missiles could cause the death of 80 million Americans.

October 22. The *Cuban Missile Crises* explodes and the US establishes a quarantine and a blockade of Cuba.

October 26. The USSR agrees to retire the missiles if the US agrees not to invade Cuba. The Crises ends.

December 18. Cuba and the US agree on an exchange of Cuban prisoners from the Bay of Pigs invasion for a rescue figure of US $62 million.

1963

March 25. After two years in the Mexican embassy, Manuel Urrutia, first president imposed by the Cuban Revolution in 1959, is allowed to go into exile in Mexico.

November 13. The Cuban government establishes a *Compulsory Military Service* for all males between 15 and 45 years of age. Young Cubans find the possibility of exile closed.

1964

January 1. The Cuban government establishes the *Military Units to Aid Production* (UMAP), where it sends thousands of religious priests and nuns, adversaries, and homosexuals.

March 26. Castro begins a purge of communist militants. The first victims are Marcos Rodríguez, Joaquín Ordoqui and Edith García Buchaca.

1965
February 2. Cuban exiles continue their attacks on Castro's forces inside Cuba and supply lines to the communist government of Cuba.
March 12. Works by Mao are confiscated in Cuban bookstores and libraries.
April 19. Ernesto Guevara, after visits to many African nations, arrives in Tanzanía with 200 Cuban soldiers chosen by him.
August 10. Anti-Castro Cubans are executed at *La Cabaña* fortress.
October 10. After negotiations with the US, hundreds of Cubans are allowed to escape the island through the port of Camarioca.
November 5. 88 Protestant pastors are condemned to 3 to 30 years sentences.

1966
January 15. Castro welcomes hundreds of leftists in Havana for a *Tricontinental* revolutionary movement.
June 22. Castro confiscates the Catholic Seminary *El Buen Pastor*.
December 12. Castro denounces and starts a violent persecution against several anti-communist groups: la *Rosa Blanca*, el *Movimiento Demócrata Cristiano*, el *Movimiento 30 de Noviembre*, el *Directorio Revolutionario Estudiantil*, el *Frente Revolucionario Democrático*, el *Movimiento Revolutionario del Pueblo* y el *Movimiento de Recuperación Revolucionaria*
December 18. Increased attacks against Catholics. Several priests, including future Cardinal Jaime Ortega Alamino, are sent to the UMAP.

1967
April 11. Ernesto Guevara urged all revolutionaries to create in the Americas «*dos, tres, muchos Vietnams.*»
August 4. Cuba signs an alliance with the US *Black Power* movement.
October 8. Without material or moral support from Castro, Ernesto Guevara is captured and executed in the mountains of Bolivia.

1968
January 25. Second purge of Cuban communists not loyal to Castro, categorized as pro-soviets, led by Anibal Escalante. Over 40 members of this "*microfraction*" are condemned from 3 to 15 years in prison.
March 13. A new *Gran Ofensiva* is announced by Castro. Over 50,000 small business are confiscated, leaving no private businesses in all of Cuba.
August 17. Each worker is Cuba is presented with a *Tarjeta de Trabajo*, where bosses will enter details of their behavior and political attitudes.

1969
January 2. Sugar begins to be rationed in Cuba. The government proposed a goal of producing 10 million tons of sugar in 1970.
April 10. The Cuban Episcopate publishes a Pastoral Letter siding with the communists and opposing the *American Embargo*.
July 21. Cuba's TV ignores the landing of an American vessel in the moon.
December 12. Pro-Castro Cubans living in the US arrive in Havana to help with the goal of producing 10 million tons of sugar.

After 10 years of Communist rule in Cuba the revolution has eliminated all private education, from elementary to university, all private business enterprises, any and all radio and TV communications, non-communist associations, private hospitals, private clubs, private home property, and all demonstrations except those organized by the Communist government.

The Cuban Revolution
1959 to present

At the end of 1958 there were six and a half million residents in Cuba. Until the 1930s, most of them had lived in the countryside but by 1959 more Cubans lived in cities than in the country. The only larger populations in the Caribbean area were Mexico with 32 million and Colombia with 13 million. Altogether Hispanic countries had 190 million residents, slightly higher than the US.

Several interesting demographics were particularly unique to Cuba. In 1958 there were a very small number of men above 60+ years of age. It was cause for concerns for historians since it was believed that men over 60 lended stability to populations.[141]

By 1959 the size of a typical Cuban family was very similar to that of US families; in 1902 it had been different. According to the 1902 exit census by the US government, 80,000 women had given birth to ten or more children during the last years of the XIX century, particularly in the countryside. The census of 1902 also reveled that during those years 660 women had given birth to 20 or more children. Of these, unexpectedly, more that 400 had been white women. That was no longer the case after Cuba reached more than 50 years of independence by 1958.

In 1959 twenty one cities in Cuba had populations of over 25,000 residents, a remarkable growth since only five cities exceeded that number in 1902. Marianao, for instance, had 5,000 residents in 1902 and by 1959 it had grown to have 200,000; in the same interval, Havana had grown from under 245,000 people in 1902 to 800,000 in 1959.

In Cuba's countryside most people lived within the perimeter of the area they cultivated rather than in small villages or *aldeas* as in Spain. Two thirds of the houses in towns and cities in Cuba had electricity in 1959; in the countryside the figure was only 11%.

Except for London and Vienna, Havana had the largest percentage of population living in the capital of the country. More

---

[141] This was attributed to the number of men lost to the island due to the very expensive price the Cubans had paid for their independence between 1895 and 1898.

A picture of the brief *Cuban revolution of 1933* which made the front page of the *New York Times* Sunday magazine;

Fidel Castro shown in the pages of Communist newspaper *Hoy*, *acussed* for the murder of University student leader Manolo Castro (no kin);

Young Fidel Castro in his days as *professional agitaror*, reprimanded by Chief of Police General Quirino Uría, at the corner of L and 9th streets in Havana.

Students from the University of Havana protesting the lack of human rights during the government of Fulgencio Batista; miliary tanks surrounding the Presidential Palace after the ***attemp on Batista's life in 1957***; thousands of Batista followers on a ***solidarity march*** after he survived the attack on his life in 1957.

Three views of Cuba before the advent of the 1959 revolution:
The colosal mountains of **Sierra Maestra**; **slums** in several places around the capital of Havana; strong and active **commercial life** across most of Cuba.

than any other capital city in the world, Havana had attracted within its borders the largest percentage of wealth of the country.

Havana, in fact, had 18 daily newspapers, 32 radio stations, 5 TV channels, of which 4 were in color; 23% of its cars had air conditioners, a luxury which was also prevalent in hotels, movie houses, theaters, business offices and many private residences. Compared to Havana, cities like Kingston, San Juan, Caracas and Bogotá looked unsophisticated. [142]

By most criteria in December of 1958, Cuba was the most progressive country in Hispanic America. Income per head surpassed US $500 per year.[143] In general terms Cuba's economy was stagnant but not underdeveloped.

On a percapita basis, Cuba had double the number of physicians and seven times more dentists than Mexico. There were no municipalities in Cuba, small or minuscule, without a physician. Havana, however, had four times as many doctors per 1,000 residents than the rest of the island and ten times more hospital beds than those available per capita outside the capital. Cuba, in spite of its indisputable limitations and the scourge of corruption, had vanquished diseases like Tuberculosis, Smallpox, and Malaria; it had progressed from 110 infant mortality in 1902 to 35 per thousand in 1958.

These figures, of course, did not reflect entirely the Cuban reality at the time. There was a substantial divergence between the status of the rich and that of the rest of the population. There was evidence of poverty among Cubans, particularly in the countryside. [144]

At the bottom of the social scale there were some 200,000 peasant families in abject poverty in the countryside, few of them owning, renting or squatting in less than one *caballería* (33 acres) of land.

Slightly higher in the social scale there were 700,000 sugar workers which had jobs only during half of the year. Of these per

---

[142] There were 4,500,000 TV sets in the entire Hispanic America in 1959; Cuba had 10% of those for a population that barely surpassed 3.4% of total Hispanics in the continent.

[143] The income per year in the US in 1959 was US $2,572.

[144] Havana, for instance, had the largest percapita ownership of Cadillacs that any city in the US or the rest of the world.

Cuba before the advent of the 1959 Communist revolution:
two views of *Havana* and two views of life in the *countryside*.

haps only 100,000 had positions within the sugar factories and were idle only for three months of the year.[145]

In the same social class as the sugar workers, there were about 650,000 permanent unemployed who lived in shanty towns typical not only of Cuba but of almost all Hispanic countries.

At the top of the social scale were 53,000 high school graduates with clerical or trade skills, 86,000 professionals with university degrees, including over 50,000 teachers, and 400,000 civil employees, military men and small business owners.

Right under the top of the social scale there were a growing middle class working very hard to make it to the top rungs of the scale. They were the strongest upwardly moving citizens of any Hispanic country in the Americas.

The middle classes in Cuba were barely caught up during the many booms and busts of the economy. They simply worked very hard to make things better for their children. They were the strong citizen reserves of an increasingly mobile social framework. They could not count with voluntary organizations or benevolent societies that could help them as their US counterparts did. They had to trust their North American businessmen, the Spanish and Cuban merchants or the Cuban government to provide jobs and opportunities. Politicians came once every few years to seek their votes. Other than that they were on their own. Together with the professionals, the aristocrats, the educated, the clergymen and the politicians they were surprised by the strength of a revolution that came to their doors in the middle of a festive night at the wee hours of the last day of the year 1958.

The revolution that arrived at such inopportune time had its cradle in the *Sierra Maestra*, a mountain range running across the South coast of Oriente, the easternmost province of Cuba. The *Sierra* is a heavily forested area crossed here and there by deep river valleys, volcanic dykes and impassable rows of *mogotes*,[146] where abrupt fault lines make crossing from one valley to another incredibly difficult. It is territory tailor made for guerrillas, rebellions, resistance and sanctuary. In the XVI century it was the place where *Taíno* tribes tried to escape and live in peace away from the

---

[145] 600,000 sugar cane cutters were idle during the *tiempo muerto* (every year, after the sugar crop was harvested and the new canes were not ready for pickup).

[146] ***Mogotes*** or *Karsts* are what remains after the dissolution of soluble rocks such as limestone, dolomite and gypsum leave behind tall columns of wheather resistant rocks composed by quartz, feldspar (alumino-silicates) and mica.

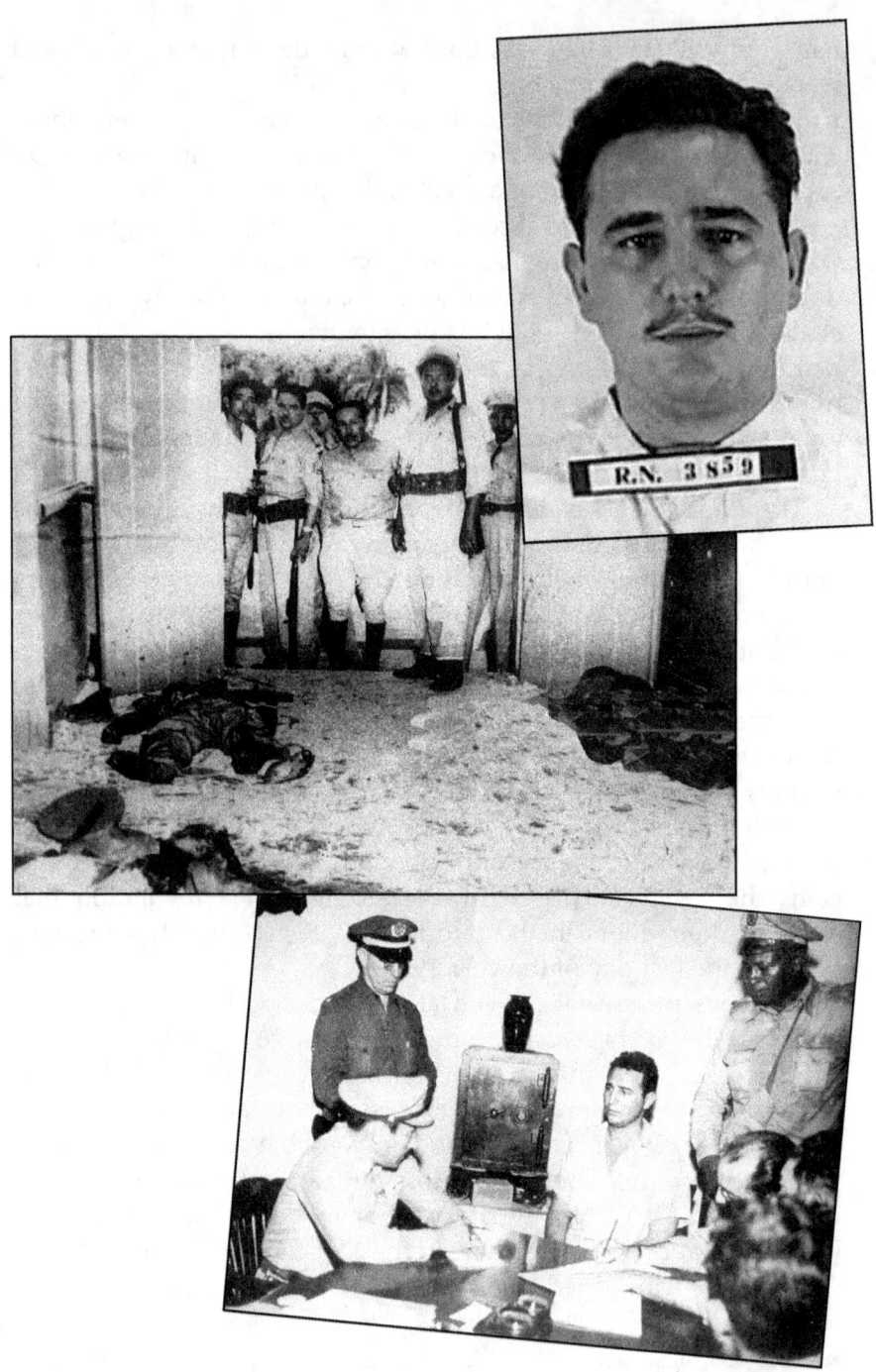

Fidel Castro as *leader of the attack on the Moncada Barracks* in Santiago de Cuba on 26 July, 1953. Castro planned the operation and recruited the assailants but there is proof that he *did not participate actively or fired a single shot*.

conquistadores. In the XVII and XVIII centuries it was the hiding place for *Cimarrones*;[147] in the XIX century it was the scenario of the *Cuban Wars of Independence*, in 1868 and 1895. In the XX century it was first the hiding place of Castro after his failed attempt to take over the *Moncada Barracks* in Santiago de Cuba on July 26, 1953, and later the stage where he decided to nurse his revolution.

In the period between 1902 (independence of Cuba) and 1958 (imminent victory of Castro's rebels from the Sierra Maestra), Cuba was constantly going from one period of instability to another with a succession of revolts, *Coup d'États*, US military interventions and quasi-civil wars. Fulgencio Batista, a former soldier who led a failed *1933 Revolution* of military men and students, took advantage of a power vacuum, assumed the reins of government for seven years and served as the elected president of Cuba from 1940 to 1944; regardless of its genesis, those years became a period of stability and progress. Unfortunately, he forced his way into a second presidential period with a bloodless military *Coup* eight years later, in March 1952. To stay afloat in power during this illegitimate period, he developed a powerful security apparatus to silence political opponents and turned Cuba into his personal fiefdom.

To strike a blow against Batista, a twice incarcerated[148] Fidel Castro gathered a group of Catholic students turned political fighters and carried out a multi-pronged attack on an important but vulnerable military installation. On 26 July 1953, his rebels attacked the *Moncada Barracks* in Santiago de Cuba, only to be decisively defeated by government soldiers. Castro, observing the carnage from a safe distance, took refuge in the Sierra Maestra when the defeat was imminent. [149] It was his first encounter with what later became his revolutionary sanctuary.

After receiving a sentence of 15 years in prison, Castro was freed by Fulgencio Batista and went into exile in Mexico.[150]

---

[147] The term *Cimarrones* refers to either runs of wild cattle or horses, or a group of runaway slaves.

[148] For *delinquency*, not for political reasons.

[149] When aprehended Castro refused to take a *Gun Shot Residue* test to determine if he had discharged a firearm; no one near the Moncada Barracks was able to testify that he had been seen near the fight.

[150] ***Batista pardoned Castro*** after serving only 2 years of his sentence. Historians have tried to explain this benevolence: pressure from civil leaders, petitions from Jesuits that had educated Castro in his youth, considerations to the Castro family that Batista had known as neighbors in his young days in Oriente.

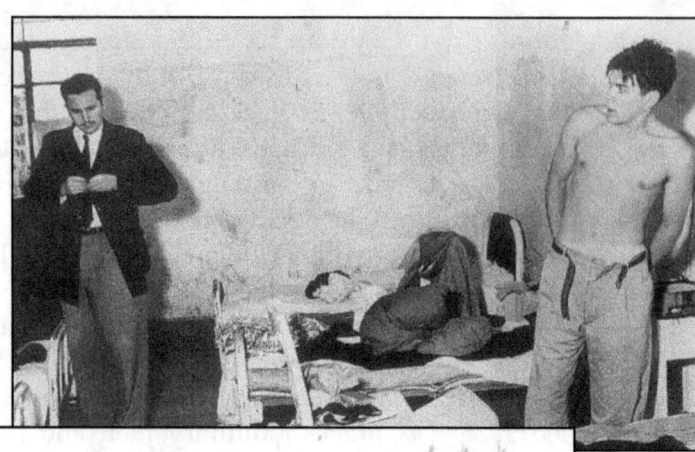

Castro and *Guevara* in Mexico after the attackers of the *Moncada Barracks* were granted an amnesty by Batista.

The only photo of the landing of the yatch *Granma* on the coasts of Oriente, Cuba.

The brothers Castro, Raúl and Fidel, with Efigenio Almejeiras on the days of their presence in the *Sierra Maestra* mountains in Cuba.

In Mexico, Castro met Ernesto "Ché" Guevara, an Argentine dentist and drifter who joined their forces. Alberto Bayo, a former military leader of the failed republican fighters in the Spanish Civil War trained them in guerilla tactics. The group returned to Cuba on December 2, 1956, on a small yacht named *Granma* and found their way into the *Sierra Maestra*.[151] Shortly after their trek began they were attacked by soldiers from the Cuban army; only two dozen escaped, among them Fidel Castro, his brother Raúl and Ernesto Guevara.

From 1956 through the middle of 1958, Castro, with the aid of occasional recruits from the island, staged successful attacks on small Batista garrisons first in the *Sierra Maestra* mountains and later in the *Sierra de Cristal* in northern Oriente and *Sierra del Escambray* in central Cuba.[152] Batista forces undertook bloody repressions to retain control of the cities in the island; an impasse was reached. The cities and towns remained under Batista's control, the mountains in Oriente and Las Villas in eastern and central Cuba became strongholds of the insurgents.

By the middle of 1958 Batista had 30,000 to 40,000 soldiers trying to secure the mountains while Castro's forces were quite small, somewhere between 200 and 800 rebels. Evidently the Cuban military were amazingly ineffective.[153] Aside from their low morale, a decisive blow to the Batista forces was an arms embargo imposed by the US government against Batista on March 14, 1958.

By the end of 1958, with weapons captured from the regular Cuban army and smuggled in by planes from Miami, the insurgency began to soundly defeat the *casquitos*.[154] They split their meager forces into four fronts in Oriente while Guevara proceeded westward towards the provincial capital of Santa Clara.

[151] The *Granma* took 82 Castro followers to Cuba. It was a 60 foot diesel powereed cabin cruiser built in 1943; it had been bought in Mexico for US $15,000 by former Cuban president Carlos Prío.

[152] At the **Escambray mountains,** an anticommunist revolutionary force, the *13 of March Movement*, composed mostly by university students, were well entrenched and had been fighting Batista's forces well before Castro's guerillas arrived. These two contingents never got along.

[153] In July of 1958 at the **Battle of La Plata**, for instance, Castro's guerillas defeated an entire batallion of the Cuban army, capturing 240 prisoners while loosing only 3 men. Two weeks later, at the **Battle of Las Mercedes**, 300 rebels were thoroughly surrounded by over 2,000 men of the Cuban army, yet they managed to escape without a single loss of life.

[154] The professional Cuban army at that time was reinforced by poorly trained unemployed youngsters earning US $33.33 a month. Because the headware they used they were called the *Casquitos*.

Cubans *clashing with Batista's police* in Havana during the early stages of the revolution; insurgents on the deep woods of *Sierra Maestra*; the zone in *Southwestern Oriente* province where the rebels fought against Batista's army.

Two photos of the **Cuban regular army** in the access areas to the mountains of **Sierra Maestra**; the assault to a train reinforcing Batista's army in Santa Clara province, almost at the end of the revolt.

The ***destrucion of bridges*** and means of communication in central Cuba that prevented Batista from reinforcing his army in 1958. Top photo, the bridge over the *Falcon river*, bottom, *assaulted trains.*

Bottom photo, the carnage resulting fron the attack to the ***Goicuría Carracks*** in Matanzaas province.

In spite of their differences and under great confusion, the city of Santa Clara was taken on December 31, 1958 by the combined forces of Ernesto Guevara and Camilo Cienfuegos (Castro's lieutenant commanders) and Rolando Cubela, Juan Abrantes and William Alexander Morgan (commanders of the *Directorio Revolucionario* and the *13 of March Movement*). News of the fall of Santa Clara brought panic to Batista and the Cuban army. Batista fled Cuba for the Dominican Republic before sunrise on January 1, 1959. Castro began to negotiate the occupation of Santiago de Cuba at the foot of the Sierra Maestra mountains.[155] Knowing of Batista's escape on January 1, the city military commander surrendered without firing a shot and Castro took the city. Within a week Havana was in the hands of Guevara, Castro made a victory march across a quiet and perplexed Cuba that culminated on January 8 in the capital and the *Directorio Revolucionario* had reconciled itself to a compliant position under Castro's undisputed authority.

Cheering crowds all across Cuba celebrated Batista's downfall, but not necessarily the triumphant victory of Castro's revolutionary forces. No one in Cuba thought that a revolution was required or had supported a «*forcible overthrow of a government or social order in favor of a new system.*» In the words of Julio Lobo:

«*We didn't care who overthrew Batista provided someone did.*»

It was unimaginable that a band of hunted men that never exceeded 1,000 strong had defeated a well equipped and trained national army. In the midst of euphoria Cubans every now and then had to ask themselves... Is this real?

Cuban intellectuals saw in the fall of Batista and the victory of the insurrection a compensation for the defeats of Céspedes and Martí in their quests for a Cuban republic «*con todos y para el bien de todos.*»

The rest of the masses of Cubans saw a respite from years of violence, repression and abuses and thought of Castro as a man with courage that had risked everything to rescue the republic from its oppressive *Batistianos*.

---

[155] ***Castro did not participate*** on the westward move of his insurgent force across the unprotected fields in Camagüey province towards central Cuba or in the *Battle for Santa Clara*. He presumably kept in touch from his refuge in *Sierra Maestra* through radio communications.

The press across Cuba and in the US on the first days of 1959, after **Batista's escape to the Dominican Republic** on the last day of 1958.

Most of Hispanic Americans, weary of the economic and political superiority and self assurance of the US, saw in the victory of Castro's rebels a well deserved flogging and whipping of the ever arrogant Americans.

As commented by British historian Hugh Thomas, «*Castro became for Eisenhower's America what Lawrence of Arabia had been for England.*» Very skillfully Castro ignored the cooperation of the *Directorio Revolucionario*, the presence of the *13 of March Movement* in the mountains of central Cuba, the funding received from ex-president Carlos Prío, the military and moral support of *Auténticos* and *Ortodoxos*, the backing from the signers of the *Pacto de Caracas* and the lobbying in Washington by trusted democratic figures like Miró Cardona and Felipe Pazos. Castro's position was:

«*Let everybody believe that I alone had won the war.*»

Within a few days after his arrival in Havana thousands of Cubans believed he could do no wrong. He was the new Bolivar of the Americas; first in Cuba, later in the rest of the continent. Castro became the political *Clavelito*[156] that Cubans so much longed for.

Castro's victory, however, was not as heroic as Cubans believed. Batista suffered divisions and politicking in his army. Discipline had been lost because of favoritism by Batista's old army guard from the 1930s: Tabernilla and Pedraza, as well as Carratalá and Ventura in the police ranks. By 1958 it was almost impossible to recruit young decent men for any of the services. The armed forces lacked good equipment.[157] At the front, Batista's army lost probably not more than 300 men, yet there were always some secret support and defections to Castro's insurgents. Morale, of course, declined after the US imposed an embargo to the Cuban official army. A further decline resulted when Batista appointed Francisco Tabernilla as Chief of Staff and Supreme Commander and resorted to promotions *en masse* of hundreds of officers.

---

[156] *Clavelito*, Miguel Alfonso Pozo (1908-1975) was a popular radio personality in Cuban radio and TV, that asked his listeners to set up a glass of common water on top of the set, ask for a gift of any kind and it would be granted by virtue of his magical powers.

[157] *Soldiers in the Cuban army* were equipped with vintage 1903 *Schneider* rifles from World War II; in the city's defenses, the regular batteries consisted of *Ordoñez* cannons from Spanish times.

Hundreds of Cubans with expressions of *support to the revolutionary forces* as they marched from remote places across the island to Havana in January of 1959

To make things easier for Castro to take over as the ruler of Cuba, the point was reached in mid-1958 when Batista began to pay more attention to his personal affairs than to the war. So did Tabernilla.[158] What finally gave Castro the uncontested glory of overthrowing Batista was the evident squalor and degradation of all other opposition elements. The *Auténticos* were discredited after having decided to play Batista's game and agreed to participate in elections that were the means Batista had found to exit graciously from Cuban political life. Prío had become an irrelevant operative, more so since he had already lost one battle to Batista on March 10, 1952 and he was comfortably waiting in Miami for someone else to rescue the republic that he had lost. The *Ortodoxos* had squabbled bitterly and had split into four different tendencies, one of which was Castro's; the others were all words and no action, except Raúl Chibás, who was wearing Castro's uniform and showing up in photos in the Sierra Maestra. Grau San Martín, of course, did not want at his age to change his comfortable home in Miramar for a foul-smelling tent in the mountains.

So it was that Castro and his frayed and tattered army entered Havana and took over the destiny of Cuba. He soon found out that he had two choices:

- *To join the bourgeoisie that had fallen in love with his rhetoric and install a safe path to democracy in Cuba, as he had promised over Radio Rebelde from the Sierra Maestra, in which case he had a limited time access to power and no assurance that he could institutionalize a social revolution, or*
- *To entertain people with siren voices during the time necessary to openly advocate and install a dictatorship of the proletariat.*[159]

The Castros were very reserved about the future in those first days of 1959; not so Ernesto Guevara who by the end of January, during a presentation at the *Sociedad Nuestro Tiempo*, stated:

«*As rebels in Sierra Maestra we became converted to the need of an agrarian reform and the parallel need of an urban reform; but the most pressing issue was to cleanse the minds of Cubans of their US inspired prejudice against socialism, and that could only be accomplished by total control of education, the press and the means of production.*»

---

[158] Julio Lobo, for instance, was asked for ***triple originals*** of his invoices for supplies to the army (sugar, meat and poultry), knowing that Tabernilla would change the invoice numbers and pay himself for triple the invoiced amount.

[159] According to Ernesto Guevara, both he and the Castro brothers new since their days in the Sierra Maestra that there would be a very violent progress of the revolution towards a ***Marxist-Leninist system***.

Castro negotiating the ***surrender of Santiago de Cuba*** with the chief of the Army in that city, Colonel José Rego Rubido; ***Camilo Cienfuegos*** with his parents after the end of the armed conflict; the ***cavalcade of Don Tomas Estrada Palma*** from Bayamo to Havana in 1902, an event that Castro waáted to emulate as he took 8 days in car to reach the capital of Cuba in January of 1959 .

As the Castro rebels approached Havana in their long victory march, [160] a fourth revolutionary figure emerged to compete for press time against Fidel Castro, Raúl Castro and Ernesto Guevara. He was a jovial and warm young man, the most *barbudo* of the *barbudos*, with a permanent smile in his face: Camilo Cienfuegos, the son of Spanish anarchists that had taken refuge in Cuba after the Civil War in Spain. To many Cubans who hardly knew him except for the chronicles of the *Sierra Maestra*, he was a warm hearted anti-Communist, a cool child-friendly hero that you would welcome at your home, particularly trustworthy because he did not seem to be as close to Fidel Castro as Guevara and Castro's brother were. Castro evidently had other opinions of him:

> «*Camilo is a revolutionary soul, made of 100% pure Communist timber, as can be seen in the books he reads, his infrequent writings and his friendly spirit of trying to unite and accommodate everybody.*»[161]

Practically all Cubans, during the Santiago-Havana march by Castro in 1959, forgot that he had been a member of *Unión Insurreccional Revolucionaria (UIR)* in the 1940s, an organization founded by Emilio Tró Rivero (1917-1947),[162] who had characterized the *UIR* as «*una organización que creía febrilmente en la violencia como método.*» The *UIR* competed for control of the University of Havana with the *Federación Estudiantil Universitaria (FEU)*, whose president Manolo Castro (no kin) was assassinated on February 22, 1948.[163]

---

[160] In his ***victory march across Cuba*** Castro was evoking the triumphal march of DonTomás Estrada Palma, Cuba's first president, from his home town of Bayamo, in Oriente, to the capital in 1902, as well as the famous whistle-stop train journey of Abraham Lincoln from Springfield to Washington for his inaugural festivities in February of 1861.

[161] ***Camilo Cienfuegos*** (1932-1959), of course, became a nuisance to the Castros as he competed for popularity among Cubans. He would dissappear on a Camagüey-Havana flight scheduled by the Castros during Camilo's mission to place Huber Matos under arrest; Matos was a very popular revolutionary that had sound the alarm that the Cuban revolution was tending Communist in October of 1959.

[162] ***Emilio Tró Rivero*** was a notorious revolutionary gangster during the 1940s in Cuba, famous for been unmerciful with his enemies and for having always his finger on the trigger. Castro knew and admired him during the years he registered but never attended classes at the *University of Havana*. Tró was killed during a gang fight known as the *Sucesos de Orfila* (September 21, 1947)

[163] ***Fidel Castro in 1948*** was acussed for the murder of *Manolo Castro* as his victim exited the *Cinecito* movie theater in Havana, as well as the murder of police *Sergeant Fernandez Caral* who was investigating the events at the *Cinecito*. He already had a police record accused of having killing *Leonel Gómez*, his opponent in a contested student election at the University.

Several views of the *route taken by Castro* to reach Havana from his center of operation in Eastern Cuba in January of 1959.

The reception given to Castro in Havana on January 8, 1959, had no precedents in the history of Cuba. People with flags on the roofs of buildings waved ecstatically; many came out onto the streets to celebrate mostly the fall of President Fulgencio Batista but also the advent of a regime of freedom, honesty and prosperity. People in cars formed long caravans welcoming men with long beards, dirty uniforms and menacing weapons, all with stunned faces contemplating the adoring masses. All across town, undisciplined and unruly gangs were breaking and burning the belongings of Batista's supporters, attacking and destroying buildings, parking meters and casinos run by Batista's hoodlums. Hundreds of youngsters, grown men and women had the number 26 painted on their foreheads, hats and clothes. Convoys of captured tanks and trucks had to weave their path through the stampeded crowds in the streets. Here and there a few discontent members of mobs and gangs fired into the crowd from behind pillars, but medics and civilians were ready to help the few wounded; it did not affect the celebrations.

All of a sudden, from an open jeep, Castro waved to the people. Several dozen photographers and cameramen recorded the events, as Castro side by side with his bearded and presumably anti-communist rebel commander Camilo Cienfuegos headed for *Columbia Military Camp*. Soon he was at the podium ready to address a large crowd.

All along his seven day trip from Santiago to Havana Castro had presented a preview of what he was to say at the Columbia Camp on January 8. In Santiago, on January 1, he had said:

«*The eyes of America are on Cuba. We deserve to be one of the best countries in the world because of our valor, intelligence and firmness. The revolution will not be an easy task. It will not come in one day but it will be achieved and we will be free for the first time in 400 years.*»

In Camagüey, on January 5, he had said:

«*We have fought so there will never again be censorship in Cuba. We know the kind of revolution we desire and that revolution will advance as rapidly as the objective conditions of its development would permit.*»

In Matanzas, on January 6, he had said:

«*We are going to attack illiteracy, graft, vice, gambling and disease.*»

Every one of these speeches ended with the slogan «*¡Patria o Muerte, Venceremos!*»[164]

---

[164] It was an expression borrowed from **Giuseppe Garibaldi** (1807-1882), the central figure in the XIX century movement of Italian unification. Until then, the *Mambi's* motto had always been «*¡Independencia o Muerte!*» and in the years of the Cuban Republic (1902-1958) it was «*¡Patria y Libertad!*»

Time magazine, first praising **Batista** in its April 21, 1952 issue, also praised **Castro** with its front cover on January 26, 1959; photos at center and bottom, riots and chaos in the streets of Havana once it became know that Batista had fled. People ***burning casinos and breaking parking meters*** simply because they had been approved and installed during the government of Batista.

These statements, of course, complimented to what he had said to Karl Meyer, a member of the editorial board of the *New York Times* during his days in the *Sierra Maestra* in September of 1957: [165]

> «I am not interested in belonging to a revolutionary government. Personally, power does not interest me. Let no one think that I have pretensions to go above and beyond a future President of the Republic. Fortunately I am immune to ambitions and vanities.»

Such words evidently contradicted those Herbert Mathews heard from Castro but did not report in his article of February of 1957: [166]

> «I swore to myself that the Americans were going to play dearly for what they were doing. [NR: selling war materiel to Batista] When this war is over, a much wider and bigger war will begin for me: the war that I am going to launch against them. I am saying to myself that this is my true destiny.»

Finally, the time came to climb up a well prepared podium and address the Cuban people; thousands were glued to their TV sets to listen and see for the first time the man that had taken over the destinies of Cuba. His words had the appearance of being prophetic and the overwhelming majority of his listeners were profoundly impressed and deeply optimistic.[167] As he delivered his speech, two white doves landed on his shoulders as he several times asked his companion and not his listeners, «¿*Voy bien Camilo?*»

---

[165] **Karl E. Meyer** (1937-) was at the time an award-winning journalist with the *Washington Post*. After retirement in 1998 he became a visiting professor at Yale and Princeton Universities.

[166] **Herbert Mathews** (1900-1977), was a run-of-the-mill *NYTimes* editorial writer whose strong friendship with the Times publisher Arthur Hays Sulzberger allowed him to expand and extend his career beyond his personal abilities. He was the first to report that Castro was not a Communist but a romantic revolutionary and in many ways contributed to the success of Castro. In fact, during the 1960s, the New York Times advertisement in the subways of the city consisted of a photo of Castro with the heading *«I got my job through the New York Times.»* By 1958, Times editors were already growing uncomfortable with Matthews's pro-Castro bias, and by 1959, when Castro himself credited the articles with helping to bring him to power, the remarkable access afforded Matthews began to quickly vanish.

[167] More than any other title, Castro's speech on that night became known as the *¿Armas para qué? Dissertation*. Time proved that other than trying to rationalize the need of disarming the people... «*because with the Revolution, the former dictatorship had gone away and there was no need to have weapons since the Revolution would take care of the safety and security of the population,*» the rest of the 8 hour presentation was full of misrepresentations. He lied to his teeth to the low level information crowd that was adoringly listening.

On the photo on top, Castro *interrogating one of his men* at his camp in Sierra Maestra. There was no pity for anyone suspected of having second thoughts about the revolution.

On the center, Castro *addressing Cubans in his first televised speech* Columbia Military Camp in Havana.

On the bottom, Castro finally *meeting again with Ernesto Gerava and Raúl Castro* after the consolidation of their forces in Havana.

A short summary of this speech follows.

> «Mi gran preocupación es que en el extranjero, donde esta Revolución es la admiración del mundo entero, no tenga que decirse dentro de tres semanas, o cuatro semanas, o un mes, que aquí se volvió a derramar sangre cubana para consolidar esta Revolución, porque entonces no sería esta Revolución un ejemplo.»
> [My big concern is that abroad, where this revolution is the admiration of the world, people would not have to say in three weeks, or four weeks, or a month, that they had to shed Cuban blood to consolidate the revolution, because then this revolution would not be the example that it is.]

> «Yo les digo que hay elementos de determinada organización revolucionaria que están escondiendo armas, que están almacenando armas y que están contrabandeando armas; nosotros no hemos cargado camiones con armas para esconderlas en ninguna parte, porque esas armas deben estar en los cuarteles. El que no pertenezca a las fuerzas regulares de la República, donde tiene derecho a pertenecer todo combatiente revolucionario, que devuelva las armas a los cuarteles, porque aquí las armas sobran cuando ya no hay tiranía y está demostrado que las armas solo valen cuando se tiene la razón, y se tiene al pueblo; de lo contrario, no sirven más que para asesinar y para cometer fechorías. ¿Armas, para qué?, ¿Para qué?»
> [I tell you that there are certain elements of revolutionary organizations that are hiding weapons; they are stockpiling weapons and they are smuggling weapons; we have not loaded trucks with weapons to hide them anywhere, because these weapons should be in the barracks. Those who do not belong to the regular forces of the Republic, to which any revolutionary fighter has the right to belong, should return weapons to the barracks, because these weapons are not needed when there is no tyranny and it is proven that guns only are necessary when you have reason on your side, and have the trust of the people; otherwise they serve only to murder and to commit crimes. Guns, what for?, What for?]

> «Cuando todos los derechos del ciudadano hayan sido restablecidos, se va a convocar a unas elecciones en el más breve plazo de tiempo posible.»
> [When all the rights of citizens have been restored, we will call an election in the shortest time possible.]

> «Ahora no hay censura, y la prensa es enteramente libre, más libre de lo que ha sido nunca, y tiene además la seguridad de que lo seguirá siendo para siempre, sin que vuelva a haber censura»
> [Now there is no censorship, and the press is entirely free, freer than it has ever been, and you have the assurance that we will remain forever without being censored again.]

> «Hoy todo el pueblo puede reunirse libremente; hoy no hay torturas, ni presos políticos, ni asesinatos, ni terror. Hoy no hay más que alegría; todos los líderes traidores han sido destituidos en los sindicatos, y se va a convocar inmediatamente a elecciones en todos los sindicatos.»
> [Today all the people can meet freely; today there is no torture or political prisoners, nor murders, nor terror. Today there is only joy; all traitors have been dismissed in the unions, and we will immediately convene elections in all unions.]

A multitude of students received Castro at the **University of Havana**; the *Diario de la Marina*, the most conservative Cuban newspaper, *praised him* and wished him a good role in Cuba's future; Castro established his headquarters at the most luxurious hotel in Havana, the recently inaugurated **Havana Hilton**, property of the Cuban aastronomic Union.

«*Jamás incurriremos en la grosería de ostentar por la fuerza una posición, porque repugnamos eso; es por algo que hemos sido los abanderados de esta lucha contra una asquerosa y repugnante tiranía.*»

[Never will we forcibly hold a position of power, because we detest that; it is something for which we have been the leaders in the fight against a filthy and disgusting tyranny.]

«*El día que el pueblo nos ponga mala cara, nada más nos ponga mala cara, nos vamos; si no fuera así, después de todas las muestras de cariño que yo he recibido del pueblo y de toda esa manifestación apoteósica de hoy, lo mejor sería irse, retirarse, o morirse; porque después de tanto cariño y de tanta fe, ¡miedo da el no poder cumplir como uno tiene que cumplir con este pueblo!*»

[The day that the people give us a dire face, we will go; after all the affection that I have received from the people and all that outstanding demonstration today, it would be best to leave, retire, or die; because after so much love and so much faith, we would be devastated failing to fulfill what one must abide by with these people!]

«*A nosotros no nos interesa controlar ningún poder por la fuerza; a un prisionero jamás se le debe asesinar, a un herido jamás se le debe abandonar, un preso jamás se debe golpear. En nuestros institutos armados jamás ni uno solo de sus hombres volverá a golpear a un prisionero, ni a torturarlo, ni a matarlo. Igual les digo que el que haya asesinado, no lo salva nadie del pelotón de fusilamiento.*»

[We are not interested to control any power by force; a prisoner must never be killed in jail, a wounded person should never be abandoned, a prisoner must never be hit. In our armed forces never will one of the men strike a prisoner, not to torture or kill him. I also want to tell you that if you have killed someone, no one will save you from the firing squad.]

«*Hoy yo quiero advertir al pueblo, quiero advertir a las madres cubanas, que yo haré siempre cuanto esté a nuestro alcance por resolver todos los problemas sin derramar sangre. Agotaré siempre todos los medios persuasivos, y todos los medios razonables, y todos los medios humanos para evitar que se derrame una sola gota de sangre más en Cuba.*»

[Today I want to tell the people, I want to tell Cuban mothers, that I will always do everything in my power to solve all problems without spilling a drop of blood. I will always use all persuasive means, and all reasonable means, and all human means to prevent a single drop of blood spilling over in Cuba.]

«*En casi todas las revoluciones, después de la lucha, viene otra, y después viene otra y observen la historia de todas las revoluciones, en México y en todas partes. Sin embargo, parece que esta va a ser una excepción, como ha sido una excepción en todo lo demás; ha sido extraordinaria en todo lo demás, y quisiéramos que también fuera extraordinaria en el hecho de que no se disparara más un tiro aquí; y creo que se logrará, creo que la Revolución triunfará sin que se dispare más un tiro.*»

[In almost all revolutions, after the initial fight, comes another, and then comes another, as you can see in the history of all revolutions, in Mexico and elsewhere. However, it seems that ours will be an exception, as has been an exception in everything else; it has been extraordinary in everything else, and we would also be ex traordinary in the fact that no more shots will be fired here; I think this will be achieved. I believe that the revolution will triumph over without firing a shot]»

The initial days of the revolutionary government in January of 1959:

President **Manuel Urrutia** with Ernesto Guevara and Camilo Cienfuegos;
José Miró Cardona, prestigious lawyer and professor, descendant of veterans of the Independence Wars, selected *Prime Minister*;
Roberto Agramonte, notable sociologist, designated *Minister of Foreign Relations*.
On the right, **Faure Chomón**, a student leader distrusted and despised by Castro, *sent abroad* for diplomatic missions.

> «Yo no soy militar profesional, ni de carrera, ni mucho menos; yo estaré aquí el tiempo mínimo, y cuando termine aquí voy a hacer otras cosas; sinceramente, yo no voy a hacer falta aquí mucho más tiempo.»
>
>> [I am not a military professional, or much less a career soldier; I'll be here the minimum time, and when I finish here I will do other things; honestly, I will not be staying here much longer.]

Within 36 hours after this allocution, the *Directorio Estudiantil*, who had taken the weapons, sheepishly returned them. They were undoubtedly persuaded by Castro's well staged speech at the Columbia Barracks. Faure Chomón,[168] one of the leaders of the weapons-snatching operation, was submitted to the humiliation of Castro's words as a group of mothers appealed to him to stop the bloodletting that the revolution had created.

> «My purpose is that neither this group or any other group should prolong the state of war. You will see how this is resolved. Your visit shows that public opinion is an irresistible force in a democracy.»

Up to that point Castro's base of power lay in his blindly loyal rebel army, most of whom were illiterate peasants.[169] He realized that he would need the help of educated people to actually run the country. He chose José Miró Cardona, one of his former professors, to be Prime Minister; another college professor, Roberto Agramonte, chairman of the *Ortodoxos*, became Foreign Minister; and Manuel Urrutia, the judge that had helped his troops during the *Sierra Maestra* days, became president. Castro himself was content to be supreme commander of the armed forces, while keeping his closest allies in the background.

Behind the scenes, Castro began to lay the foundation of a parallel system of power, in which he held complete control. Under the name *Bureau for Revolutionary Planning and Coordination*, Castro brought together many of his old friends from the July 26 Movement, including Raúl Castro, Ernesto Guevara and Camilo Cienfuegos. They met regularly at Castro's headquarters, in the top three floors of the *Havana Libre Hotel* (formerly the Havana Hilton,

---

[168] **Faure Chomón Mediavilla**, a former main organizer of the attempted magnizide in the presidential palace in 1957 during Batista's presidency, was the leader of the expedition that established a *Segundo Frente* at the Escambray mountains in central Cuba in late 1950s. Castro cast him aside by sending him abroad for several years as ambassador to the Soviet Unión, Vietnam, Bulgaria and Ecuador. He became a non-person in Cuba after returning from these posts.

[169] At the request of the revolutionary government, hundreds of these **campesino-soldiers** were accomodated in private homes by people in Havana that had great sympathy for the *revolucionarios*. Most of them had never sat at dinner tables or had ever properly used a bathroom.

Three men that had impacted the thinking of Castro during his younger years:

Herminio Portell Vilá (1901-1992), a notable historian who had been his teacher at the Universioty of Havana; **Augusto Cesar Sandino** (1895-1934), a Nicaraguan revolutionary, enigmatic leader of varios movements against anything having to do with the US; **Jorge Eliézer Gaitán** (1903-1948), a charismatic leader of a populist movement in Colombia.
On the bottom, a picture of Castro at the riots that became known as the **Bogotazo**, occuring in Bogotá, Colombia, after the assasssination of Gaitán on April 9, 1948.

managed by the Hilton chain but property of the Cuban Gastronomic syndicate).

The type of revolution that Castro had in mind had to be consistent with his heroic self-definition and the continuous tension that he needed to be happy and fulfill his destiny. He absolutely needed to identify an enemy, now that Batista was gone from his life. At first he continuously referred to the "*counter revolutionaries,*" but that did not completely satisfy his want for a much larger dragon to slay. He was familiar with the best-sellers from Herminio Portel Vilá, Ramiro Guerra and Fernando Ortiz, all of whom had chastised and reprimanded the US government for its ambitions to control the meager Cuban economy.[170] He openly declared his fantasies at one of the meetings of the *Bureau for Revolutionary Planning and Coordination*:

«Una revolucion que no fuese atacada, en primer lugar no sería positivamente una verdadera revolución. Además, una revolución que no tuviera delante un enemigo, correría el riesgo de adormecerse.»
[A revolution that is not attacked would not be positively a true revolution. Moreover, a revolution that is not facing an enemy, risks falling into slumbering.]

Castro saw in challenging the US the answer to his need to cultivate his heroic fortunes and keep the revolution *en vilo* (on pins and needles). Besides, all Cuban popular leaders in the past (Estrada Palma, José Miguel Gómez, Gerardo Machado, Fulgencio Batista, Ramón Grau San Martí, Carlos Prío), had sooner or later lost their luster and became causes of disconcert for the people. He needed to make sure that his leadership would outlast every person that had ever lived in Cuba; as a bonus, he had a not so secret ambition to bring his name at the top of world leaders, greater than Garibaldi, Stalin and Lenin and much greater that Juan Perón, Augusto César Sandino or Jorge Eliécer Gaitán. He decided to cast his chips with Marxism, knowing that US aid, technical assistance, investments, commerce, favorable treaties and favorable status with the US would have been good for Cuba but not so good for himself.[171] In other words, he decided to reveal himself as a *bona fide*, card-carrying Marxist-Leninist.

---

[170] In spite of this, the ***Americanos*** had always been more popular in Cuba than they were anywhere else in Hispanic America. The American government intentions, however, were always suspicious, particularly those of the very ritual, precise and exacting Eisenhower's government.

[171] ***Castro's ancestral hatred*** for the US, according to his friends, had been exacerbated when in the American TV series *The 64,000 Question*, a contestant had won the top price in 1956 by answering Walter Reed and not Carlos Findlay to the question *"Who found the cure for yellow fever?"*

Several initial leaders of the 1959 Cuban revolution:

Armando Hart Dávalos (1930-), Cuban Communist, grandchild of a US lawyer, first *Minister of Education* of the revolutionary government, member of the Politburo; **Faustino Pérez Hernández** (1920-1992), doctor in medicine, born in Zaza del Medio, Las Villas, son of Canario immigrants, landed in Cuba abord the *Granma Yatch* with Castro; **Augusto Martínez Sáenz** (1926-), intimate friend of Castro, *Minister of Defense* in the first days of the revolution; **Humberto Sorí Marín** (1915-1961), lawyer, member of the *Partido Auténtico*, served Castro as *Minister of Agriculture* for four months, resigned and began to conspire against the revolution. He was executed after the *Bay of Pigs* invasion.

The first government established in Cuba in 1959 was a dream that no other republic in Hispanic America had enjoyed. Most Cubans were in an extraordinary positive mood. The dictator had escaped, his fawning dependants had deserted, clean young men were in charge, a brave struggle had finished with and unbelievable and unprecedented success, the entire world had nothing but praise for the quixotic adventure the Cubans had lived, kindness and generosity were in everyone's mind; this was it, there were no limits to what could be accomplished.[172]

Among the members of the initial revolutionary government were Judge Manuel Urrutia Lleó (1901-1981), a decisive and brave man, became the provisional president; José Miró Cardona (1902-1972), a man that had resisted the Batista clan, professor of Law at the *Universidad de La Habana*, and president of the *Colegio de Abogados de La Habana* became Prime Minister; Roberto Agramonte (1904-1995), dean of the *Escuela de Filosofía y Letras* of the *Universidad de La Habana*, became Foreign Minister; Rufo López Fresquet (1911-1986), one of the best Cuban economists, became Minister of the Treasury; Raúl Cepero Bonilla (1920-1962), an early Batista opponent and historian, became Minister of Commerce; Felipe Pazos (1912-2001), brilliant economist, former Cuban delegate to the *Bretton Woods Conference* in 1946 and founder of the *Cuban National Bank* in 1950, returned to that post, among others.

These new ministers were acknowledged and confessed *bourgeois*; they had no qualms about sharing their functions with other less known and less qualified figures, such as: Faustino Pérez (1920-1992), one of the 82 insurgents that had landed with Castro in Oriente in 1956, appointed Minister of Confiscated Property; Armando Hart Dávalos (1930-   ), a communist combatant in the *Sierra Maestra*, appointed as Minister of Education; Humberto Sorí Marín (1915-1961), the *abogadito*, author of the laws authorizing summary courts-martial and executions in the Sierra Maestra, appointed Minister of Agriculture; Augusto Martínez Sánchez (1923-2013), a close friend of Castro and late comer to the fight against Batista, appointed Minister of Defense, and others.

Castro, having reserved for himself the position of Commander-in-Chief of the Army, was never comfortable with the *bourgeois*

---

[172] Citizens and companies were willing to pay their taxes in advance; volunteer organizations had hundreds of new applicants, teachers were willing to teach *pro bono* in their spare time, medical doctors would see poor patients without charge, workers were willing to extend their tasks with no additional pay, families were opening their homes to feed and accomodate the freedom fighters from the mountains. Every one was looking for how to do their part to improve things in Cuba.

Scenes from **summary executions** during the days of the insurgents fighting Batista's forces in *Sierra Maestra*. They were a prelude of thousands of executions carried out by the revolution after taking over the government of Cuba, many of them *instigated* by the Argentinian Ernesto (Ché) Guevara.

ministers but very friendly to the young ministers with a history of armed involvement in the revolution, particularly Armando Hart and Martínez Sáenz. The most important task initially was to purge the ministries of *botelleros* (sinecures). 800 were expelled from Treasury; 260 from Agriculture; 580 from the Health Department; 180 from Commerce; 320 from Education, even 121 from the University of Havana, and so on.

Together with the legitimate cleansing of public agencies came private vendettas, false accusations and political vengeance, as well as pressure from *Sierra* veterans to be accommodated in the empty public payroll slots. Nothing was more distressing, however, than what was occurring in the search and punishment of Batista accomplices. The task was organized and directed in Havana by Efigenio Almejeiras (1931-), a Granma passenger in December of 1956 that was appointed chief of the *Revolutionary National Police*. In other cities across Cuba, the search and punishment was in the hands of local military chiefs and newly appointed civil provincial prosecutors.

The forces of order became the enforcers of the policy of retribution. Days after days, starting January 3, there were arrests of officers of the old armed forces, many of whom had not made any attempts to conceal their identities. In a mock imitation of the WWII Nuremberg trials, the *barbudos* were pitiless looking for those who had committed abuses or crimes, even if they had been following the orders of their superiors, which were already on safe ground outside Cuba.

There was no precedent for these raids of the guilty in the history of Cuba, not even in the midst of the reaction of the masses to the fall of Machado in 1933.[173] Much more, there were no precedents for the summary public trials in many city squares, parks and athletic facilities across the island and the increasing number of speedy guilty verdicts which were followed by immediate executions. The only devastating precedent were the sentences and death penalties imposed by Raúl Castro and Ernesto Guevara to about one hundred discontents, disobedient and deserters in the days of Sierra Maestra.

---

[173] **Roberto Agramonte** as Foreign Minister, argued to ambassadors and journalists who began to visit Cuba that the trials were expedited to prevent relatives of those murdered by the Batista government to take the law into their own hands, an argument that was quite difficult to sustain by the noble ex-professor of philosophy from the University of Havana and author of 17 books on sociology; Agramonte presented his resignation in June of 1959 and sought asylum in the US, where he died in 1995. There were no private settlement of scores in Cuba in 1959 like it had ocurred after the fall of Machado in 1933.

The man who did most to **export the revolution** out of Cuba into the world was Enesto Guevara. The man on the photo on top left is ***Orlando Pantoja Tamayo*** (aka Olo and Antonio, 1933-1967), one of Guevara's loyal followers. They fought together in the failed experience in *Congo*, Africa and in *Bolivia*, where both were hunted and executed. On the photo below, ***Félix Rodríguez Mmendigutía*** (1941-), the man who captured Guevara in the jungles of Bolivia . The photo is dedicated to ***Miguel Uría***, brave combatant on the *Brigada 2506* that tried to overthrow the Castros in 1961.

Initially, during the first days in January of 1959, there were about 100 trials and executions conducted by tribunals composed of several members of Castro's army who had absolutely no expertise in the law. Some of these tribunals had a lawyer acting *pro bono* to help the prosecution (not the accused) to follow as much as possible the regulation and methodology of the law. Most of them were Castro followers that would later assume important positions in successive revolutionary governments.[174] By the end of January the trials were conducted with more discipline in large public arenas, many of them under the TV cameras. Turned into Roman circuses, conditions were not propitious to render fair sentences. Every day there were news on the papers of atrocities that had become the norm in Cuban jurisprudence. By the end of January the number of executions had reached over 200, many of them but not all, for mistreatment or torture of prisoners.[175]

It seemed for a while that the revolution was executing ex-Batista sympathizers *in loco* of the true delinquents and gangsters in the dictator's staff that had escaped.[176] For a while, the excessive number of executions led to a timid formal protest from the US Department of State complaining that «*Cuba needs to have a profe-*

---

[174] One of these "advisors," for instance, was **Captain Orlando Pantoja**, an aid to Guevara in the *Escambray* mountains in 1958, who was later killed on the side of Guevara in *La Higuera*, Bolivia, on October 9, 1967.

[175] On a *1960 TV interview*, when asked why so many of the accused were executed for acts which had not resulted in anybody's death, Castro answered that had they been imprisoned and fulfilled their sentences or escape, they would have certainly or most probably perpetrated some private acts of vengeance.

[176] **Rolando Masferrer** (1918-1975), a guerrilla leader, lawyer, Cuban congressman (1949 and 1954), newspaper publisher (*Tiempo* and *Libertad* in Santiago de Cuba), member of the old Communist party, gangster, enforcer and political activist, rival of Castro in the bloody 1940s feuds at the University of Havana, killer of priests (a Franciscan father in Manzanillo, 1956), thief of public funds (US $10 million in 1957), and staunch supporter of Batista, was happily living in Miami, where he arived aboard his yatch in 1959. He became a good friend of *Jimmy Hoffa* and *Santo Trafficante* and, rumor was, a bodyguard of *Howard Hughes*. In 1961Masferrer had an inconclusive meeting with John F. Kennedy to talk about a mission to kill Castro. In 1975 he was killed by a car bomb in Miami.

Colonel **Esteban Ventura Novo** (1913-2001), one of the top political assassins during Batista times, chief of the *Cuban Bureau of Investigations* (1954), apointed by Batista as Chief of the *Fifth Police Station* (Calle Belascoain in Havana, 1956) and the *Ninth Station* (C and Zapata streets, Vedado, 1957), responsible for over 12 known murders of Batista's political enemies, left Cuba on the same plane as the dictator towards the Dominican Republic on January 1, 1959. He created in Miami *Ventura Security Services*, a private organization to protect businessmen and condominium buildings. He died a wealthy man of a heart attack on May 21, 2001.

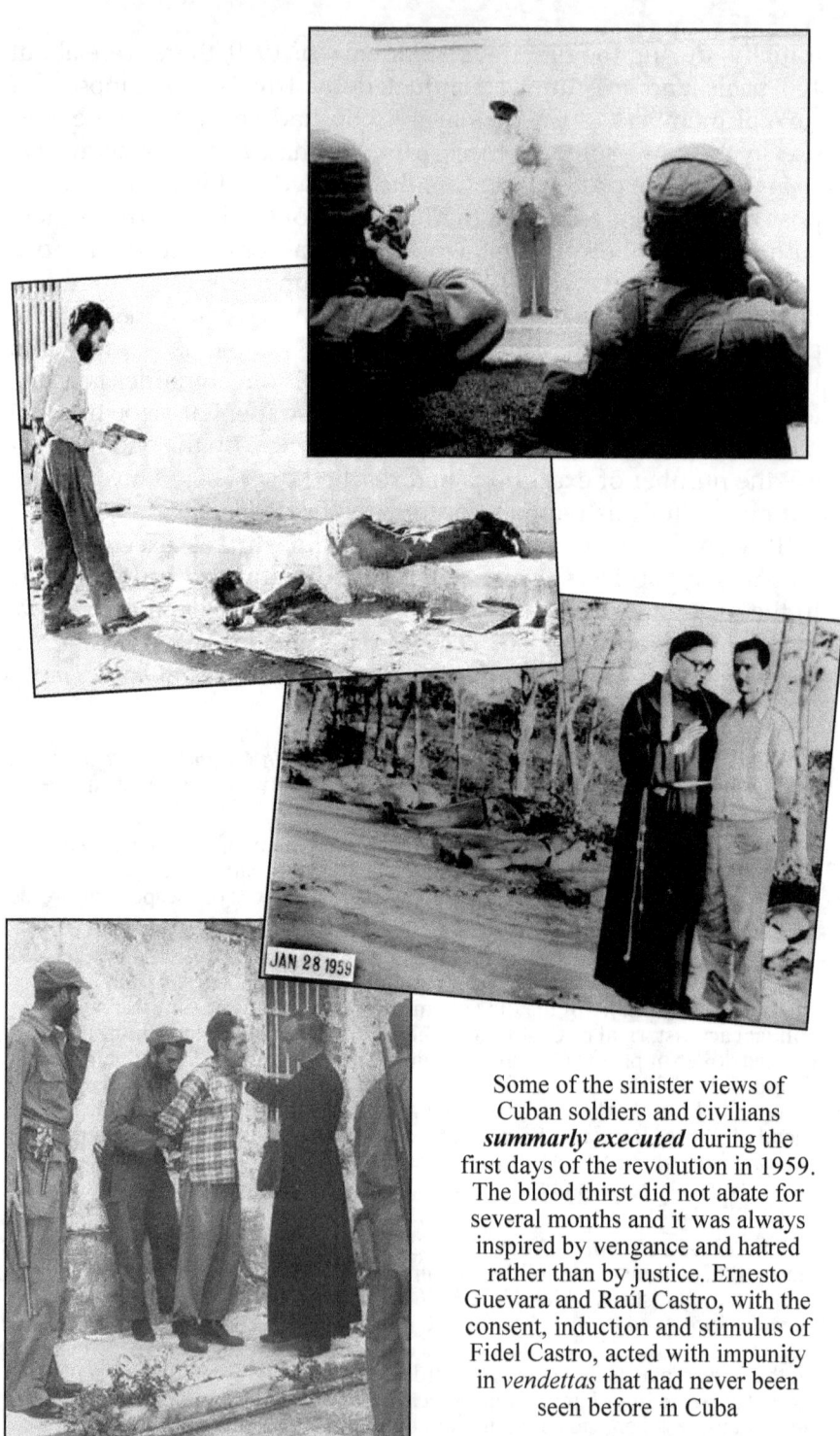

Some of the sinister views of Cuban soldiers and civilians **summarly executed** during the first days of the revolution in 1959. The blood thirst did not abate for several months and it was always inspired by vengance and hatred rather than by justice. Ernesto Guevara and Raúl Castro, with the consent, induction and stimulus of Fidel Castro, acted with impunity in *vendettas* that had never been seen before in Cuba

Throughout the initial days of the Cuban Revolution, the man that did the most to destroy capitalist Cuba was the Argentinian Ernesto (Ché) Guevara. Shamefully, over the years he became a quintessential capitalist brand. After his death in the jungles of Bolivia, deserted by his Cuban comrades and hunted by the Bolivian army and the American CIA, he became a heroic protest symbol for the trivially uninformed masses around the world. His likeness, still to this day, adorns mugs, baseball caps, couture bags, hoodies, tank tops, flags, student's books, club shirts, denim jeans, socks, and of course those ubiquitous T-shirts with Alberto Korda's photograph showing Ché in his beret as the embodiment of the revolutionary chic and the personification of romantic teenagers' infatuation and heartthrob.

The man so depicted was honored by Robert Redford in his film *The Motorcycle Diaries*, which missed an important Guevara quotation from the book on which the motion picture was based:

«*The Negro is indolent and lazy, and spends his money on frivolities, whereas the European is forward-looking, organized and intelligent... I plan to do for blacks exactly what blacks have done for the human race: nothing.*»

None of the ignorant worshipers of Ché have read the man's idea of justice as expressed in 1967 at his *Message to the Tricontinental* in Havana:

«*Hatred as an important element of our struggle; unbending hatred for the enemy, which pushes a human being beyond his natural limitations, making him into an effective, violent, selective, and cold-blooded killing machine.*»

Or the following phase on both a letter to his mother and another to his former wealthy girl friend Chichina Ferreira in October of 1967:

«*I felt my nostrils dilate savoring the acrid smell of gunpowder and blood of the enemy; revolution without firing a shot? You're crazy. It was all a lot of fun; the bombs were the main distraction to break the monotony I lived in.*»

Or his remarks of January 29, 1957 about his landing in Cuba:

«*Finally, there I was in the Cuban jungle, alive and bloodthirsty.*»

During his days in the Sierra Maestra and after the entrance to Havana, Guevara held summary trials where he murdered and executed scores of people; enemies, suspected enemies, and poor souls who were in the wrong place at the wrong time. His instructions to Ramiro Valdés, his personal slaughterer were «*When in doubt, kill them.*» On the way to Havana over 30 *casquitos* fitted that definition. After he took over the Cabaña prison, in a manner chillingly reminiscent of Stalin's Lavrenti Beria, Guevara became the one-man appellate board after the midnight revolutionary tribunals. Dozens of men were executed every week without Guevara ever looking over or overturning a sentence. Sometimes, for almost 30 weeks, there were 50 or 60 executions on a single day.

In Bolivia, after his capture, Guevara told Félix Rodríguez, the CIA man who captured him: «*I think that about 2,000 men saw justice from my hand at La Cabaña between January and June of 1959.*»

After a visit to Russia in August of 1962, Guevara bragged that:

«*Cuba was willing to risk everything in an atomic war of unimaginable destructiveness to defend its principles.*»

This is the real story of the man whose portrait is worn by dimwitted men like Carlos Santana and is tattooed in the abdomen of Mike Tyson.

The top leadership of the traditional Communist Party in Cuba:

Top to bottom, left to right: ***Salvador García Aguero*** (1907-1965), founder of the Partido Socialista Popular (PSP), Senator of the republic in the first Batista government in 1944 and ***Juan Marinello Vidaurreta*** (1898-1977), president of the PSP since its founding; ***Antonio Nuñez Jiménez*** (1923-), graduate from the Universities of Havana and Moscow; the trio ***Lazaro Peña***, ***Blas Roca*** and ***Juan Marinello***; ***Edith García Buchaca*** and her second husband ***Joaquín Ordoqui Mesa***, ***Anibal Escalante*** and ***Carlos Rafael Rodríguez***, first husband of Edith García Buchaca..

sional government that respects the laws and the basic tenants of justice.» Castro took the opportunity to dismiss any advice from the US pointing that *«your recommendations to Batista led to the defeat of his troops during our revolutionary insurrection.»*

All through those days of January 1959 a notable absence in the political life of Cuba were the Cuban Communists.[177] On an interview with Joseph North, editor of the US Communist newspaper *The Daily Worker*, Ernesto Guevara told him that he had not met any Cuban Communists in *Sierra Maestra*. The same observation was told by Camilo Cienfuegos to a reporter from the Mexican newspaper *Excelsior*. Guevara, however, had ordered his *edecán* Antonio Nuñez Jiménez (1923-1998), to enter the offices of the *Bureau of Anti-Communist Activities (BRAC)* and take over the files and documents that had been compiled since 1954 by its director, Colonel Mariano Faget, and the head of the CIA in Havana, Lyman Kirkpatrick. Once the lists of party membership suspects were in Guevara's hands, there was little possibility that any future appointments to the revolutionary government could be vetoed as going to a Communist sympathizer. From 1957 to the end of 1958 only very low level members of the Communist youth had joined Castro with instructions of *«standing by for the outside possibility the revolt succeeds; be gracious, helpful and ask for nothing but friendship.»* The party could now incorporate his bigger hitters to the revolution.

Notwithstanding the absence of home bred Communists, thanks to Guevara and Raúl Castro some prestigious international figures had a presence by phone, radio or other means of communication with Fidel Castro in the Sierra Maestra; well known activists like Pablo Neruda, Rafael Alberti, Gus Hall and Frank Marshall Davis, among others.

For a long time after January of 1959 Castro kept insisting he did not want anything to do with the old Cuban Communists:

«I am really not afraid of falling into the orbit of International Communism. Have I sought support from any of these old Communists?. The answer is a clear No. I am only seeking the backing of public opinion of the peoples of Hispanic America.»

---

[177] During the entire fight against Batista the Cuban Communists had played a smaller role than the **Juventudes de Acción Católica**, who lost three of its leaders in the April 9 strike against Batista, which was opposed by the Communists. Only in October of 1958 had the party sent Carlos Rafael Rodríguez to the *Sierra Maestra*. There, he had to compete for Castro's attention with *Ortodoxos* like Bisbé, Catholic priests like Father Llorente, Cuban economists like Felipe Pazos and many others strong anti-Communists that were supporting the rebel leader.

Scenes -somewhat similar to those during Roman times or the French revolution- from the summary public trials carried out at the *Palacio de los Deportes* during January 1959. On the top right, the acussed colonel **Jesús Sosa Blanco** (1908-1959), former military officer, during his trial of February 16, 1959 before 17,000 spectators.
On the bottom, two inocent student martirs executed by Castro to eliminate any risks of potential competition for the loyalty of students in Cuba. **Alberto Tapia Ruano** (1939-1961) and **Virgilio Campanería** Ángel (1938-1961), both very popular Catholic university students.

The time eventually came, however, when he thought he had to finish the executions of his *Batistiano* enemies and end the process of inducing fear in the heart of anyone planning to oppose his revolution. He decided to stage a monumental public trial in the largest sports arena in Havana. [178] The first prisoner chosen to be judged was Army Major Jesús Sosa Blanco (1907-1959); he had been arrested and accused of having committed 108 murders during his service in the Batista army. His *abogado de oficio* (court appointed defense lawyer) was Dr. Aristides de Acosta, a man of enormous academic distinction and many years of experience in criminal jurisprudence.

A report by the *International Commission of Jurists* in Geneva, in November of 1962, reached the following conclusions:

«*Dr. Acosta was coerced and threatened, not only by the prosecutor but also by the president of the court himself.*»

«*The accused was harassed and insulted; moreover the court appointed defense counsel was treated in the same way.*»

«*There was such a scandal at the Coliseum that all the newspapermen and lawyers were ordered out and the public hearings were suspended. The trial was continued in camera at the fortress of La Cabaña. The result was a death sentence for Sosa Blanco and imprisonment for Dr. Acosta.*»

«*During his services as Mayor Jesús Sosa Blanco court appointed defense lawyer, Dr. Acosta was in prison three times. In 2 cases, the first two, he was taken away from the court room itself and taken to the G-2 building in Havana on Fifth Avenue and Fourteenth Street. The third time he was taken to his offices at a building in the corner of Empedrado and Montserrate streets. When they arrived with Dr. Acosta they broke into the chambers where his brother and other lawyers were working and arrested the entire staff at his offices and at his chambers and locked them up in his own cell at the G-2 building.*»

Under those challenging conditions justice had no possibility to surface and much less to prevail; Major Jesús Sosa Blanco was sentenced to die and executed within hours. No one will ever know if he deserved to be condemned to die or if he was worthy to receive a lesser sentence.

Another case investigated by the *International Commission of Jurists* in Geneva was the trial of Dr. Armando Escoto.

---

[178] The **Palacio de los Deportes**, also known as the *Coliseo de la Ciudad Deportiva*, had been built by Batista in 1957 with a seating capacity of 15,000 places, site at the intersection of the *Avenida de Rancho Boyeros* and *la Via Blanca*. The base of the building was a 103 ft circular concrete slab with over 20,000 square meters of surface. At the center, it was over seven meters high. It had been designed by Civil Engineer Luis Arroyo and his wife Ángela.

Scenes of the ***interminable summary executions*** of military men and civilians during the early months of 1959. In spite of numerous international requests for the executions to be halted, the government continued for months and even invited foreign personalities from the left to witness what they called "*revolutionary justice*." The executions were stopped when the Russian government declared that "*enough is enough*."

Dr. Armando Escoto was one of the most vigorous public defenders of Cuban citizens who were sentenced for anti-communism activities. In March of 1959 Dr. Escoto challenged Fidel Castro's decisions on two successive occasions and stood up to him with the outmost public spirit. He believed firmly that the rights of the accused he was defending were violated in what constituted a break with normal democratic principles that had always been observed in Cuba. Castro, present at the trials, became furious.

In the middle of one of Dr. Escoto allegations during a trial, Castro advanced towards him and tried to strike him; when Dr. Armando Escoto defended himself he was attacked, restrained and wounded by Castro's guards.

After his encounter with Castro, Dr. Escoto was arrested and sent to a jail in Pinar del Rio. A friend of Escoto, who was also a lawyer named Dr. Portillo, acted as his public defense counsel, assisted by a second lawyer; Dr. Escoto was charged as if he were a criminal. The defense of Dr. Escoto by his two lawyer friends, acting as his public defenders, was ignored. The prosecutor and the members of the court bullied them and jeered that they were *derrotistas* (defeatists) and counterrevolutionaries just like the accused. Dr. Escoto was sentenced to death. Both of his two lawyer friends, residents of Havana, were also tried and shot in Pinar del Rio, where they had no friends and had never practiced.

On the report by the *International Commission of Jurists*, several hundreds of other similar cases were summarized. At the end, the Commission stated five main trends that the revolutionary Cuban justice had introduced in detriment of the accepted norms of criminal law in democratic countries:

«*(1) Retroactivity of criminal legislation has been applied to the detriment of the accused.*

(2) The death sentence could be imposed for simple political offenses.

(3) Total confiscation of property has been ordered against political offenders by a court sentence and in many cases by extra-judicial administrative proceedings.

(4) Those indicted for political offenses are deprived of the right of habeas corpus.

(5) Those indicted for political offenses are denied any appeal before any higher Court of the land in violation of guarantees contained in Cuba's historical constitutional legislation.»

After reading this report, Castro went on TV on December 16, 1960 to say that the Judiciary was parasitical, that it would be better for magistrates and judges to resign because if they did not they would find themselves out of a job anyway; that their salaries were three times as high as those of Army Majors who had fought

Every now and then, Ernesto (Ché) Guevara would show up at places where the revolution was executing its opponents and try his own hand at shooting several condemned prisoners, in a fashion reminiscent of a sports event.

for two years in the *Sierra Maestra*, and that civilian magistrates were *botelleros* (sinecures) drawing their pay without doing any work. Following this speech, eight members of the Supreme Court drafted a joint letter of resignation, which they submitted to a plenary session of the Court.

Two weeks later, a cell normally used by those awaiting trial, in the building housing the Supreme Court in Havana, was guarded by *milicianas* (militia women) armed with sub-machine guns. Inside were about 40 women employed until that day in the Court offices. In another adjoining cell were about 50 incarcerated men, including Dr. Justiniani Duval, Secretary for Administrative Disputes and Special Legislation and Dr. Rafael Galeano, a high level official of the Supreme Court.

Lawyers in the building were informed of the following:

- *Each court, by decision of the highest army command, would be reduced to only 3 magistrates, with at least 1 or 2 of them members of the militia.*
- *Police organizations can ignore their obligation to bring arrested persons before a court within 24 hours of their arrest, nor do they need to allow arrested persons to communicate with their lawyers. People under arrest can be kept incommunicado for up to 2 months without being permitted to see a lawyer or being brought before a court.*
- *Milicianos (Militiamen) are from now on authorized to assume the role of President of the court, with their militiaman's uniform underneath their gowns and carrying weapons. Prosecutors will also be militiamen, dressed in exactly the same way and also armed, with their gowns over the militia's uniform.*
- *Defense lawyers shall only be informed of the charges against the accused a few minutes before hearing was due to begin (with the result that, in most cases, they were unable to prepare their defense and debate the charges against his clients). Due notice of the dates on which cases were to be tried need not be given to either the accused nor his defense counsel.*
- *Changes can be made in the charges; when the original indictment could not be proved, a new version can be written and put forward.*
- *Lawyers who energetically defended their clients can be subject of imprisonment and could even be shot as counter-revolutionary criminals.*
- *Interviews with prisoners, when possible at all, always should take place in the presence of guards, who need to be members of the army or the militia.*

The atrocities committed in Cuba by the revolution had begun at the *Sierra Maestra*, where firing squads were used to enforce discipline, punish disloyalty or treason and to intimidate those who wanted to go home after having naively joined the insurrection. Once the revolution took over the reins of the nation, it began a reign of terror only comparable with the revolutions in France in 1792, Mexico in 1910 or Russia during Stalin's and Beria's purges.

Serious historical scholars have documented 3,615 firing squad executions in Cuba from January 1, 1959 to the end of 1960. None of the accused enjoyed the due process guarantees found in every Western-style democracy. Most of Castro's firing squad victims

A step by step depiction of the *trial and summary execution* of a young Cuban soldier named *Evelio Otero* in 1959.

were afforded only a perfunctory show trial, the outcome of which was predetermined; most didn't even get that. Ernesto Guevara was Castro's chief enforcer and had a personal hand in at least 100 firing squad executions, often delivering the *coup de grace* personally. [179] In response to questions about Castro's firing squads, Guevara once reiterated:

> «*To send men to the firing squad, judicial proof is unnecessary. These procedures are an archaic bourgeois detail. This is a revolution, and a revolutionary must become a cold killing machine motivated by pure hate. We must create the pedagogy of the paredón.*»

Having given free rein to Guevara and his brother Raúl Castro in the business of quickly executing any potential opponents to the stability and security of the revolution, Fidel Castro turned his attention to the business of controlling every aspect of life in Cuba: the economy, education, the military, foreign relations, what to do with traditional Communists and with members of his 26 of July Movement that did not agree with the increasing evidence of sovietization of the island.[180] He had to first resolve, however, what became known as *el asunto de los pilotos*, the issue of the pilots.

During a prominent revolutionary trial on February of 1959, more than 40 of the aviators, pilots, gunners and mechanics of the former Cuban Air Force, were charged with the crime of genocide in Santiago de Cuba, province of Oriente. They were accused of

---

[179] Invited in 1980 by the Sandinistas to observe the quickness of revolutionary justice and the deployment of the anarchist tactics of Ernesto Ché Guevara, was one young US bona fide Marxist revolutionary and professionally trained anarchist sympathizer from New York; his name was **Bill de Blasio**, elected as the 109th Mayor of New York city in 2014.

[180] Even in the days at the Sierra Maestra Castro began to clash with insurgents that were in disaccord with the harsh tactics of the revolutionary movement. One clear example was the collision with **Frank País**, who having survived the failed uprising during the *Granma* landing in December of 1956, became the leader of the guerrilla movement in the cities, a much more difficult and dangerous operation. A well-built, good-looking, and charismatic leader, he was one of the few people who dared to confront Castro's leadership, and he often clashed with Fidel. Frank País came from an upper-class background and was passionately anti-Communist and a devout Catholic. He wanted to stop Castro's strict authoritarian style with a more decentralized structure. He was being followed closely by Batista's army and for several months pleaded for support from Castro, who was relatively safe in the impenetrable mountains surrounding Santiago de Cuba. País was ultimately found in one of his city hiding places and killed by Batista's forces. Castro immediatelly turned his discontened follower into an icon of his revolution and shamelessly began to use him for his benefit. He even had the audacity of naming the forces under his brother Raúl Castro the *Frank País Second Front*.

The infamous Trial of the Pilots in February of 1959.

On March 2, 1959, 43 members of the **Cuban Air Force** were found inocent and absolved of al charges by a Revolutionary Tribunal composed of two Rebel Commanders and a Rebel Captain. The tribunal ordered all to be set free immediately. Instead they were taken to the **Boniato Prison** after their acquital. Castro spoke on TV that night announcing he would not accept that decision. On March 5, 1959 a new Tribunal was convened in the absence of the acused; the house was packed with an audience that chanted, yelled and physically threw the defense lawyers out of the room. The second trial lasted 8 hours, with the Tribunal not reaching a decision. Castro went again on TV on March 8 and **ordered that 19 pilots be sentenced** to 30 years of forced labor, 9 gunners to 20 years and 14 mechanics to 2 years. His will was done.

indiscriminate bombing of the area where the insurgents were located, with a number of rebels and civilians killed. Castro demanded the death penalty by firing squad for all of them. A Military Court composed of three rebel officers of the revolutionary forces was arranged, presided by Major Felix Lugerio Peña, with two other officers acting as associate judges: Pilot Antonio Michel Yabor, Castro's chief of the Rebel Air Force while at the *Sierra Maestra* and Adalberto Paruas Toll, a lawyer and a judge advocate. After two weeks of deliberations, disclosure of documents, declarations by character witnesses and peasants living in the area of interest, as well as controllers and dispatchers from the Cuban Air Force, the Court found the aviators innocent of the crime of genocide as charged by the revolutionary prosecutor.

When Fidel Castro heard news of the verdict, he went berserk in front of national TV and accused the Military Tribunal members as counter-revolutionaries, demanding an investigation of the proceedings and a new trial. Fearing for his life, judge Antonio Michel Yabor sought exile in the US and Major Felix Lugerio Peña, the chief judge, committed "suicide" at Camp Columbia.

A second Military Tribunal ordered by Castro, ignoring all the judicial principles of double jeopardy and the "sanctity of a judgment," was convened. The first absolutory sentence was revoked and the aviators were found guilty as charged and condemned to thirty years of hard labor, "generously" sparing them from the death penalty. In this second Military Tribunal the accused aviators were not permitted to be present, under the pretense that they could influence the jury. All 40 and more of the aviators served their prison sentences of more than 20 years, under the most severe conditions. Three of them mysteriously died in jail.

At the conclusion of this Military Tribunal, having established a precedent, additional pilots were brought in front of other revolutionary trials, under the same charges, in Courts assembled in Santa Clara, La Havana and Camagüey. In total more than seventy-five pilots served over 20 years of imprisonment.

Starting on April 1959, several former pilots of the Cuban Air Force had unusual fatal "accidents" due to unforeseen mechanical defects during takeoff or landing; two cases took place at Camagüey's and three at Santa Clara's airports. Other "irregularities" took place. In a inexplicable incident on August 9 of 1959, a C-46 coming from the Dominican Republic was intercepted and shot as it touched the ground, killing the pilot.

Castro eventually ordered the discharge of all former members of the Cuban Air Force still on active duty; a new era started as

Cuban pilots began to receive training in the Soviet Union, Communist China and the Czechoslovakia Republic.

The reactions to the executions and the annulment of the first trial of pilots produced a storm of criticism across the Americas. Castro could not understand that avalanche of disapproval. He immediately thought that the State Department was behind the "campaign" against him and the revolution. He declared to *Bohemia* magazine «*If there should be intervention, 200,000 Gringos will be killed.*» The story hit the headlines around the world. In Washington they began to consider him not a statesman but a clown.

Forced by the circumstances, Castro decided to visit New York, Boston, and Washington to temper the negative impressions and seek the benevolence of public opinion. American reporters, after all, adored him and his tales of the days spent fighting a guerrilla war in Cuba; they loved the fatigues and combat boots he favored, and were spellbound by the bushy beard that cut his striking figure. In April 1959, Castro looked for, secured and accepted an invitation from the *American Society of Newspaper Editors* to visit New York City. His trip did not count with an inauspicious start when it became clear that President Dwight D. Eisenhower had a golf engagement and showed no intention of meeting with Castro. Instead, Castro settled for a talk to the *Council on Foreign Affairs*, a group of influential private citizens and former government officials interested in U.S. international relations, and scheduled a meeting with the Editorial Board of the New York Times on April 24.

During both sessions Castro was confrontational, indicating that Cuba would not beg the United States for economic assistance. Angered by some of the questions from Council members, he abruptly left the meeting. Finally, before departing for Havana, he met with VP Richard Nixon, who candidly hoped that his talk would push Castro "in the right direction." Nixon later declared that Castro...

> «Was either incredibly naive about Communism or was a card holding member of the Party; I tend to believe the former.»

Back in Cuba, Carlos Rafael Rodríguez, Carlos Franqui and Juan Marinello were communicating every detail to their Russian benefactors, who believed that their friends, particularly Guevara, were once again associated with the powers that be in Cuba.[181]

---

[181] *Carlos Rafael Rodríguez* was a full blown *barbudo* who had been minister in Batista's 1940-1944 government. *Guevara* had a long history of Communist militancy. The *Castros* were known to be good loyal burrowing moles that had no need to expose themselves for the time being.

After the ceremonial speeches, Castro attended a political meeting at New York's Central Park. There were 30,000 people in attendance, most of them curious bystanders. He spoke in broken English for more than 2 hours. A police detachment of 500 men on foot and 33 in horseback took care of security, at one point detaining a man trying to throw a bomb to the speaker. From New York he travelled to Boston, where McGeorge Bundy, dean of Arts and Sciences at Harvard received him. At a Q&A session, the students proved to be more interested in the issue of executions than in his left-leaning credo. Before returning to Cuba Castro visited Houston, Montreal, Brasilia, Buenos Aires and Brazil. His impressions were that «*Hispano America loved him, the US was considering an invasion of Cuba and Nixon was a jackass,*» according to Carlos Franqui. On the day of his arrival in Cuba, CBS ran a program (Studio 56) that stated:

«*The new government is rife with Communists and there will be a blood bath in Cuba because the anti-Communists feel they have no recourse but fight violence with violence.*»

Jules Dubois, the Latin American correspondent for the *Chicago Tribune*, considered as "the world's most widely known and most decorated reporter of Latin American affairs," had a different opinion:

«*There is Communist infiltration in Cuba but not Communist domination; whatever few they are, they can easily overcome the influence of Guevara. When it comes to Raúl, a visit behind the iron curtain at age 20 does not make anyone a Communist.*»

Unexpectedly, the NY Times reported that same week that...

«*American labor groups in the US are alleging that free trade unions in Cuba are now dominated by infiltrated communists.*»

It was very difficult to assess who knew the situation best. That night, on a six hour speech, Castro told thousands of Cubans at the *Plaza de la República* that Cuba had the respect of the entire continent.

Next day the *University of Havana* opened for classes after two years of idleness. About 30 tenured professors had been purged. Any credits earned by students that went abroad during the period when the University was closed, were declared void and null. Castro began to call his insurgency in Cuba a *Humanist Revolution*.

On July 13, Manuel Urrutia was dismissed by Castro as President of Cuba. A well known Communist from Cienfuegos, Osvaldo Dorticós Torrado, took over his post.

In April of 1959 Castro began an ***11 day visit to the US***. Whenever he went he wore rumpled green fatigues rather than civilian clothes. Eisenhower snubbed him but VP Nixon and Secretary od State Cristian Herter agreed to see him. At a sesion of the *Council on Foreign Relations* he stormed out, angry with some of the questions after his speech. He ***refused to eat anything prepared by Americans*** and had his staff fry chichen parts in his room at Harlem's *Hotel Theresa*.

Relations between the US and Castro deteriorated rapidly following his April visit. In less than a year, thousands of Cubans took the route of exile and began to turn the easygoing and bucolic town of Miami into a world class destination city.[182] Within weeks of Castro's visit, President Eisenhower ordered the CIA to arm and train the youngest among the Miami group of Cuban exiles and prepare to attack and invade Cuba.[183] Castro, on his part, began to consolidate his power by increasing the tightness of his claws around the population in the island.[184] His next project was to secure control of the University students in Havana and to stop the potential uprising of former school teacher Huber Matos (1918-2014), the combat commander of the Antonio Guiteras Ninth Column in the rebel army's Sierra Maestra operations; Matos had denounced the pro-Communist direction of the revolution from his base of operations in Camagüey in July of 1959.

On September 9, 1959, Castro imposed Rolando Cubela as President of the *Federación de Estudiantes Universitarios (FEU)* over the clear popular candidate Pedro Luis Boitel. It was part of a clever scheme to secure the control of Cuba's university students, a force that had always weighted in favor of democracy in Cuba.

Cubela (1932-) had been the founder of the *Directorio Revolucionario Estudiantil (DRE)* and a military leader of the Escambray mountain front in the fight against Batista, where he received the rank of Commander, the highest in the Revolutionary Army. He had been implicated in various assassination attempts against Batista's ministers but enjoyed the absolute confidence of Raúl Castro as head of the Armed Forces.

---

[182] Incredibly, the ***Washington Post*** editorialized that things were improving in Cuba upon Castro's return and ***CBS*** ran the second part of its series *Is Cuba going Red?*, reporting that it was not.

[183] The ***Eisenhower*** well calculated, organized and US supported efforts to destroy Castro and prevent Cuba from going Communist were shattered by the inexpert, abashed and diffident decisions of his succesor, John F. Kennedy who , lacking self confidence, timidly stopped the air support to the trained Cubans at the Bay of Pigs invasion, causing the irreperable damage of depriving the Cubans the opportunity to stop Communism in the American continent.

[184] ***Upon receiving Fidel Castro back in Cuba***, his brother Raúl became worried that he could have been seduced by the Americans. He had to prove Fidel that he could not govern without the help of the Communists. Raúl had no charisma, sympathies or following of any kind in Cuba, but he decided to risk producing a schasm in the movement by sending Lazaro Peña, a long time old-fashion Communist, to Moscow, to ask the Soviets for help in the organization of intelligence work. He inmediately began to execute people that were not war criminals and organize mass arrests of ideological and activist counter-revolutionaries. From that moment on, the old Cuban Communist Party, the PSP, with the help of Raúl, began to open chapters in every town, union and school in Cuba.

Rolando Cubela Secades (1932-) and *Pedro Luis Boitel* (1931-1972), student university leaders. *Hubert Matos* and *Camilo Cienfuegos* on a visit to the *University of Havana*. *Major Pedro Luis Díaz Lanz* ,(1926-2008), former commander of the Rebel Air Force who deserted and turned against Castro.

Boitel (1931-1972) was a Cuban poet and opponent of the Batista government who became involved in the July 26 Movement and was their candidate for President of the *Federación de Estudiantes Universitarios (FEU)*. He was leader of the students that feared the militarization of the *FEU* if an army officer like Cubela was installed as President.

The Castro brothers could not risk the defeat of Cubela and on the day of the election to the presidency of the *FEU* Castro showed up at the meeting and addressed the students, feigning impartiality. He asked the students to *«Do away with party factional rivalries and agree on the unanimous proclamation of a single candidate.»*

Unexpectedly, a few hours before the elections, Boitel withdrew his candidacy and Cubela was elected unanimously as the sole candidate. Cubela's first decision, in accordance with Castro's plans, was to organize student militias asking students to *«fulfill their heroic mission by becoming sworn members of the militias and proudly wearing the uniform of militia members.»*[185]

From there on the University of Havana was overwhelmed with military fanfare as day and night little bands of militia garbed students strutted through university grounds, fully armed and in military formation, singing revolutionary slogans and following the stentorian shouts of their officers. The University of Havana ceased to be an academic community dedicated to the pursuit of knowledge and the preservation of culture.[186]

---

[185] By **coercing student leaders** to swear loyalty to the militias, the Castro brothers had instituted a mechanism by which any deviation from the party line on the part of any student that had joined the militia was considered treason and was punishable by death. It forever silenced the university students in Cuba.

[186] Never was the sense that **every revolution eats its own children** more notable; Castro got rid of Rolando Cubela some time later and on March 10, 1966, he was sentenced to 25 years in prison for plotting the assassination of Castro.

The revolution also **never forgets its enemies**; Boitel went on to organize the *Movimiento de Recuperación Revolucionaria (MRR)*. He was detained and sentenced as counter-revolutionary. Tortured and beaten incesantly during his 42 years imprisonment in the dreaded *Castillo de Principe* penitentiary, he died there on May 24, 1972, after a 53 days hunger strike. He was buried in an unmarked grave in the Colon Cemetery in Havana. Clara Abraham, his mother, had been holding a vigil at the prison guardpost for weeks, hoping to see her son. She was taken forcibly in a patrol car to the Political Police Headquarters at *Villa Marista*, where she was notified that *«your son is dead and buried.»* She was not given any details of his burial place. When she attempted to find it at the common graves area in the cemetery she was intercepted, insulted and attacked by a group of women armed with wooden clubs wrapped in newspapers. With the women there was a Dr. Gallardo, a man posing as the doctor that took care of Boitel in prison who was actually an infiltrator from the Political Police.

The case of Huber Matos was easier to solve for the Castro brothers. He had clear revolutionary merits; for years he had been in contact with the revolutionaries stationed in *Sierra Maestra* mountains and had helped them with his contacts with President José Figueres of Costa Rica, who supported Cuban rebel aims and helped Matos obtain and air-drop weapons and supplies to the rebels. When he joined them at Sierra Maestra he was given the rank of Commander. In January 1959, he rode into Havana atop a tank in a victory parade alongside Castro and other revolutionaries. When he was assigned to be Commander of the Army in the province of Camagüey he became concerned about the Communist infiltration in the government in Havana and first began to complaint and make openly anti-Communist speeches and later, in September of 1959, tendered his resignation in a letter to Castro. His words were:

> «*Communist influence in the government has continued to grow. I have to leave power as soon as possible. I plan to alert the Cuban people as to what is happening.*»

Castro immediately went into a frenzy and on October 21 sent revolutionary leader Camilo Cienfuegos to Camagüey to arrest Matos. As Cienfuegos and Matos met, Matos warned Cienfuegos that his (Cienfuegos) own life was in danger, since Castro resented his popularity and had probably expected that Matos' troops would kill him rather than allow Matos to be taken prisoner. Cienfuegos did not pay heed to the warning and relieved Matos of command and arrested him and his entire military staff. [187]

On that very same day, former Air Force Chief of Staff Pedro Luis Díaz Lanz, now a Cuban exile, flew from Florida and dropped leaflets in Havana calling for the removal of all Communists from the government. Castro became furious and set up a massive rally where he promised a revolutionary trial for both Matos and Díaz Lanz. The multitude screamed ¡*Paredón!*, ¡*Paredón!*(to the gallows!). Next day Castro called a meeting of Ministers to at least determine Matos' fate. Three of the ministers were hesitant to condemn Matos without a thorough investigation. They were immediately, right at the meeting, dismissed from their

---

[187] On the way back to Havana, the plane of Camilo Cienfuegos plummeted in the Caribbean sea. The pilot of an escort aircraft following Camilo's also dissapeared; so did the plane's mechanic who reported that on that day the plane's machine guns were inoperative (he was run over by a car in Havana). A fisherman that claimed he had seen Camilo's plane under gun fire from another aircraft was never seen again by his family. An Air Force inspector looking into the case was gunned down as he was flying to Cienfuegos to interview potential witnesses.

positions. So were five captains and eleven lieutenants that had expressed reservations about Matos' execution at a meeting in Columbia.

When the trial was opened on December 13, 1959, Castro delivered a seven-hour speech accusing Matos and the others of campaigning against the revolution and promoting the interests of the US government, the confiscated Cuban large landowners, and Batista. The prosecution asked for the death sentence. On December 15, 1959, the court found Matos guilty of counter-revolutionary activity and sentenced him to twenty years in prison. He served his sentence to the last day in Havana's *La Cabaña* Prison. Sixteen of those years were spent on solitary confinement. He died in Miami in 2014, at age 95.

Pedro Luis Díaz Lanz, the former commercial pilot with *Aerovias Q* who supplied Castro's forces at Sierra Maestra with numerous risky deliveries of weapons and had become head of the Revolutionary Air Force in January 1, 1959, testified for several hours at US Senate hearings after the day he dropped leaflets in Havana with impunity. He was recruited by the CIA and worked for the US government for several years. In 2008, after years of poverty and depression, at the age of 81, he took his own life with a gunshot wound to the chest.

The last months of 1959 could be characterized as "the days of the final decline of the moderates." Humberto Sorí Marín, Minister of Agriculture, main drafter of the 1959 Law of Agrarian Reform, creator of the INRA, the *Instituto Nacional de la Reforma Agraria*, the chief judge of the military tribunal that tried and condemned Major Sosa Blanco and a close friend of the Castros, ended up resigning his post and joining a subversive campaign to eliminate the Communist influence in the government and the Armed Forces. When he landed in Celimar, near Havana, on March 13, 1961 with a cache of arms and explosives, he escaped detection but a few days after he Bay of Pigs invasion failed, he was executed.

Foreign Minister Roberto Agramonte resigned his post in May 1960 because of the Communist tilt of the government. He was replaced by Raúl Roa García, a notable card-carying Communist, friend of Rubén Martínez Villena and Julio Antonio Mella, founders of the Cuban Communist Party, and Pablo de la Torriente Brau, the rabid Marxist who died as a Commissar of the International Communist Brigades during the Spanish Civil War.

On November 7, 1959, Manuel Artime Buesa (1932-1977), a devout Catholic physician that had joined the rebel army in the *Sierra Maestra* and had become the second in command of the *Instituto*

At the top, a solidarity march across Havana, presided by (left to right) **Fidel Castro, Osvaldo Dorticos, Ernesto Guevara, Augusto Martínez Sánchez, Antonio Nuñez Jiménez** and **Willian Morgan.**
Bottom left, **Humberto Sorí Marín**. On the right, a newspaper announcing the law confiscating most large extensions of land in Cuba, whether productive or not. *Henry Morgan* and *Sorí Marín* were eventually tried and executed for actions against the revolutionary government.

Nacional de la Reforma Agraria (INRA) in Manzanillo, resigned his post on the same grounds of Humberto Sorí Marín, his boss. His letter of resignation appeared in the front page of the newspaper *Avance*; having a spotless record as a physician, a revolutionary and a teacher of many insurgents at *Sierra Maestra*, his leaving the revolution had an enormous impact on the prestige of the Castro government.[188]

As the moderates began to fall one by one during the last weeks of 1959, it became increasingly clear that the swing away from the US was set in motion irreversibly almost from the day Batista left power. The process, of course, accelerated with the resignation of Prime Minister José Miró Cardona and his whole cabinet on February 13, 1959. The US learned on that day not only that all of the moderates they had recently been praising were gone, but also that Castro replaced Cardona as the Prime Minister. Taking that position was not enough for Castro; he also altered the law in order to give himself, as the new Prime Minister, drastically increased power. The US Embassy in Cuba, on a memo to Washington stated:

> «*Castro will totally dictate the policy of the government and dispatch all administrative matters with an appointed puppet president.*»

Castro indeed proceeded to suspend elections for two years and within a month had effectively neutralized the moderate section of the government and had given the U.S. a preview of similar changes to come. But the mayor point of conflict was his *Reforma Agraria*, a mayor radical change in the land tenure system of Cuba. Its regulations, as per a memo dated May 21, 1959 were:

- All landholdings over 99 acres are subject to expropriation by the Cuban government.
- Within one year, all private corporations would lose the ability to exploit sugar cane fields unless they had registered the name of their stockholders and proven they were all Cuban citizens.

---

[188] **Manuel Artime** with the help of the US embassy in Havana, left Cuba on a Honduran ship. He became involved with the CIA in a counter-revolution supported by former ministers and Cuban anti-Communist leaders like Tony Varona, José Miró Cardona and Aureliano Sánchez Arango. On 17 April 1961 he went ashore with *Brigade 2506*, the assault contingent of Cuban exiles, at *Playa Larga* in the **Bay of Pigs Invasion**. He was captured and jailed by Castro's forces and released from prison on December 24, 1962. He died of cancer in November of 1977. As in the case of another prominent leader of the Cuban exiles, **Jorge Mas Canosa** (1939-1997), founder of the *Cuban American National Foundation*, his death was attributed to a clever assassination scheme designed by the Castro brothers.

- All expropriated landowners would be subject to compensation but it would be in the form of 20-year bonds with no more than 4.5 % interest.

The Agrarian Reform Law resulted in the immediate expropriation of 50,000 *caballerías* (1.6 million acres) of American owned land.[189] On June 30, the US National Security Council was informed by the CIA that...

> «*Cuban Soldiers have occupied cattle lands in Camagüey province following Castro's declaration that immediate nationalization of excess cattle land would occur in response to US cattlemen's opposition to agrarian reform.*»

Surprisingly, many officials of the Kennedy administration believed there was little concrete evidence to support the accusations of Communist inspiration; some, however, admitted that the seed of doubt regarding the Cuban government's political ideology had been planted.[190]

Worse than the Agrarian Reform, the Cuban situation took a dark turn from which it would never come back: the CIA began to get word that heavy arms shipments, as well as 23 Soviet-made fighter jets and small arms had begun to be funneled into Cuba from the United Arab Republic. Military hardware was been swapped with discounted sugar shipments.[191] It was the drop that overflew the bucket; from there on the US changed his Cuban policy from observant and wait-and-see to hard-line and aggressive.

Eisenhower was particularly inflamed by these developments. On July 6, 1960 he cut the Cuban sugar quota from 2,150,000 tons per year to 700,000 tons. At the same time he declared:

> « *This action amounts to economic sanctions against Cuba; now we must look ahead to other economic, diplomatic and strategic moves. There is no hope that the US will ever be able to establish a satisfactory relationship with any Cuban government dominated by Fidel Castro or his close associates.*»

---

[189] On a telegram from the US Department of State to its Embassy in Cuba, dated May22, 1959, Castro was cited as saying «*this will not affect in any way the relations between Cuba and the US.*»

[190] The US State Department identified this action as an strictly and isolated case, even though by the end of the year total scale expropriation was in full swing.

[191] Five million tons of Cuban sugar over a three year period was approved for exchange for 100 million dollars in Soviet trade credits. No one could predict at the time that this bond formalized on May 7, 1960, would commercially and politically tie Cuba with the Soviet Union until the end of the Cold War.

It was then Castro's time to be inflamed. Cuba seized all US-owned lands on the island and threatened violent mob action against all US property or personnel in Cuba. Castro added that...

«He would take everything from Americans in Cuba, down to the nails in their shoes, if Cuba's sugar quota in the US market were cut one pound more.»

The Soviet Union took advantage of the dispute by offering to buy enough additional sugar from Cuba to compensate the lost quota from the US, an offer that Castro gladly accepted.

Emboldened by his ability to get away with decisions the Communists in Cuba had never dreamed were possible, as pointed out by Anastas Mikoyan (1895-1978), USSR Prime Minister in a visit to Cuba,[192] Castro accelerated in 1960 the pace of transformation of the republic.

On March 31, all private Radio and TV stations in the island were confiscated.

On May 11, all newspapers, magazines and book publishing houses were nationalized.

On June 29, all petroleum refining operations property of Esso, Texaco and Shell were intervened by government troops, declared national property and forced to refine crude oil from the USSR.

On September 17, all private banks and financial institutions were seized and impounded.

On October 13, every private business in Cuba was appropriated by government agents, many of whom were recruited from the business own personnel.

On October 15 all real estate property in Cuba was taken away from their legitimate owners. Tenants and lodgers were told to send their rent checks to government offices. Property owners would keep only the home where they lived.

Castro's strategy continued to be pandering to the needs of sub-developed countries and securing world sympathy and moral

---

[192] As early as September of 1959, the Soviets had sent to Cuba a KGB agent called Vadim Kotchergin to find out how they could profit from the chaos. According to Khrushchev in 1965, neither the *Soviet Party Central Committee* nor the *KGB* had any notion of who Castro was. **In 1960 Khrushchev sent Mikoyan to Havana**; he returned to Moscow saying *«Cuba in 1960 reminds me of my childhood in 1905 Russia.»* While in Havana to open an exposition, Mikoyan attempted to deposit flowers at the Martí statue in Havana's Central Park; he was rebuffed by Catholic students from the University of Havana, which were beaten by the police. Acccording to Juan Manuel Salvat, one of the protesters, *«We went there to protest the presence in Cuba of the man who was responsible for the 1956 Soviet massacre in Hungary and to express the danger of the Cuban government becoming more Communist each day.»* The incident was highlighted on a photo in the cover of that week's *Life Magazine*.

A newspaper in Miami announcing the end of diplomatic relations and total rupture between the US and the revolutionary government of Cuba; a symbolic embrace of *Nikita Khrushchev* (1894-1971) with Castro in 1961. *Khrushchev,* a survivor of Stalin's purges, was in the inner circle of Stalin but denounced him and was retired by Brezhnev with the help of the KGB. He died in 1971.
Photos below, the *El Encanto* before and after Carlos González Vidal, a counter-revolutionary arsonist, placed a bomb that burned it to the ground on April 13, 1961.

support from left leaning governments. His efforts were particularly important *vis-a-vis* Latin America's guerrilla movements and the 18 African countries that at the time were achieving independence. In an ambitious project well beyond the economic and human capabilities of Cuba, on September 8 Castro sent hundreds of Cuban soldiers and volunteers to Africa to reinforce the *Front de Libération Nationale* (National Liberation Front, FLN) from Algeria against French troops.[193] He lent similar help to Kwame Nkrumah, leader of the recently independent Republic of Ghana. The year 1960 closed with Castro's declaration that «*All his life he had been a card-carrying Communist.*» The US responded canceling all pending sugar delivery contracts from Cuba.

Up to that time, more than 1,350 Cubans had been executed by the government; more than 120 union leaders have been condemned an average of 22 years in prison; more than 100,000 Cubans had taken political refuge in the US.

As Castro tightened more and more his control of the business of government, he was successfully changing many fundamental laws of the republic. Reaction to his reckless disregard for laws and traditions was soon forthcoming.

On April 13, 1961, the city of Havana suffered from an act of sabotage like no other that had ever been seen in Cuba; *El Encanto*, the best department store in Hispanic America, was completely destroyed by fire. The five story merchant of luxury had been built in 1888 at the corner of San Rafael and Galiano in central Havana and had been nationalized a few months earlier. One person died, 18 people were injured in the blaze and 930 employees had lost their employ. The arsonist had placed two packs of *Eden* cigarettes filled with C-4 explosives inside bolts of cloth in the tailoring department. He was sentenced to death and executed. Two days later, on April 15, four B-26 planes from Guatemala bombarded several military airports in Cuba. A furious Castro denounced the action[194] and took the opportunity to proclaim the irrevocable socialist character of his revolution. It was just the preliminary step of a much serious action by the opposition.

On April 17, the *Bay of Pigs* invasion was launched from training camps in Guatemala by Cuban exiles living in the US. Thousands of people were arrested all over Cuba. Priests, lay Catholics

---

[193] When ***Algeria became independent*** in 1963, it received aid from Cuba in the form of a 50 strong delegation of physicians and medical staff that were essential to the meager health services in Cuba.

[194] It was well known that Castro and his advisers had found out about the raid and had moved the Rebel Air Force planes out of harm's way.

Some photos from the failed invasion of Cuba by Cuban exiles from Miami. The action by the Brigade 2506 was probably the final act of a determined struggle to restore Cuban to democracy. Photo at the center, the invasion leaders, Civilian **Manuel Artime Buesa MD** (1932-1977, on the left), Brigade Commander, **José Pérez-San Román**, (1930-1989, in the center) and Second-in-Command **Erneido Oliva González** (1932-).
Below, the **Museum of the Brigade** in Miami.

and thousands of internal opponents were taken to cells in secret police headquarters. Dozens of suspects were shot at *La Cabaña* fortress in retaliation. By April 20, however, US President Kennedy retracted his promise of general support to the invaders and retired the logistic, intelligence and US aerial protection to the exiles' Air Force; the invasion was defeated. The indecisiveness of Kennedy[195] allowed Castro to dispose for good of all present and future opposition to his Communist exploits.

Once again the quick summary trials began to marshal dozens of Cubans in front of the *paredones* (execution walls). In a dozen of prisons in Havana, at the *Coliseo de Deportes*, as well as at many other locations with large empty spaces (like the *Teatro Blanquita*, baptized by the revolution as the *Karl Marx Theater*) dozens of prisoners from the *2506 Brigade* and likely sympathizers were humiliated and abused. Out in the cities of Cuba, several thousand common citizens were arrested and aggressively coerced to condemn the invasion. For almost 15 days, nothing of any merit was done across the island. As before, the Castro regime was more interested in vengeance than in justice.

On June 16, the Castro government began to send Cuban students to the USSR and other countries behind the iron curtain. Weeks later Castro would announce that any professional that had left the island or had plans to do so would be considered as resigning his/her Cuban citizenship; they would not be allowed to ever set foot on the island again. At the start of the new school year the government passed a norm prohibiting any teacher in Cuba, under the threat of imprisonment, to teach anything having to do with religion, whether history, dogma, practices or statistics.

In a final blow to personal independence in Cuba, Castro declared all currency in circulation null and worthless. Only 400 pesos of the old currency per person would be accepted for exchange with new paper money printed on the sly and stealthily in Czechoslovakia. Thousands of business went bankrupt and thousands of people and entire families went hungry. The era of "control through scarcity" had arrived. It had the possibility to sustain the Communist government in Cuba for years to come. Finally, to deprive people of compassionate or moral support and presuma-

---

[195] Kennedy later commented that the CIA plans for the Bay of Pigs invasion was *«too large to be clandestine and too small to be successful.»* Kennedy was never forgiven by Cuban exiles or anti-Communists the world over for **his wavering and lack of resolve** when confronting Communism. His dithering at the *Bay of Pigs* was probably the main reason why the Russians would test him again the following year during the Cuban Missile Crisis in October 14, 1962.

bly to provide an end to what Lenin had called «*the opium of the masses,*» all across the island a raid on cathedrals, parishes and small churches yielded over 130 priests and nuns that were corralled and taken to the *Covadonga*, a ship anchored in Havana harbor, ready to take their precious cargo away from the island. Altogether the year 1961, which the government had designated as "*the Year of Education*," had become a lesson for all liberal democratic peoples across the Western world.

Most historians agree that the hopes of freeing Cuba from Communism were demolished after the resounding failure of the *Bay of Pigs* invasion. The scant number of democratic fighters in Cuba were decimated. By and large, countries in Hispanic America saw in the Bay of Pigs a victory of the Third World over the irritating impositions of the rich countries. Europeans and Africans, far from the theater of the crimes, began to fall for the quixotic tales of Castro and Guevara as redeemers of the oppressed. The extreme left in the US, Malcolm X, aka *el-Hajj Malik el-Shabazz*, Elijah Muhammad, aka Elijah Robert Poole, and Louis Farrakhan, aka Louis Eugene Wolcott, began to dream visions of a broad coalition of Cuban revolutionary Marxists and American blacks; businessmen in the US kept an eye on Cuba hoping that the devastation of Cuba offered a good prospect for American business.

The political, human and economic decline of Cuba has had no end since the days of the 1961 episode.

> In 1961 rumors spread in Cuba about the government seizing the *Patria Potestad* (rights of protection and custody) for children between the ages of 5 and 16. Cuban bishops and volunteers organized the evacuation of 14,000 of children out of Cuba in what had become known as *Operación Pedro Pan*.
>
> In what became a massive demographic engineering experiment, entire families in Cuba began to be relocated against their will to serve the national interests.
>
> To secure the loyalty of the USSR, Cuba agreed to deploy Intercontinental Ballistic Missiles in its territory capable to reach with nuclear bombs a large portion of the US.
>
> In 1963 Cuba established a Compulsory Military Service for all males between 15 and 45 years of age, after which young Cubans found the possibility of exile closed.
>
> In 1966 a large number of Catholic priests and lay people, including future Cardinal Jaime Ortega Alamino, were sent to forced work camps known as the UMAP *(Military Units to Aid Production)*.
>
> Since 1960 Cuba has had a network of Committees to Defend the Revolution (CDR) in every city block, every municipality, every factory and every office, whose purpose is to detect and de-

nounce anti-Communist activities. By 2010, 8.4 million Cubans, out of a population of 11.2 million, were registered as CDR members.

In conclusion, the paradise that the Cuba revolution promised... was never there. There was never a link between justice, equality, liberty and human rights since the advent of the revolution. There have never been any social achievements that were not attainable with the liberal democratic model. Cuba confirmed the prognostications of many world class intelligent minds that with Communism the island would become a hellhole. Cubans have paid a colossal price for their experiment in its Marxist-Leninist government model; a price that will probably never be recovered.

Far from being a beacon of resistance to American imperialism, Cuba has forever suffered the most colossal drain of talent that any civilized country has ever experienced. In its roster of dedicated leaders, Cuba can only show world class bloodthirsty losers and murderous slayers in the category of Ernesto Guevara and the brothers Castro.

People across the world can be deceived and bamboozled about Cuban progress in health, education, culture, child care and the status of women; the crude reality is that almost 2 million Cubans have abandoned the island and hundreds more continue to try to escape, many times at the risk of their own life.

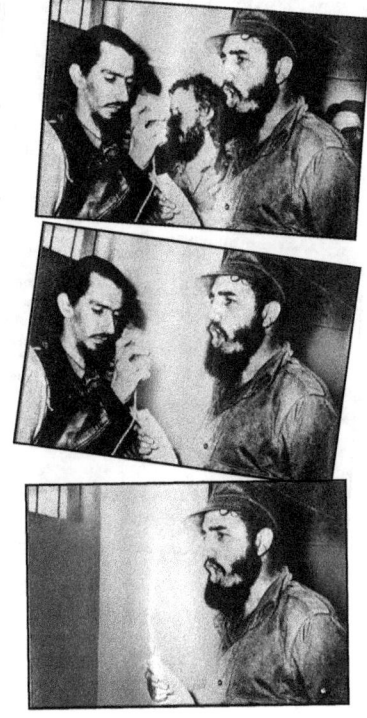

By all accounts, Cuba has been since 1959 in the hands of greedy exploiters of human fantasies that have made Cubans believe in a magical world that has never materialize in half a century and never will; it has guarantee for the Castro brothers and their comrades, however, a lifetime of power, luxury, opulence and material comforts.

Following the Russian tradition of erasing former supporters turned opponents from photos, **Carlos Franqui** first and **Enrique Mendoza** later, dissapeared from the original picture in which they were shown with Castro. One by one they were erased from Cuba's revolutionary history.

Castro and the press have always had a ***great affinity for each other***, in spite of his known crimes against his adversaries and humanity in general.

For half a century people of all clases have ignored the brutality and criminal behavior of **Ernesto (Ché) Guevara** and have venerated and praised him as a romantic revolutionary. On the photos, **Carlos Santana** at the 2005 Oscars, the **Rev. Jessie Jackson** on one of his visits to Cuba, Shawn Corey Carter, the famous rapper also known as **Jay Z**, and even the first black president of the US **Barack Hussein Obama**.

In a speech in front of the United Nations in 1964, Guevara proudly admitted: «*yes, we have executed, we are executing, we will continue to execute.*»

By the thousands, Cuban have been risking their lives since 1959 to escape the revolutionary paradise. The photos show, on top, the *launching of a balsa* (rudimentary floting device) on the coasts of Cuba. In the center, the balsa across the gulf of Mexico *trying to reach the coasts of Florida*.
On the photo below, faces of some of the 41 Cubans *deliberatly drowned* as their tugboat "13 de Marzo" was attacked by the Cuban Coast Guard on July 13, 1994, as they attempted to leave the island.

The 1959 Castro revolution has turned Havana from a modern and beautiful city into a delapidated and dirty slum. These photos present some of the thousands of buildings that have suffered the neglect and humiliating ***abandonment of property taken from their legitimate owners*** and given to residents of Havana as the only place where they could live and work.

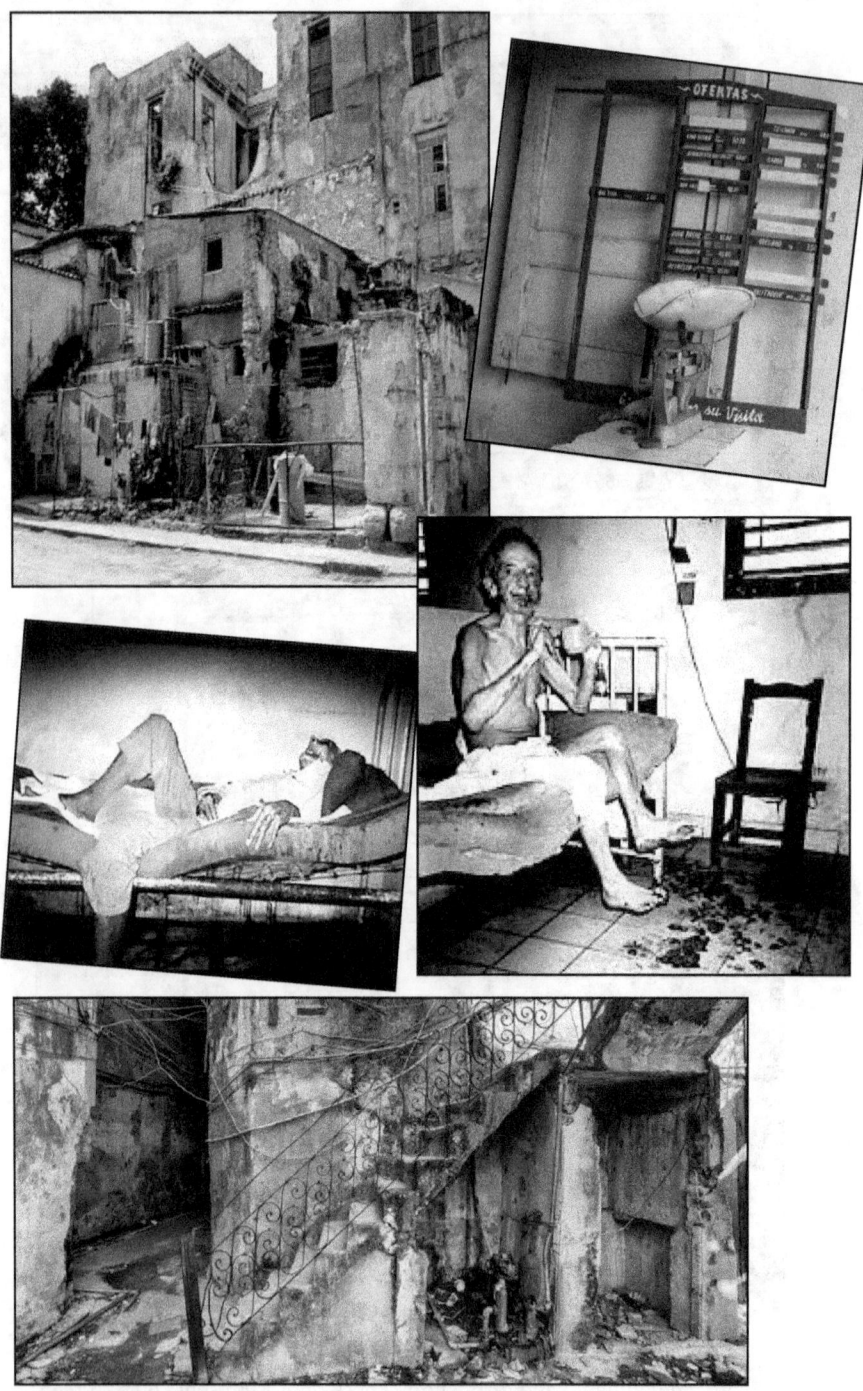

These photos show the *interior of residential buildings, commercial property and hospitals* taken from their owners and made of compulsory use to residents in Cuba. Very little is left of what the revolution inherited from Cuba before 1959.

A historical summary of the Cuban Revolution "accomplishments"

- Over 4,500 Cubans were summarily executed. None of them were granted due process of the law as guaranteed by all civilized political systems.
- Close to 2 million Cubans went into exile into Europe and the US. Their personal and family properties were confiscated.
- All private businesses in Cuba have ceased to legally exist.
- All schools, radio and TV stations, newspapers and every means of communications have been taken over by the state.
- Religious institutions are continuously harassed unless they conform to Marxist norms. The public practice of any and all religions is forbidden.
- Cubans are prohibited to leave the island except with licenses from the revolutionary government. Cubans outside the island are not allowed to return unless they register and comply with the same requirements as foreigners.
- All books and materials exposing non-Marxist doctrines are banned. Possession of them is severely castigated.
- No popular expressions of discontent, such as marches, rallies, speeches and writings are tolerated.
- No political parties other than the Communist party are allowed. No free elections ever occur at any level, except with single candidates imposed by the Communist party.
- Competing (non-Marxist) labor organizations are illegal.
- Tourism and the life style of all Marxist leaders take priority in the consumption of goods and services over the needs of the general population.
- Every home, workplace, neighborhood and human interaction is under constant surveillance by Committees for the Defense of the Revolution that denounce all actual or potential deviations from the credo of the Marxist revolution.
- The lack of pride of ownership has resulted in disregard and disappearance of good housing in most of Cuba. Decent homes have been turned into tenements. Many Cubans dress, live, socialize and communicate like very dispossessed people do in primitive societies.
- Young people have lost any illusions of growing as individuals and progress economically in the restraining society created by the Communist government. They have risked their lives for over half a century trying to escape from the place of their birth into a modern civilization.
- The "humanistic" 1959 revolution of Cuba, soon turned into a Marxist adventure, ended up as a despotic scheme controlled by an organized criminal gang. Marxism is ready to perpetuate itself for several generations in the island. The world now visits Cuba with the same curiosity that many people enjoy going to zoos to see almost extinct animals.

Not content with a prior failure in their 1933 revolution, Cubans relapsed thirty years later into a revolutionary fervor that demolished for good their young democracy and any hope to been able to cast off the Communist plague.

Epilogue

The ominous question when it comes to revolutions, revolts and insurrections is Why do they almost always fail? Those implicated don't ever see failures of strategies, but rather the result of poor tactics, issues that weren't dealt with correctly or the inability of people to perform at the level they were trusted to do for the success of the Revolution. Historians that look at revolutions see the ever present failures from a different perspective. The main failure of turning revolutionary dogma into action, is the inability of revolutionaries to see beyond the attainment of power.

All political systems, whether they are theocracies, democracies, communism, fascism, capitalism, feudal governance, or what have you, must address a most basic tenet: power not only has to be acquired but it must also be made continuously viable. Revolutions, revolts and insurrections are usually strong on defining the path to victory but are generally very weak on what sustaining path needs to be taken once victory is attained. The French were very successful dethroning Luis XVI, but not one of the revolutionaries knew how to govern afterwards. Once the Mexicans sent Porfirio Díaz to exile in France, they had to wait twenty years for men like Obregón and Cárdenas to set the country in a path to progress. The followers of Lenin never brought peace to Russia and eventually the empire collapsed in front of well managed Western countries. Castro was probably very astute in overthrowing Batista, but his regime has for half a century scored one miserable failure after another.

Political, economic and social power, is wasted or even destructive unless it is exercised from within a trusting and convivial society. Revolutionaries, rebels and insurgents can easily create an ideological battlefield and, of course, you can't destroy an ideology. But the issue is that once a revolution's exercise of force has brought power as a reward, the most difficult tasks begin: to alter the mores and beliefs of society in consistency with the revolutionary beliefs; revolutionaries, rebels and insurgents must discard the delusion that their earned power is an accomplishment by itself, and engage in an unwavering path to make both the citizens and the State grow under better and healthier conditions. Anything else would be a source of contempt and deception. Despite the lofty and poetic dreams of liberation, freedom, participation, justice and self determination, the outcome of revolutions must be intimately linked to prosperity, growth, human, societal and economic development. It was not achieved in the French, Mexican, Russian and Cuban revolutions, and that's why they were miserable failures and people ended up cursing their leaders... *Damn the Revolution !*

Appendices

I	Declaration of the Rights of Man and Citizen, 26 August 1789	318
II	The Revolutionary Tribunal's Use of the Guillotine	321
III	Primary Documents of the Mexican Revolution	323
IV	Excerpts of Several Articles of the 1917 Mexican Consitution	325
V	The Abdication of Nicholas II (1917)	328
VI	Excerpts from Lenin's Political Testament (1922)	329
VII	A Capitalist, a Marxist-Leninist and an Anarcho-Syndicalist analize the subversion of the Cuban Revolution	331
VIII	A selection of quotes from the writings and speeches of Ernesto (Ché) Guevara	335

Appendix I
Declaration of the Rights of Man and Citizen
26 August 1789

Once they had agreed on the necessity of drafting a declaration of rights, the deputies of the National Assembly still faced the daunting task of composing one that a majority could accept. The debate raised several questions: should the declaration be short and limited to general principles or should it rather include a long explanation of the significance of each article; should the declaration include a list of duties or only rights; and what precisely were "the natural, inalienable, and sacred rights of man"? After several days of debate and voting, the deputies decided to suspend their deliberations on the declaration, having agreed on seventeen articles. These laid out a new vision of government, in which protection of natural rights replaced the will of the King as the justification for authority. Many of the reforms favored by Enlightenment writers appeared in the declaration: freedom of religion, freedom of the press, no taxation without representation, elimination of excessive punishments, and various safeguards against arbitrary administration.

-0-

«*The representatives of the French people, constituted as a National Assembly, and considering that ignorance, neglect, or contempt of the rights of man are the sole causes of public misfortunes and governmental corruption, have resolved to set forth in a solemn declaration the natural, inalienable and sacred rights of man: so that by being constantly present to all the members of the social body this declaration may always remind them of their rights and duties; so that by being liable at every moment to comparison with the aim of any and all political institutions the acts of the legislative and executive powers may be the more fully respected; and so that by being founded henceforward on simple and incontestable principles the demands of the citizens may always tend toward maintaining the constitution and the general welfare.*

In consequence, the National Assembly recognizes and declares, in the presence and under the auspices of the Supreme Being, the following rights of man and the citizen:

1. Men are born and remain free and equal in rights. Social distinctions may be based only on common utility.

2. The purpose of all political association is the preservation of the natural and imprescriptible rights of man. These rights are liberty, property, security, and resistance to oppression.

3. The principle of all sovereignty rests essentially in the nation. No body and no individual may exercise authority which does not emanate expressly from the nation.

4. Liberty consists in the ability to do whatever does not harm another; hence the exercise of the natural rights of each man has no other limits than those which assure to other members of society the enjoyment of the same rights. These limits can only be determined by the law.

5. The law only has the right to prohibit those actions which are injurious to society. No hindrance should be put in the way of anything not prohibited by the law, nor may anyone be forced to do what the law does not require.

6. The law is the expression of the general will. All citizens have the right to take part, in person or by their representatives, in its formation. It must be the same for everyone whether it protects or penalizes. All citizens being equal in its eyes are equally admissible to all public dignities, offices, and employments, according to their ability, and with no other distinction than that of their virtues and talents.

7. No man may be indicted, arrested, or detained except in cases determined by the law and according to the forms which it has prescribed. Those who seek, expedite, execute, or cause to be executed arbitrary orders should be punished; but citizens summoned or seized by virtue of the law should obey instantly, and render themselves guilty by resistance.

8. Only strictly and obviously necessary punishments may be established by the law, and no one may be punished except by virtue of a law established and promulgated before the time of the offense, and legally applied.

9. Every man being presumed innocent until judged guilty, if it is deemed indispensable to arrest him, all rigor unnecessary to securing his person should be severely repressed by the law.

10. No one should be disturbed for his opinions, even in religion, provided that their manifestation does not trouble public order as established by law.

11. The free communication of thoughts and opinions is one of the most precious of the rights of man. Every citizen may therefore speak, write, and print freely, if he accepts his own responsibility for any abuse of this liberty in the cases set by the law.

12. *The safeguard of the rights of man and the citizen requires public powers. These powers are therefore instituted for the advantage of all, and not for the private benefit of those to whom they are entrusted.*

13. *For maintenance of public authority and for expenses of administration, common taxation is indispensable. It should be apportioned equally among all the citizens according to their capacity to pay.*

14. *All citizens have the right, by themselves or through their representatives, to have demonstrated to them the necessity of public taxes, to consent to them freely, to follow the use made of the proceeds, and to determine the means of apportionment, assessment, and collection, and the duration of them.*

15. *Society has the right to hold accountable every public agent of the administration.*

16. *Any society in which the guarantee of rights is not assured or the separation of powers not settled has no constitution.*

17. *Property being an inviolable and sacred right, no one may be deprived of it except when public necessity, certified by law, obviously requires it, and on the condition of a just compensation in advance.»*

Appendix II
The Revolutionary Tribunal's Use of the Guillotine

This description of the proceedings of the revolutionary tribunal, and of the physical setting of the *Place de la Révolution* where the guillotine stood, by an unsympathetic English observer gives the flavor of the workings of revolutionary justice. The site of hundreds if not thousands of executions, this public space is now called the Place de la Concorde, "the place of peace," and is situated between the Ministries of the Army and Navy and the new meeting place of the National Assembly.

«*In the centre of the hall, under a statue of justice, holding scales in one hand, and a sword in the other, with the book of laws by her side, sat Dumas, the president, with the other judges. Under them were seated the public accuser, Fouquier-Tinville, and his scribes. Three colored ostrich plumes waved over their turned-up hats, à la Henri IV, and they wore a tri-colored scarf. To the right were benches on which the accused were placed in several rows, and gendarmes, with carbines and fixed bayonets by their sides. To the left was the jury.*

Never can I forget the mournful appearance of these funeral processions to the place of execution. The march was opened by a detachment of mounted gendarmes—the carts followed; they were the same carts as those used in Paris for carrying wood; four boards were placed across them for seats, and on each board sat two, and sometimes three victims; their hands were tied behind their backs, and the constant jolting of the cart made them nod their heads up and down, to the great amusement of the spectators. On the front of the cart stood Samson, the executioner, or one of his sons or assistants; gendarmes on foot marched by the side; then followed a hackney-coach, in which was the Rapporteur [recorder] and his clerk, whose duty it was to witness the execution, and then return to Fouquier-Tinville, the Accusateur Public [public prosecutor], to report the execution of what they called the law.

The process of execution was also a sad and heart-rending spectacle. In the middle of the Place de la Révolution was erected a guillotine, in front of a colossal statue of Liberty, represented seated on a rock, a Phrygian cap on her head, a spear in her hand, the other reposing on a shield. On one side of the scaffold were drawn out a sufficient number of carts, with large baskets painted red, to receive the heads and bodies of the victims. Those bearing the condemned moved on slowly to the foot of the guillotine; the culprits were led out in turn, and, if necessary, sup-

ported by two of the executioner's valets, as they were formerly called, but now denominated élèves de l'Executeur des hautes oeuvres de la justice [students of the executor of the great works of justice]; but their assistance was rarely required. Most of these unfortunates ascended the scaffold with a determined step—many of them looked up firmly on the menacing instrument of death, beholding for the last time the rays of the glorious sun, beaming on the polished axe; and I have seen some young men actually dance a few steps before they went up to be strapped to the perpendicular plane, which was then tilted to a horizontal plane in a moment, and ran on the grooves until the neck was secured and closed in by a moving board, when the head passed through what was called in derision, la lunette republicaine [the republican telescope]; the weighty knife was then dropped with a heavy fall; and, with incredible dexterity and rapidity, two executioners tossed the body into the basket, while another threw the head after it.»

Appendix III
Primary Documents of the Mexican Revolution

Plan of San Luis of Potosí
Attributed to: Francisco I. Madero
Date proclaimed: October 5, 1910

In the 1910 presidential elections, Francisco I. Madero was arrested for daring to challenge Mexico's longstanding ruler, Porfirio Díaz. Madero escaped from prison and fled to San Antonio, Texas where he proclaimed the Plan de San Luis Potosí, declaring the 1910 elections illegal and calling for armed rebellion against the federal government. The Plan abstractly cited effective suffrage and no-reelection as the primary goals of Madero's An Educator's Guide to the Mexican Revolution 86 movement. Strikingly absent were calls for substantive land or labor reform, foreshadowing Madero's failure to adequately incorporate those principally important issues into his short-lived presidency.

Plan of Ayala
Attributed to: Emiliano Zapata
Date proclaimed: November 25, 1911

Disenchanted with the recently installed President Madero's slow-moving social reforms in 1911, Zapata proclaimed the Plan de Ayala, calling for immediate and comprehensive land reform. The Plan was proclaimed in Ayala, in Zapata's home state of Morelos and reportedly authored by Zapata and a local schoolteacher named Otilio Montaño. The Plan demands restitution of indigenous lands taken during the Porfiriato. It does not distinguish Madero from Díaz, recognizing that false men and traitors make promises like liberators and then forget those promises upon arriving in power. Zapata and his followers would pursue the aims of the Plan de Ayala by taking arms against the next three Mexican presidents.

Plan of Guadalupe
Attributed to: Venustiano Carranza and Álvaro Obregón
Date proclaimed: March 23, 1913

In 1913, Victoriano Huerta overthrew and executed the revolutionary President Francisco Madero in a coup. Venustiano Carranza proclaimed the Plan de Guadalupe, denouncing the traitor, Huerta, and declaring himself the interim President of Mexico. The Plan had no proposal for any type of social reform whatsoever. Plan of Agua Prieta Attributed to: Álvaro Obregón Date proclaimed: April 23, 1920 Description: Obregón proclaimed the Plan in Agua Prieta, a border town in Sonora. To produce and proclaim it, he allied with two other Sonorans: Adolfo de la Huerta and Plutarco Elías Calles. Together, they promoted the Plan as a way to give the Sonoran-led Obregonistas a reason to rally. The Plan's primary thrust was to repudiate the Carranza administration, accusing it of making a farce of suffrage, violating the political sovereignty of the states, and of betraying the original principals behind the Revolution. The Plan furthermore declared that Adolfo de la Huerta would be the supreme chief of the army. Within two weeks, Carranza had fled the capital and Obregón was in charge of the country.

During the first decade of the 20th century, the anger of the Mexican people towards the dictatorship of Porfirio Díaz was growing, and with no legal options open to him, Francisco I. Madero wrote and published a document calling for the destruction of Diaz's authoritarian presidency and the re-institution of democracy through violent direct action. The publication of the famous document immediately started the Mexican Revolution.

Image: Carranza, Obregón, Madero and Zapata, around the Monument to the Mexican Revolution, built in Mexico City in 1936.

Appendix IV
Excerpts of Several Articles of the 1917 Mexican Constitution

Excerpt of Article 3 of the Constitution of 1917:

Freedom of religious beliefs being guaranteed by Article 24, the standard which shall guide such education shall be maintained entirely apart from any religious doctrine and, based on the results of scientific progress, shall strive against ignorance and its effects, servitudes, fanaticism, and prejudices. Private institutions devoted to education of the kinds and grades specified in the preceding section must be without exception in conformity with the provisions of sections I and II of the first paragraph of this article and must also be in harmony with official plans and programs. Religious corporations, ministers of religion, stock companies which exclusively or predominantly engage in educational activities, and associations or companies devoted to propagation of any religious creed shall not in any way participate in institutions giving elementary, secondary and normal education and education for laborers or field workers.

Excerpt of Article 27 of the Constitution of 1917:

Ownership of the lands and waters within the boundaries of the national territory is vested originally in the Nation, which has had, and has, the right to transmit title thereof to private persons, thereby constituting private property. Only Mexicans by birth or naturalization and Mexican companies have the right to acquire ownership of lands, waters, and their appurtenances, or to obtain concessions for the exploitation of mines or of waters. Religious institutions known as churches, regardless of creed, may in no case acquire, hold, or administer real property or hold mortgages thereon; such property held at present either directly or through an intermediary shall revert to the Nation. . . . .

Excerpt of Article 130 of the Constitution of 1917:

The federal powers shall exercise the supervision required by law in matters relating to religious worship and outward ecclesiastical forms. Other authorities shall act as auxiliaries of the Federation.

Congress cannot enact laws establishing or prohibiting any religion. Marriage is a civil contract. This and other acts of a civil nature concerning persons are within the exclusive competence of civil officials and authorities, in the manner prescribed by law, and shall have the force and validity defined by said law. Ministers of denominations shall be considered as persons who practice a profession and shall be directly subject to the laws enacted on such matters. Ministers of denominations may never, in a public or private meeting constituting an assembly, or in acts of worship or religious propaganda, criticize the fundamental laws of the country or the authorities of the Government, specifically or generally. They shall not have an active or passive vote nor the right to form associations for religious purposes. A minister of any denomination may not himself or through an intermediary inherit or receive any real property occupied by any association for religious propaganda or for religious or charitable purposes. Ministers of denominations are legally incapacitated as testamentary heirs of ministers of the same denomination or of any private person who is not related to them within the fourth degree.

Excerpt of Article 123 of the Constitution of 1917:

Workers, day laborers, domestic servants, artisans (obreros, jornaleros, empleados domésticos, artesanos) and in a general way to all labor contracts: The maximum duration of work for one day shall be eight hours. The maximum duration of night work shall be seven hours. The following are prohibited: unhealthful or dangerous work by women and by minors under sixteen years of age; industrial night work by either of these classes; work by women in commercial establishments after ten o'clock at night and work (of any kind) by persons under sixteen after ten o'clock at night. The use of labor of minors under fourteen years of age is prohibited. Persons above that age and less than sixteen shall have a maximum work day of six hours. For every six days of work a worker must have at least one day of rest. During the three months prior to childbirth, women shall not perform physical labor that requires excessive material effort. In the month following childbirth they shall necessarily enjoy the benefit of rest and shall receive their full wages and retain their employment and the rights acquired under their labor contract. During the nursing period they shall have two special rest periods each day, of a half hour each, for nursing their infants. The minimum wage to be received by a worker shall be general or according to occupation. The former shall govern in one or more economic zones; the latter shall be applicable to specified branches of industry or commerce or to special occupations, trades, or labor.

After much heated debate congress adopted the 1857 constitution, however there was continued debate and anger over many of the articles, particularly those that were viewed as against the Catholic Church.

Appendix V
The Abdication of Nicholas II (1917)

The abdication of Nicholas II, signed in Pskov on March 15th 1917 (March 2nd in the old Julian calendar). Nicholas abdicated power to his brother, Grand Duke Michael, however within one day he too had relinquished power to an elected representative assembly:

«By the Grace of God, We, Nikolai II, Emperor of All Russia, Tsar of Poland, Grand Duke of Finland, and so forth, to all our faithful subjects be it known:

In the days of a great struggle against a foreign enemy who has been endeavoring for three years to enslave our country, it pleased God to send Russia a further painful trial. Internal troubles threatened to have a fatal effect on the further progress of this obstinate war.

The destinies of Russia, the honor of her heroic Army, the happiness of the people, and the whole future of our beloved country demand that the war should be conducted at all costs to a victorious end. The cruel enemy is making his last efforts and the moment is near when our valiant Army, in concert with our glorious Allies, will finally overthrow the enemy.

In these decisive days in the life of Russia we have thought that we owed to our people the close union and organization of all its forces for the realization of a rapid victory; for which reason, in agreement with the Imperial Duma, we have recognized that it is for the good of the country that we should abdicate the Crown of the Russian State and lay down the Supreme Power.

Not wishing to separate ourselves from our beloved son, we bequeath our heritage to our brother, the Grand Duke Mikhail Alexandrovich, with our blessing for the future of the Throne of the Russian State. We bequeath it our brother to govern in full union with the national representatives sitting in the Legislative Institutions, and to take his inviolable oath to them in the name of our well-beloved country.

We call upon all faithful sons of our native land to fulfill their sacred and patriotic duty of obeying the Tsar at the painful moment of national trial and to aid them, together with the representatives of the nation, to conduct the Russian State in the way of prosperity and glory.

May God help Russia.»

Appendix VI
Excerpts from Lenin's Political Testament (1922)

The document known as Lenin's political testament was in fact a series of short letters, written to the Congress of Soviets over the course of a week in December 1922. He expressed concern about a potential split in the Bolshevik Central Committee, in large part because of divisions between Stalin and Trotsky:

«*I would urge strongly that at this Congress a number of changes be made in our political structure. I want to tell you of the considerations to which I attach most importance.*

At the head of the list I set an increase in the number of Central Committee members to a few dozen or even a hundred. It is my opinion that without this reform our Central Committee would be in great danger if the course of events were not quite favorable for us... I think it must be done in order to raise the prestige of the Central Committee, to do a thorough job of improving our administrative machinery and to prevent conflicts between small sections of the Central Committee from acquiring excessive importance...

By stability of the Central Committee, of which I spoke above, I mean measure against a split, as far as such measures can at all be taken. For, of course, the white guard in Russkaya Mysl (it seems to have been S.S. Oldenburg) was right when, first, in the white guards' game against Soviet Russia he banked on a split in our Party, and when, secondly, he banked on grave differences in our Party to cause that split.

I have in mind stability as a guarantee against a split in the immediate future, and I intend to deal here with a few ideas concerning personal qualities.

I think that from this standpoint the prime factors in the question of stability are such members of the Central Committee as Stalin and Trotsky. I think relations between them make up the greater part of the danger of a split, which could be avoided. [This could be avoided] by increasing the number of C.C. members to 50 or 100.

Comrade Stalin, having become Secretary-General, has unlimited authority concentrated in his hands – and I am not sure whether he will always be capable of using that authority with sufficient caution. Comrade Trotsky, on the other hand, as his struggle against the Central Committee on the question of the People's Commissariat of Communications, has already proved [his] outstanding ability. He is personally perhaps the most capable man in the present Central Committee – but he has displayed excessive self-confidence and preoccupation with the purely administrative side of the work.

These two qualities of the two outstanding leaders of the present Central Committee can inadvertently lead to a split, and if our Party does not take steps to avert this, the split may come unexpectedly."

"Stalin is too rude and this defect, although quite tolerable in our midst and in dealing among us Communists, becomes intolerable in a Secretary-General. That is why I suggest that the comrades think about a way of removing Stalin from that post and appointing another man in his stead who in all other respects differs from Comrade Stalin in having only one advantage, namely, that of being more tolerant, more loyal, more polite and more considerate to the comrades, less capricious, etc. This circumstance may appear to be a negligible detail. But I think that from the standpoint of safeguards against a split and from the standpoint of what I wrote above about the relationship between Stalin and Trotsky it is not a [minor] detail, but it is a detail which can assume decisive importance.»

Lenin died at 18.50 hrs, Moscow time, on Jan 21, 1924, aged 53, at his estate at Gorki settlement.

Appendix VII
A Capitalist, a Marxist-Leninist and an Anarcho-Syndicalist analize the subversion of the Cuban Revolution

Over the last half century the world has witnessed the gradual degeneration of the Cuban Revolution from a Marxist-Leninist experiment into a totalitarian dictatorship led and maintained by an ill-intentioned group of greedy and violent mobsters.

The revolution, within the first few weeks, began to hoodwink thousands of naive and idealistic political romantics around the world. Over time, few of these initial supporters have accepted the disappointing reality of Castro's Cuba; to this day they continue to befriend the gang of felons that governs Cuba.

We present here the opinions and vision of three men who were fanatical Castroites at first but, facing the enormous glaring personal motives and ambitions of Castro's gang, they were no longer willing to camouflage and cover-up the unpardonable criminal excesses of his revolution.

Herbert Matthews (1910-1977), foreign correspondent and later senior editor of the New York Times, the man that published the sensational interview with Fidel Castro in the *Sierra Maestra* on February 17, 1957:

> «*Castro is a dictator. His revolution was clearly "autocratic." He made the mistake at his Moncada trial in 1953 and in the Sierra Maestra in 1957, of promising to implement the liberal democratic constitution of 1940. He did not make a mistake. He knew full well and later openly confessed* [in his "I am a Marxist-Leninist" speech, Dec. 1, 1961] *that Batista could be overthrown and Castro's clique could come to power, but only on the basis of a democratic program acceptable to the Cuban bourgeoisie, the Church and other non-radical forces. In the Cuban political tradition, it was an impossibility to get them to accept a Marxist revolution... He was an astute politician. He did not make the mistake of antagonizing these elements by prematurely initiating expropriation of property, executing anyone and other radical measures. He waited until his regime was strong enough to neutralize, and if necessary, smother the opposition.*»

«*During the summary nature of Cuban trials, Castro's prosecutors, many with criminal records, were the executioners at La Cabaña fortress in Havana ... I remember soldiers in Ché Guevara's column that were acting like butchers killing cattle in an abattoir ... within days these courts lost all of their authority. Lawyers who defended those accused of being counter-revolutionaries, ran the danger of prosecution themselves... Habeas corpus was no longer functional in late 1959. Many times the evidence would not stand up in a Western court of law, but this was a bogus court of law in the midst of a perilous revolution. The prisons were filled to overflowing. The interrogation rooms of the G2, Castro's secret police, were scarcely less vile than the torture chambers of Batista's SIM ... there were more prisoners in February of 1959 than Batista ever had.*»

Rene Dumont (1904-2001), French Communist sociologist and environmental politician, a former friend of Castro's revolution who throughout Europe praised Castro's effort and was invited several times to visit him Cuba.

«*The number one man in Cuba is Castro. Castro is Prime Minister of the Revolutionary Government, Commander in Chief of the Armed Forces, and First Secretary of the Cuban Communist Party. As an official, one's job depends upon Castro's confidence and on personal connections. Leadership of the essential agencies is placed in the hands of men in whom the Boss [Castro] has confidence. Cuban society remains authoritarian and hierarchized; Fidel maneuvers it as he sees fit. The result is a militaristic society.*»

«*In public everybody is for Castro. In private his partisans are less numerous. Everybody goes to the demonstrations in the Plaza de la Revolución. It is obligatory... Castro has confidence only in himself. He is no longer content with claims to military and political fame. He has to feel himself the leader in both scientific research and agricultural practice* [about which he knows next to nothing.] *Nobody dares oppose him if he wants to hold his job. When he throws his beret on the ground and flies into one of his rages, everybody quakes and fears reprisals.*»

«*There exists vigilance* [spying] *with the increasing control of neighborhoods by the Committees for the Defense of the Revolution* [CDRs] *standing in for and helping the police. Everybody belongs to the CDRs, unless he wants to miss out on many advantages. Capitalism robs the worker of his dignity, police inquisition in the Cuban Revolution again denies it to the poorest worker, the censored press CONSTANTLY lies. No one can challenge Granma to publish what Castro wants.»*

«In Cuba the military have taken over command of the economy ... it is becoming clearer and clearer that the army is transforming Cuban society. Militarization was urged not only to eliminate inefficiency and disorganization, but to cope with the passive resistance of a growing number of workers... it became increasingly difficult to distinguish between the Communist Party and the army, since they both wore uniforms and carried revolvers ... This sort of Cuban communism is devilishly close to army life ... This military society ... follows a path leading away from participation of the people; it leads to a hierarchized society with an authoritarian leadership headed by Castro who decides all problems, political, economic and technical.»

Abelardo Iglesias (1914-1972), prominent Cuban veteran anarchist, friend of Camilo Cienfuegos, follower of Mikhail Bakunin, regular writer for *Guangara Literaria*, the Cuban anarchist magazine.

«Apart from byzantine discussions, there are these objective facts about the Cuban Revolution which no one can deny. I have listed briefly the main points:
- *The so-called revolutionary regime is essentially a corrupt oligarchy dominated by a handful of mobsters accountable to no one for their actions.*
- *In line with their sectarianism and convenience they have abolished all individual rights.*
- *They have centralized political and economic power to an extent never known before in Cuba.*
- *They constructed an apparatus of terror immensely more efficient than Batista's repressive agencies.*
- *The land has not been distributed to the peasants, for individual, family, collective or cooperative cultivation, but has become the 'de facto' property of the state agency, the Institute for Agrarian Reform (JNRA), working for the benefit of the chieftains and not for those who work the land..*
- *The nationalization of private enterprises has not benefited the workers or the state. The industries are administered not by capable individuals or members of the workers' unions, but have been taken over by brainless lackeys of Castro that only seek to reinforce the power of the state, converting the former wage slaves into slaves of the state machine.*

- *Public education has become a state monopoly. The state arrogates to itself the right to impose its kind of education upon the young, regardless of the opinion of the parents.*
- *The legitimate necessity to prepare against counter-revolutionary aggression has been the pretext for the unnecessary militarization of children and adolescents as in Russia and other totalitarian states.*
- *The right to strike has been abolished and the workers must, without complaint, obey the decrees imposed upon them in their work places. The unions have lost their independence and are actually state agencies, whose sole function it is to cajole or force the workers to obey the commands of the state functionaries without protest.*
- *There are no genuine judicial tribunals. Opponents are punished not for alleged offences, but for their convictions and anti-revolutionary ideas.*
- *Fidel Castro's government is conducted in accordance with Mussolini's notorious dictum:*
  Nothing outside of the State!!
  Nothing against the State!!
  Everything for the State!!
- *Castro purged, jailed, banished and tortured hundreds of his adherents, who had distinguished themselves for bravery in the Revolution, only because they were too independent; he replaced them with traitors, mobsters, gangsters, crooks, felons, outlaws and former enemies, who, for a few grains of power, repented and recanted and became his main support as fanatical disciples.»*

Herbert Mathews, the *capitalist*, **Rene Dumont**, the *Marxist-Leninist* and **Abelardo Iglesias**, the *anarcho-syndicalist*, three men offering their analysis of the Cuban Revolution.

Appendix VIII

A selection of quotes from the writings and speeches of Ernesto (Ché) Guevara

«*I am not Christ or a philanthropist, old lady, I am all the contrary of a Christ.... I fight for the things I believe in, with all the weapons at my disposal and try to leave the other man dead so that I don't get nailed to a cross or any other place.*»

LETTER TO HIS MOTHER (JULY 15, 1956).

«*The situation was uncomfortable for the people and for Eutimio, so I ended the problem giving him a shot with a .32 pistol in the right side of the brain, with exit orifice in the right temporal lobe. He gasped for a little air while going dead. Upon proceeding to remove his belongings I couldn't get off the watch tied by a chain to his belt, and then he told me in a steady voice farther away than fear: "Yank it off, boy, what does it matter!" I did so and his possessions were now mine.*»

DIARY ENTRY FROM SIERRA MAESTRA ON THE EXECUTION OF EUTIMIO GUERRA AS AN ANTI-REVOLUTIONARY SPY (JANUARY 1957).

«*We must carry the war into every corner the enemy happens to carry it: to his home, to his centers of entertainment; a total war. It is necessary to prevent him from having a moment of peace, a quiet moment outside his barracks or even inside; we must attack him wherever he may be; make him feel like a cornered beast wherever he may move. Then his moral fiber shall begin to decline. He will even become more beastly, but we shall notice how the signs of decadence begin to appear.*»

«*How close we could look into a bright future should two, three or many Vietnams flourish throughout the world.*»

«*Hatred as an important element of our struggle; unbending hatred for the enemy, which pushes a human being beyond his natural limitations, making him into an effective, violent, selective, and cold-blooded killing machine.*»

MESSAGE TO THE TRICONTINENTAL, SENT FROM HIS JUNGLE CAMP IN BOLIVIA; PUBLISHED ON APRIL 16, 1967.

«*I knew you were going to shoot me; I should never have been taken alive. Tell Fidel that this failure does not mean the end of the revolution, that it will triumph elsewhere. Tell Aleida to forget this, remarry and be happy, and keep the children studying. Ask the soldiers to aim well.»*

LAST WORDS OF GUEVARA TO ARNALDO SAUCEDO, HEAD OF INTELLIGENCE OF THE US ARMY. OCTOBER 9, 1967.

«*The Negro is indolent and lazy, and spends his money on frivolities, whereas the European is forward-looking, organized and intelligent... I plan to do for blacks exactly what blacks have done for the human race: nothing.*»

CHÉ GUEVARA, THE MOTORCYCLE DIARIES.

«*I felt my nostrils dilate savoring the acrid smell of gunpowder and blood of the enemy; revolution without firing a shot? You're crazy. It was all a lot of fun; the bombs were the main distraction to break the monotony I lived in.*»

LETTER TO HIS MOTHER, OCTOBER OF 1967.

«*Finally, there I was in the Cuban jungle, alive and bloodthirsty.*»

REMARKS OF JANUARY 29, 1957, UPON LANDING IN CUBA.

Three images of Ernesto (Ché) Guevara:
The commercialized image produced by **Alberto Korda** on March 5, 1960,
The somber face when he was **captured in Bolivia** and begged for his life,
and the 2003 poster by **Reporters without Borders** denouncing his crimes.

Index

1
13 of March, 247, 251, 253

A
Abdication, 328
Abrantes, 251
Acción Católica, 279
Acosta, 281
Adams, 45, 89
Agramonte, 231, 267, 273, 297
Aguascalientes, 139
Alamino, 235, 306
Alberti, 279
Alexander II, 161, 163, 165
Alexander III, 161, 163, 165
Ancien Régime, 18
Artime, 297, 299
Austria-Hungary, 177, 179, 181
Auténticos, 253, 255

B
Barbudo, 257, 290
Bastille, 15, 17, 35, 41, 43, 63
Batista, 231, 245, 247, 251, 253, 255, 259, 261, 267, 269, 271, 273, 275, 279, 281, 287, 290, 293, 295, 297, 299, 315, 331, 332, 333
Batistianos, 251
Bay of Pigs, 233, 234, 293, 297, 299, 303, 305, 306
Beregere Clinic, 219
Bisbé, 279
Bloodthirsty, 277, 307, 336
Bloody Sunday, 151, 169
Bolsheviks, 151, 152, 163, 167, 187, 189, 191, 195, 197, 199, 201, 205, 211, 215, 219, 221
Botelleros, 273, 285
Bourgeoisie, 15, 21, 203, 223, 255, 331
Buchaca, 234

C
Calles, 84, 125, 129, 131, 133, 135, 137, 143, 324
Camarioca, 235
Capitol, 8
Cárdenas, 125, 137, 143, 315
Carranza, 83, 84, 99, 115, 117, 119, 121, 123, 125, 127, 128, 129, 137, 139, 324
Casquitos, 247, 277
Catholic Church, 21, 39, 79, 125, 133, 135, 137, 139, 327
CDR, 306, 233, 234, 332
Celaya, 84, 121
Chapultepec, 103
Cheks, 201
Chibás, 231, 255
Chouan, 53, 73
CIA, 231, 234, 277, 279, 293, 297, 299, 300, 305
Cienfuegos, 232, 251, 257, 259, 267, 279, 291, 296, 333
Ciudadela, 100, 103, 105, 107
Clergy, 25, 29, 39, 45, 47, 53, 63
Coliseo de Deportes, 305
Colorados, 101, 115
Columbia, 231, 259, 267, 289, 297
Commissar, 196, 215, 297
Communism, 221, 279, 290, 293, 305, 306, 307
Communist, 151, 152, 153, 191, 205, 209, 215, 219, 221, 231, 232, 234, 235, 257, 261, 275, 279, 287, 290, 291, 293, 296, 297, 299, 300, 301, 303, 305, 307, 313, 332, 333
Communist Party, 151, 152, 153, 191, 205, 209, 215, 219, 221, 234, 293, 297, 332, 333
Confiscated, 53, 78, 79, 89, 199, 232, 233, 235, 297, 301, 313
Congress of Vienna, 177
Constitution, 15, 16, 39, 45, 47, 49, 53, 59, 63, 69, 71, 73, 91, 121, 125, 129, 133, 143, 169, 171, 175, 231, 325, 326
Constitutionalists, 113, 119, 123
Cordeliers, 49, 57
Coup de Grace, 287
Coup d'État, 83, 89, 115, 119, 123, 191
Covadonga, 234, 306
Cristero, 133, 135
Cuban Revolution, 9, 135, 234, 237, 277, 313, 317, 331, 332, 333, 334
Cubela, 232, 251, 293, 295

D
Dacha, 205
d'Alambert, 21
Decena Trágica, 113, 115
Díaz Lanz, 296, 297
Diderot, 21
Directorio Revolucionario, 251, 253, 293
Directory, 16, 73
Doléances, 25, 27, 29
Dorticos, 232
Dubois, 291
Duma, 151, 159, 163, 169, 171, 175, 181, 328

E
Eisenhower, 231, 253, 269, 290, 293, 300
El Encanto, 233, 303
Elijah Muhammad, 306
Encyclopédie, 21
Enlightenment, 21, 77, 318
Ernesto Guevara, 235, 247, 251, 255, 257,

267, 273, 279, 287, 307
Escoto, 281, 283
Estates General, 18, 23, 25, 27, 29, 31, 33, 41, 45
Exile, 15, 21, 53, 57, 84, 89, 107, 115, 125, 137, 139, 151, 159, 167, 187, 203, 207, 217, 234, 245, 289, 293, 296, 306, 313, 315

F
Farrakhan, 306
Federales, 119
Felix Díaz, 99, 100, 101, 105
FEU, 232, 257, 293, 295
Fidel Castro, 229, 231, 245, 247, 257, 279, 283, 287, 289, 293, 300, 331, 334
Firing Squads, 135, 231, 234, 285, 287
FLN, 303
Franqui, 290, 291
Franz Ferdinand, 179
French Revolution, 9, 13, 15, 17, 18, 43, 50, 51, 55, 59, 61, 67, 69, 71, 76, 77, 78

G
Gaitán, 269
Genocide, 53, 287
Girondists, 16, 43, 57, 59
Gorki, 205
Grégoire, 39, 63
Gulag, 153, 154, 219

H
Halley's Comet, 85, 86, 87
Harvard, 201, 291
Havana, 109, 231, 232, 233, 235, 237, 241, 251, 253, 255, 257, 259, 267, 273, 275, 277, 279, 281, 283, 285, 289, 290, 291, 293, 295, 296, 297, 299, 301, 303, 305, 306, 332
Hispanic America, 233, 241, 269, 271, 279, 303, 306
Hôtel de Ville, 27, 71
Huerta, 83, 84, 97, 99, 101, 103, 105, 107, 109, 113, 115, 117, 119, 121, 123, 125, 127, 129, 131, 143, 324

I
Impounded, 301
INRA, 231, 297, 299
Intervened, 301

J
Jacobin, 15, 16, 33, 43, 45, 49, 51, 52, 71
Jeu de Paume, 31, 33
Juárez, 87, 89, 91, 95, 97, 100, 133

K
Kamenev, 153, 154, 187, 205, 207, 211, 215
Kazan, 167
KGV, 219
Kulaks, 153, 219, 223

L
Lafayette, 15, 20, 39, 41, 43, 47, 49, 51, 53, 65
Lavoisier, 78
Lenin, 151, 152, 153, 165, 167, 187, 189, 191, 196, 197, 203, 205, 207, 209, 211, 213, 215, 219, 221, 223, 269, 306, 315, 317, 329
Library of Congress, 8
Llorente, 279
Louis XVI, 15, 20, 23, 25, 29, 31, 33, 35, 39, 41, 43, 45, 47, 49, 51, 52, 53, 57, 59, 61, 63, 69

M
Machado, 269, 273
Maderistas, 93
Madero, 6, 81, 83, 87, 93, 95, 96, 97, 99, 100, 101, 103, 105, 107, 109, 113, 115, 117, 123, 125, 127, 129, 141, 143, 323, 324
Malcolm X, 306
Marat, 16, 37, 39, 49, 57, 59, 71
Mariano Faget, 279
Márquez Sterling, 107, 109
Marseillaise, 17, 51
Martínez Sánchez, 271
Marxist, 167, 221, 223, 255, 269, 287, 297, 307, 313, 317, 331, 334
Matos, 232, 257, 293, 296, 297

Menshevik, 151, 167, 169, 185, 187, 197, 211
Mexican Revolution, 9, 81, 83, 85, 95, 120, 125, 137, 139, 143, 317, 323, 324
Mikoyan, 232, 301
Milicianas, 285
Military Tribunal, 289
Mirabeau, 31, 43, 45
Miró, 231, 253, 267, 271, 299
Missile Crises, 234
Missiles, 306
Molotov, 209, 215
Moncada, 245, 331
Montesquieu, 21
Morgan, 251
Motorcycle Diaries, 277, 336

N
Napoleon, 16, 43, 52, 53, 63, 73, 76, 77, 89
National Assembly, 15, 31, 33, 39, 41, 45, 49, 51, 69, 71, 318, 321
National Palace, 99, 103, 105, 107, 120
Nationalized, 301, 303
Necker, 15, 23, 31, 35
Negro, 277, 336
Neruda, 279
Nicholas II, 151, 152, 159, 161, 165, 167, 169, 171, 173, 175, 181, 185, 193, 317, 328
Nixon, 231, 290, 291
NKVD, 153, 154, 197, 217, 219
Noailles, 20, 35, 65
Nobles, 25
Novy Mir, 207, 211
Nuñez Jiménez, 279

O
Obregón, 83, 84, 115, 121, 123, 125, 127, 128, 129, 131, 133, 136, 137, 139, 315, 324
October Manifesto, 169, 171, 173, 211
October Revolution, 151, 191, 195, 207, 211, 215, 219, 221
OEA, 234
Operación Pedro Pan, 234, 306
Ordoqui, 234

Oriente, 243, 245, 247, 257, 271, 287
Orozco, 83, 95, 97, 99, 101, 113, 115, 121, 127, 141
Ortodoxos, 253, 255, 267, 279

P

Paredón, 296
Party Congress, 207, 209, 215
Patria Potestad, 234, 306
Pazos, 231, 232, 253, 271, 279
Pedraza, 253
Perón, 269
Pilotos, 287
Pino Suárez, 83, 97, 100, 107, 109, 113
Plan de Agua Prieta, 127
Plan de Ayala, 83, 96, 97, 123, 323
Plan de Guadalupe, 83, 119, 324
Politburo, 154, 187, 201, 203, 205, 207, 209
Porfiriato, 115, 141, 323
Porfirio Díaz, 81, 83, 87, 91, 93, 95, 97, 101, 117, 125, 128, 141, 315, 323, 324
Port Arthur, 171, 173
PRI, 137, 141
Prío, 247, 253, 255, 269
Proletariat, 15, 223, 255
Provisional Government, 185, 187, 191, 193, 195, 203, 211
Public Safety, 15, 16, 57, 63, 67, 71, 73
Purges, 73, 203, 219, 221, 285

R

Rasputin, 175, 183
Reforma Agraria, 297, 299
Reyes, 93, 97, 99, 101, 103, 120
Rights of Man, 15, 17, 41, 47, 49, 59, 317, 318
Roa, 297
Robespierre, 13, 16, 18, 45, 51, 52, 53, 55, 57, 59, 61, 63, 67, 69, 71, 78
Romanov, 151, 159, 165, 173
Roosevelt, 117, 154, 173
Rouget de Lisle, 50, 51
Rousseau, 21, 71
Russian Empire, 167, 171, 181
Russian Famine, 199
Russian Revolution, 9, 149, 151, 157, 163, 173, 187, 195, 205, 211, 221, 223

S

San Luis de Potosí, 95
Sandino, 269
Sans-Coulottes, 17, 57, 71
Santa Ana, 89, 143
Santa Clara, 247, 251, 289
Santana, 277
Santiago, 103, 231, 245, 251, 257, 259, 275, 287
Sedov, 217, 219
Sedova, 211, 217
Siberia, 153, 159, 167, 177, 209, 211
Sierra de Cristal, 247
Sierra Maestra, 232, 243, 245, 247, 251, 255, 257, 261, 267, 271, 273, 277, 279, 285, 287, 289, 293, 296, 297, 331, 335
Sieyès, 25, 31, 45
Sorí Marín, 271, 297, 299
Sosa Blanco, 281, 297
Soviet, 151, 152, 153, 154, 169, 185, 187, 193, 195, 196, 197, 199, 201, 203, 205, 207, 209, 211, 217, 219, 234, 267, 290, 300, 301, 329
Soviet of Workers, 185
Soviet Union, 195, 205, 300
St. Antoine, 27, 35, 52
Stalin, 152, 153, 154, 187, 203, 205, 207, 209, 211, 214, 215, 217, 219, 221, 223, 227, 269, 277, 285, 329, 330

T

Tabernilla, 253, 255
Talleyrand, 43
Tallien, 71
Tannenberg, 183
Terror, 13, 16, 18, 29, 63, 67, 69, 71, 76, 78, 79, 153, 196, 197, 221
Texas, 87, 95, 96, 323
Thermidor, 67, 71
Tocqueville, 17, 18, 27
Triple Alliance, 181
Triple Entente, 179, 181
Trotsky, 6, 151, 153, 154, 187, 189, 205, 207, 209, 211, 213, 215, 217, 219, 221, 329, 330
Tsar, 151, 159, 161, 163, 165, 169, 171, 173, 175, 181, 191, 328
Tsarevich, 165, 193
Tuileries, 15, 39, 43, 47, 49, 52, 55, 57, 69, 73, 78

U

UIR, 257
UMAP, 234, 235, 306
University of Havana, 257, 295, 301
Urrutia, 231, 232, 234, 267, 271, 291
US Black Power, 235

V

Varennes, 15, 47, 49, 53
Veracruz, 83, 84, 86, 91, 101, 107, 109, 115, 117, 121, 125, 139
Versailles, 15, 20, 25, 29, 31, 33, 39, 41, 45, 51
Vladivostok, 171, 189

W

Wilson, 83, 84, 115, 117, 191
Winter Palace, 163, 169, 191, 195, 215

Z

Zapata, 81, 83, 84, 95, 96, 97, 99, 101, 113, 119, 120, 121, 123, 139, 141, 143, 275, 323, 324

Raúl Eduardo Chao received his PhD from Johns Hopkins University and after a brief stint in industry spent 18 years in academe, as Full Professor and Department Chairman at the **Universities of Puerto Rico and Detroit**. *In 1986 he founded a very successful management consultancy, assisting companies and government agencies to develop positive work environments and process improvement techniques as the means to secure improvements in productivity and quality.* **The Systema Group** *had as clients many Fortune 100 companies and Federal and State organizations, both in the US and abroad. As its Chairman, Chao wrote a dozen books and numerous articles in newspapers and reviewed journals. He and his wife Olga live in Coral Gables, Florida and spend long periods of time in Paris.*

The font used throughout the text has been **Palatino Linotype**, one of the classic old style serif typefaces inspired by designs of the 16th century Italian calligrapher **Giambattista Palatino**. The font was reissued in 1948 by **Hermann Zapf** for the Linotype Foundry, the company created by Ottmar Mergenthaler, a German immigrant to the U.S. who invented the revolutionary line typesetting machine that was first used in 1890 by the **New York Tribune**.

The font used in the covers, title pages, headings and ornaments is **P22 Franklin Caslon**, a faithful interpretation of the type used by Benjamin Franklin in the 1750's in his printing shop and particularly in his **Poor Richard's Almanac**. This font was developed in 2006 by the International House of Fonts for the Philadelphia Museum of Art to commemorate the 300th birthday of our most remarkable Founding Father. The font accompanying the photos and illustrations is **Verdana**; a humanist sans-serif typeface designed by **Matthew Carter** for *Microsoft Corporation*, with hand-hinting done by **Tom Rickner**, then at *Monotype*. Demand for such a clear and easy to read type-face was recognized by **Virginia Howlett** of *Microsoft's* typography group. The name "**Verdana**" is based on a mix of *verdant* (something green, as in the Seattle area and the Evergreen state of Washington), and *Ana* (the name of Howlett's eldest daughter